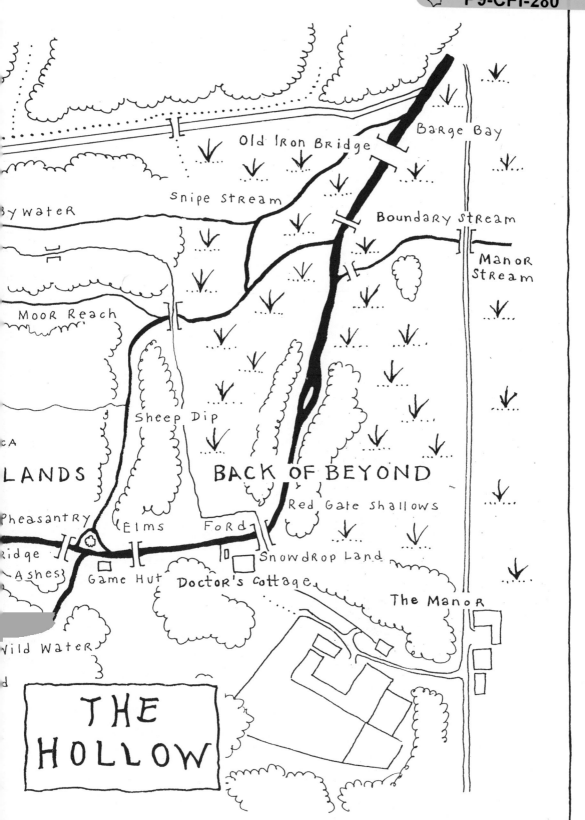

Barge Bay

Old Iron Bridge

Snipe Stream

Bywater

Boundary Stream

Manor Stream

Moor Reach

Sheep Dip

CA

LANDS

BACK OF BEYOND

Red Gate Shallows

Pheasantry

Elms

Ford

Snowdrop Land

Ridge

Ashes

Game Hut

Doctor's cottage

The Manor

Wild Water

THE HOLLOW

Chalkstream Chronicle

Chalkstream Chronicle

LIVING OUT THE FLYFISHER'S FANTASY

WRITTEN AND ILLUSTRATED BY

NEIL PATTERSON

LYONS & BURFORD

First published in the USA by Lyons & Burford Publishers, 1995
Originally published in the UK by Merlin Unwin Books, 1995
Text and line illustrations © Neil Patterson, 1995

Lyons & Burford Publishers,
31 West 21 Street,
New York,
NY 10010,
U.S.A.

ISBN 1-55821-425-9

Designed and typeset in 11 point Caslon by Merlin Unwin Books
Printed and bound by Butler & Tanner Ltd, Frome, UK.

CONTENTS

To Big Mum and the Big Kid

& to the Dry Fly

whose design is more intricate than
the most complex computer,
whose character is more infinite than
a century of men who have fished it

PREFACE

'Home is where one starts from' - T. S. Eliot

The piscatorial itchy-foot, Negley Farson, in his book *Going Fishing* wrote: 'Fishing should be the exercise of your skills - and its rewards the places it brings you to'.

The reward for his skills was to go fishing in two hemispheres. My reward - no greater, certainly no smaller - took me to the bottom of my garden.

This book hasn't rocketed from a publishing house - it has oozed from the banks of a river. A river that I have shared my home with for over twenty years. A river that has become a best friend.

For this reason, it is this river that I want to thank first; for her friendship - and for trusting me to divulge between these covers so many of the secrets that she has shared with me in the long time that I have known her.

The make-believe of a perfect fishing day is composed of many things. Often, in my case at least, very little to do with the number of trout caught. Or even the fact that I ever saw a whisker of a fin at all.

Fishing is also the people you share the river with who - like the finest formulated fly dressing - keep memories afloat long past their sail-by date.

Because this book is more than the scribblings and the scratchings of a man on a river bank solely in pursuit of its contents, I am indebted to the following people who are as much a part of my days on The Hollow as the streams, the bridges, the trees, the birds and the fish, lost, found and occasionally tricked.

Ron Clark, my very best friend and companion at all times, for ever. Vincent Meade who introduced me to the far side of fly-fishing. John Goddard who proved to me that it's possible to find energy you're not supposed to have. Stewart Canham who hasn't an unfunny thing to say about me (and vice versa) - and 'The Black Git'.

Neighbours Bernard James, Reg Windle and Eddy Starr for their friendship and patience. Hoagy Carmichael who gave me 'The Carrot'. Bill Parry-Davies, for The Camel & Pubic. Pierre Affre, Tim Benn, John Brown, Brian Clarke, Peter Drake, Peter Flint, John Ginifer, Kenny Hall, David Hopson, Preben Torp Jacobsen, Peter Lapsley, Darrell Martin, Frank Martin, Dennis Mutton, my cousin Hilary and Trevor Pharaoh, Geoffrey Rivaz, Lionel Sweet, Dick Talleur, my Uncle Doug and Uncle Ray, Barry Woodward, Len Wright, the owners of the river whose request to remain anonymous I respect, and the many rods on The Hollow, past and present, who gave me encouragement over the years to write this chronicle.

And to those people who didn't come down to the river with me, but who are always close.

To Nancy, my mother, for not letting me keep my maggots in the fridge and who therefore drove me to flyfishing. To Doris, my wife, up the track waiting for me with a towel. To Robin, my father, who is up there eternally looking down on me. To Robin, my young son, who is down there constantly looking up at me. To Gerald and Jane Robins, next door, my second parents.

To the many editors, past and present, of magazines who gave me the chance to air my thoughts and who have allowed me to publish some of these thoughts again in this book: Roy Eaton and Sandy Leventon of *Trout & Salmon*, John Wilshaw of *Trout Fisherman*, Mark Bowler of *Fly-Tying & Fly-Fishing*, Brian Harris of *International Flyfisher*, John Randolf of *Fly Fisherman*, and various editors of *The Flyfishers' Club Journal*.

To Bohuslav Martinu and Ralph Vaughan Williams who scored the soundtrack to this book, and who I recommend you listen to when reading it.

To Merlin Unwin who dared take on this book (and all the creative tantrums that were to accompany it), who took control of all the words and sketches and moulded them in the shape of the thing you hold now in your hands.

Lastly, to Nick Lyons who hounded me to put pen to paper in the first place; for so long, from so far away. If only we could spend the same number of hours together on a river bank as we have spent writing to one other.

January

RIVER IN A LANDSCAPE

The year started so quietly. The muffled sound of cotton wool tyres woke me. Bat-eyed and still in bed, I stared across the bedroom through a crack in the curtains and watched the ghostly shape of a hoary white Land Rover prowl across Sticklepath Bridge and up the track from The Hollow.

Late morning. This was the first sign of life.

I got dressed and scratched a hole in the ice on the inside of the window on my way downstairs. Across the yard, the Big House was still fast asleep behind tight curtains. The cars parked outside lay snuggled under white blankets. I had decided to walk to the village to get milk and to see if anyone was still alive after the New Year celebrations.

The back door snapped open. A star-speckled night cast in cold had set the flints in ice. My heels clanged like church bells on the track down to the bridge, my footsteps softening when I stepped onto the grass on the river bank. The gurgling behind the hut was the Meadow Stream diving head-first into ancient woodland. Oaks, beeches, ashes, sycamores, alders, chestnuts and Scots pines draped in wintriness cracked in the cold. Icicles hung like woolly mammoths' tusks from the branches. I headed up river towards the road.

Up on the Marshes, the air was clear and still. I could hear the village turning in its sleep half a mile away, and the growl of a phantom Land Rover crossing the road bridges at the head of the water meadows on its way back from the shop.

I wondered if my fish was still there.

At this time of day, at this time of year, the sun is at its strongest. Even so, there was hardly enough light to let me see if the monster red-nosed grayling I had been after every spare Saturday afternoon for the last two months was still lying deep in the Church Pool, a cold salmon-sized hatch pool at the top end of The Hollow. In my mind I could see it, wagging its tail at me on the gravels, padded out on all sides by a dozen smaller members of the shoal. I had had my last chance at him yesterday but I had seriously bodged it.

When I'm out with rod and nymphs, I normally carry a little round, plastic box with me, three inches across, two inches deep. This contains three small wooden spools of fuse wire and a selection of hooks to tie made-to-measure wire nymphs. The size of hook is dictated not by the size of insect I wish to imitate, but by the amount of weight needed to deliver it at mouth level to the fish. But with my hands pushed into gloves, it was too cold for delicate procedures.

Instead, I had a pre-tied lead-backed shrimp the weight of a snow shoe on the end of my hook. On entry, this heavyweight had my grayling finning backwards on my first cast, forwards again on my second - then sideways on my third, into a fierce rush of water the colour of a glacier, and away.

It was the last I was to see of this grayling that season.

Yesterday had been the last day of the year, and the last chance for me to go out with a fly-rod until April when the trout season opens again. Today I wasn't on the river fishing; I was out staking my claim, making sure that once again, The Hollow knew to expect me at any time in the new year.

With rod, or without.

———————

January is an important month for the river. Lifeless and black, it flows slow and heavy. Weary after a year of running without a rest, she flows back into herself to collect her thoughts. There is much to think about. Not of giving - this she has done every other month of the year. Thoughts of 'taking' preoccupy her now.

The contents of the deep scrapes in the gravels, wounds cut by trout, are left for her to nurse. Wrapped in gravel cradles, the abandoned trout eggs planted there are her children now. All she asks is one thing: to be left alone.

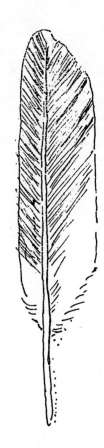

On a warm summer evening in six months' time, the shallows spread with newly-hatched fly, the surface rocking with the soundless pecks of tiny mouths - with more fish than you have casts to throw - you will remember this time when you deserted the river, leaving her alone in a frozen silence.

On my way across the Marshes, I passed half a mile of scarred shallows. At the station, I lifted the collar of my oilskin and wrapped my scarf round for a second time. Curls of feather down shook into the air. My wife and I had decided to have goose for Christmas dinner. I had ordered one from the farm. On Christmas Eve, I had spent all day in the stable plucking it, finishing up with fluff in my hair, my beard, my coat, my scarf; everywhere. The man at the garage thought there had been a fall of snow when he saw me.

The village was filled with stray zombies. A House of Hammer graveyard, the main street was haunted by floating people in misty vapours. On my way back to the Wild Wood Lodge, I decided to check my baits.

In January, there are pike to be caught.

At the end of the summer, I had lowered a galvanised tank onto the shallows of the stream by a rickety footbridge in front of the Boss's cottage. Drilled full of holes to let the water run through. This improvised cage is where I keep my pike baits. Fresh and silver, not one longer than eight inches, these baits are the spoils of many autumn grayling and dace sessions. Carefully transported back in a green canvas bag, the little fish are tipped into the tank. Ready for action at the drop of a rusty-rimmed goldfish net, they're there for whenever I can find the time to walk to the bottom of The Hollow, to the Back of Beyond.

Down in these bleak parts, on a late January afternoon, a northerly wind has a clear run at you across open meadows. It can whip up a chill that stabs like a driven nail. Only one thing is colder, that's the steely glint in the eye of a female pike making her way up through Barge Bay from the canal, where it crosses the river below an old iron bridge, up into the sheep-scattered meadows of the Back of Beyond, swirling with frosty mists straight out of Macbeth.

Sinister and silent, it's here her search begins for a mate, and a larder of soft-sided roach.

It had been the pursuit of pike in January that had first introduced me to upper reaches of this arctic, white-walled Berkshire valley - and to a river I was to abandon everything to live next to.

Tired of late nights and weekends of work, weary of London, I had decided to visit my country cousin who worked as a waitress in a restaurant in a small town close to The Hollow. She had married the chef, and settled down. Trained in Switzerland, her chef not only knew how to de-bone and cook pike, more importantly, he knew how to catch them.

On my first day, he took me and a box of sprats (so high you could have a conversation with them) to the canal just outside the town. Standing in a cloud of breath, I couldn't concentrate on the wonky sprat pirouetting in the milky waters below the lock. The sparkle of the stream running behind me, parallel to the canal, glinted in the corner of my eye.

Spinning circles the size of angels' haloes as they sipped invisible food from the surface, the stream's little fish were putting on a livelier mid-winter show than the sullen frost-bitten pike, fumbling around like blind men, looking for my bait in the dingy depths of the canal.

As I gazed over my shoulder into the crystal clarity of the forbidden stream, the strands of bronze weed tresses wove a tapestry of untold fishing tales in my imagination. Tales unknown, that needed to be spun - by me. It was a stream I had to fish.

It was there, on that frost-gripped January day, I made the decision that was to change my life. A day that is rare in anybody's life. A day that is like no other, for after it nothing that happens is ever the same.

The following Saturday, squeezing the contents of my one-bedroom flat into the back of my car, I said goodbye to Islington. An hour and a half later I was back in a vacant bedroom in my cousin's semi on a housing estate at the end of the High Street. That night I wrote a classified ad to put in the local paper. That Thursday, it appeared. That Friday, I got one reply. That Saturday I was bouncing down a farm track to the Big House. A poky one-bedroom attic flat was on offer with a bathroom, a kitchen, a hall with a round window shaped like a daisy and a sitting room with a tiny fireplace with two round-shouldered logs sleeping in it. That Sunday morning, I moved into my tree-top nest.

That evening, as I carried the last box from the car, the river winked at me across a field laced with snow.

The Big House stands in a gentle chalkstone slope that rolls down into The Hollow. Here, the backbone of the valley, the river, twists and turns through wide open meadows, dashing in and out of fox-filled woods, creating forked carriers, side-streams and drains on all sides. Wild, restless, it is a part of the South of

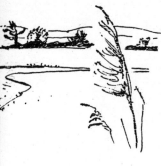

England that has not yet decided how it is going to settle down.

The Hollow is the second-last flyfishing beat on the river. On the cusp of a trout and coarse fishery, Noah would have wanted it to step aboard and come along with him as the prime example of a chalkstream's ability to 'explode' life out of sun and water - big, fat, lush, profuse; flora, fauna, flies and fishes of every freshwater kind. If, that is, he had been able to find a partner capable of the same prodigious output to accompany The Hollow onto the Ark.

In the twenty miles above The Hollow, there are more noble, more manicured, more famous beats attracting the more tradition chalkstream angler. The breed who like the tame, anaesthetised thing. The angler who gets his name on a syndicate list with a long view, who wants to sleep easy through the close season - and in many cases the season itself - knowing that when he finally gets old and frail he will be able to wheel himself up and down the steam-pressed banks of his super-trimmed, obstacle-free beat in a Bath chair knowing he need never fear the tiniest bump.

Below The Hollow, damp meadows and woodland make for better duck swamps and pheasant thickets than trout water. Below that, the river kerb-crawls through a market town before joining up with a canal and finally flowing into the Thames where, having lost every last shred of its identity, it slithers stagnantly towards the City (from whence I make my daily escape) and on to the sea.

For this reason, The Hollow is more than a trouty, flyfishing beat. It's a threatened landscape where a spirited chalkstream makes its last stand.

For over sixty years, the Big House's stables, kennels and cobbled yard had been the focus for the local hunt. But the hunting days had long gone. With it, the horses, the hounds and the people who rode with them. Like a large crumbling fruit cake, the Big House was well past its sell-by date.

Tucked away at the back of the main building, is where Lady McFarlane lives. At the time I moved in, her home had been the Big House for more than a quarter of a century. In all the years I was to know her, I never once saw her wearing slacks, jeans, tracksuit bottoms or any other trouser-like thing. Whether she was digging gardens, chopping logs or walking dogs. She was always the Lady, and always wore a skirt - and in foul weather, a distinctive crimson anorak. This was accompanied by a head scarf and black welly-boots when she walked her labrador on late, wet autumn afternoons.

Lady McFarlane was no stranger to hard work. Rosy-cheeked, cheeks blooming with health - a portrait of a woman by Frans Hals - she and her husband had once run their own dairy farm before moving to The Hollow. But her past was always to remain a mystery - mainly because I never asked about it. The other mystery was the exact length of her light brown hair which she always wore up in a bun.

With a smiling mouth and a determined eye, you knew your place with Lady McFarlane. Whereas a trout in the right place was guaranteed to patch up any neighbourly misunderstanding in the general locality, if I had ever crossed Lady McFarlane, no stupid fish - or token bunch of flowers - could have hoped to compensate for the shame and sorrow I would have felt. Fortunately, in all the twenty years I have shared The Hollow with her, we have agreed on most things.

Long before I appeared on the scene, she'd spilt the house into flats. Although her kitchen was at the back of the Big House, facing away from the action, she knew everything that went on. Even so, the day I arrived to view the Attic I don't think she realised that I was going to be a resident in her yard - for life.

Handing me the key to the front door and the Attic, she quickly let me have the bad news. The river at the end of the track was out of bounds to people who lived in the Big House. Only 'fishermen', in 'Volvos', with 'tickets' were allowed there.

The next day, through the branches of the cypress tree that framed my little window, I saw the potter who rattled around in the flat below me heading off down the track with her two dalmatians. In a hunchback position, my head following the slope of the attic roof and tilting towards the window, I watched her turn the bend at the bottom of the field and carry on past an acre of Christmas trees. Instead of walking straight on towards the farm, she turned left down the track to Sticklepath Bridge, and crossed over the river. Like a rabbit sucked into a hole, she disappeared into the forbidden woods.

'If she can do that, so can I,' I said to myself as I set off down the track the next day.

It was a late Saturday afternoon. Everyone in the Big House was wrapped round log fires, paraffin heaters, or one another. With the entire world concentrating on keeping warm, this was the safest time to go trespassing; or so I thought.

I hadn't reached the bend, when the river breathed a figure out of the trees. It walked across the bridge towards me out of the mist of its own breath.

It was the Boss. The riverkeeper.

'You must live in the Big House,' he said, his jacket wide open and the top button of his shirt undone displaying a plantation of grey hair.

I didn't have to say anything. The statement was a prelude to open season for mouth aerobics. I stood listening, watching the sun drop slowly behind his right shoulder, dissolving like a soluble asprin into a chilly winter's evening sky. In length, he told me a doctor had taken over the fishing lease from the Estate and there were plenty of vacancies on the beat. If I wanted, he would show me round and let me have a look.

'But it'll take at least four hours, mind. And you won't get to see it all.'

It was dark when I arrived back at the stable yard. Lady McFarlane was chopping logs by torch-light in one of the stable blocks. I told her I'd met the Boss and he'd volunteered to show me the river. She laughed.

'If the walk doesn't kill you, the talk will.'

———————

In the mile and a half of main river that glides through water-meadows and woodland, many fingers of water have a hand in shaping The Hollow trout fishery. Streams tangle as they slip in and out and over and under one another like a basket of silvery snakes. A criss-cross mesh of carriers, fast shallows, broad idle glides, round-shouldered woodland streams, classic wide-open water-meadow runs, sparkling riffles; and at the bottom, black, unfathomable waters holding, God knows?

The Boss had calculated that in better days when all the drains and carriers were filled to the brim, when hatches were in operation and the Estate employed drowners to regulate the flow, there would have been thirty-two miles of fishable double-bank water.

Nowadays, many of these hatches stand like gravestones in the water-meadows, marking spots where crystal clear veins that once freshened the surrounding fields had died. Fifty years on, all that remained was a network of dry bones bleached green with neglect, hanging together on the smashed ribcage of flyfishing streams of a bygone age.

The Boss's brick and tile cottage stands in the centre of the beat by an orchard and a stream that feeds his stew tanks, aerating next year's stock. According to Lady McFarlane, the Boss had lived in The Hollow for ever - at least since time began. No date was ever given; there was talk of wars; but which wars, and when? But a gentle 'rrrr' that rounded off certain words suggested that he hailed from north, rather than south, of the border.

Friend and neighbour, the Boss and I were to pass many happy days together, in the spring, summer, autumn and the winter - whenever we needed to catch up on our very different lives. No matter how far they drifted, they always met up in the one place: the river.

The greatest of countryman, the Boss had a photographic memory. He knew every flower, shrub, tree and insect on the river; the latter he knew better than the back of his hand. If news got to him that a single gudgeon had swum into The Hollow, give him an hour and he'd find it. More importantly, he understood the geography, physics and dynamics of a river better that those who called themselves experts.

His love of every fluid ounce and every woody inch of The Hollow resulted in him feeling that he was responsible for the care and attention of not just the streams in The Hollow, but the entire river valley. Total protection, he called it. His commitment ran much further, and deeper - way down into the very aquifers that fed the valley and pumped life into it. The way he saw it was that their husbandry and careful management was as important to the long-term health and flow of the river, in general, as any work he could do locally on The Hollow.

Full of shrewd advice and penetrating comment, the Boss was one of the greatest riverkeepers in England. And because my world is the river, to me he is the greatest river keeper in the world.

At either end of The Hollow there's a pub. One, just up the main street in the village, serves beer and lunch-time snacks across the bar. The other, the Manor, is on the main road opposite the farm, attached to a restaurant that has earned the highest gastronomic accolades.

Two-thirds of the way down the river is the last outpost before the Back of Beyond: a little wooden hut with a lawn that runs down to the river to a ford used by tractors from the farm. This hut belongs to the Doctor who owns the fishing rights. His practice is in the Midlands, so he has far to travel. At the end of a long day when his bed appears to be on the other side of the world, he would stay over in a sleeping-bag on the sofa. An oil lamp in the window indicated that he was in residence.

Thirty years ago, the Shed (as it's known by the farm people) or the Doctor's Cottage (as it's known by the Boss, as the custodian of the fishery's status) mysteriously caught fire destroying the roof and seriously damaging the contents which at that time housed the previous occupant's fishing library. He had also been a long-standing rod on the water.

Fate is a strange thing. Ten years later, I walked into a second-hand fishing bookstore in London. Flicking through the books on display I found one with that previous occupant's library plate stuck on the inside cover. It was a book written by another flyfisherman who had fished the surrounding area in the thirties and forties. He must have walked, even fished, the bank opposite the Doctor's Cottage.

For the second time, this book, with smoke-stained spine and sepia page-ends, is now back by the river that spawned its birth and where it ended up living. Only this time it had moved up to the middle of the beat from the bottom end: to the Attic.

It was meant to come to rest there. Just like I was meant to come to rest there.

———————

I rented the draughty tree-top attic flat for five years. My teeth chattering in the rafters waiting for my chance to pop the question to Lady McFarlane.

Now that the hunt horses were grazing on greener pastures in the sky, I presented my plan to her: to buy one of the empty stable blocks on the other side of the yard from the Big House, and turn it into my home. I had one stable in particular in mind. The one by the track. The one nearest the river.

The idea was accepted, a price agreed and, like a demented bug in a nut, I immediately started hollowing out the inside of my stable, shaping a home inside. On trains, on buses, on lunch-breaks - on and on I went, sketching my vision on backs of envelopes, cornflake packets, cigarette packs. Anywhere blank enough to accommodate my mad schemings. The stable, built of red brick and tile, was constructed at the turn of the century. Until the fifties, it housed eight horses, but now it was derelict. My plan was to convert it into a home, and a 'fishing lodge'. A meeting place for fishing friends next to the river.

With pencil and paper, I stripped out the hay loft and drew in two bedrooms upstairs, joined by a cat-walk. This way I could expose the delicate cob-web rafters of the roof to a large hall below. My idea was to create a 'town' within the four walls. Rooms leading off the large hall would be small 'buildings within a building'. In the summer, I wanted to be able to throw open the front door, the floor-to-roof hall becoming a 'town square' to gather in. With paviour floors, covered with rugs in winter.

I wanted a twin-window door set in the interior brick wall I had designed, with bricks laid to form various patterns and topped by a dog-tooth course. I wanted these doors to open into the first 'warm area' - a sitting-room. Inside, a large brick fireplace, wooden floors, a panelled ceiling and on one wall, a bookcase made out of the timbers that had once supported the roof before they were replaced by channels and piers that would need to be built-in to allow the ceiling to be lowered.

The second 'building' leading off the hall would be my study, with an uninterrupted view across fields. This would also have panelled floors and ceiling, with built-in cases made from original materials - and my 'World of Fly-tying' cabinet, with thirty drawers stuffed with more feathers, furs and silks than a Victorian millinery shop.

At the south, river-facing side of the stable, I planned building a large tiled bathroom. Leading into this, with a back door pointing down to Sticklepath Bridge, a cobbled hall, or tackle room - a Decontamination Room which I could dive into covered in anything, or followed by anyone the river introduced me to, nasty or nice. At the other end, I'd planned the area to be divided using two of the original stable doors as partitions. One area, a kitchen, the other, a dining room and library.

Upstairs, I wanted the rafters of the north-facing bedroom to be left exposed. The south-facing bedroom, overlooking the river, I wanted pine-panelled. The far end of this room looked down to the river and across the Berkshire Downs. On my plans, I sketched an arched window, leaving just enough brickwork around it to give necessary support. I wanted nothing to stand between me and the river.

That winter, I kept myself warm by throwing my arms wildly in the air with the architect by my side briefed to make all my limb circlings and facial acrobatics legal and structurally sound. My body language at dictionary's end, my handy-man skills amounting to nothing, I let the builders take over.

From base camp in the Attic, I watched them arrive in a flurry of sand and cement in the awesome shape of the Five Steves. Steve, the builder; Steve the chippie; Steve the plumber; Steve the electrician; and to make things easier, Young Steve, the general dogsbody. Walk onto the site, shout 'Steve!' and you had an instant party.

All through the winter into spring, into summer, ladders came, ladders went. Walls went up, walls came down. Roofs came off, roofs went back on again. Ceilings were raised, floors lowered. Windows came out; dogs, cats, autumn leaves piled in.

Finally, the Scots pine tree I'd marked in Robins Wood was felled, its trunk measured, stripped and pulled from the woods by four of the Steves and hoisted up as the supports for my front porch. The fifth Steve nailed the mounted antlers I'd found in a junk shop above the door.

Now all it needed was a name.

The focal point in a rolling landscape of fields, woods, hills, sky and river - an ever-changing picture impossible to frame - it was a location impossible to name, although hundreds spring to mind. But as the place that was to give me warmth and shelter when I was blown off the river, I named my new home after the woods that shielded it, and me, from the wet prevailing south-west winds.

Which is least stressful? Marriage, death - or building works? Death: at least you don't have to clean up afterwards. That Christmas, on a still winter's day - still no wood floors downstairs, still no paint on any of the walls, still no central-heating anywhere in the house, still no staircase (only a step ladder leading up to the bedroom), my wife and I moved into the Wild Wood Lodge.

The first night, we slipped between the sheets like ice-lollies back into their wrappers. Assuming the pre-natal position, I listened to a new night noise outside my window, the hush of a silver river sliding through the bare black trees of the ancient wood, hanging with chandeliers of ice. Not a warming sound, but the sound I had come to hear. A sound I wanted to get used to. A pulse I wanted to match, in time with mine.

At last I had a bed so near the river that if I was to dream of trout and fall out of bed, I'd fall in the river. But that night, I dreamed of warmer things.

Spring was a long way off. There was a lot to do.

It was January. After a year, the conversion was almost complete. To the Five Steves, this meant the windows were in. The largest, the bedroom window on the south-facing wall, stood the same height as me. With an arched top, it swung wide open on a central pivot - or you could lift the entire window frame out. Either way, I could make a huge hole in the wall leaving nothing but icy morning air between me - standing eyes closed, breast out, nostrils open - and the smells and the sound of the river jangling through the glassy, ice-bound woods.

With only two tiny eyebrow windows there previously, this side of the building had never come face to face with the river before. Now it confronted it. Sticklepath Bridge would never leave its sight again.

This bridge is the end of the line for fishermen who come to fish the top section of The Hollow. There, by a small parking area, is the Mad House, the fishing hut, where you can always find somebody willing to hear your craziest fishing story or loony tale of woe, if not at the table on the river-bank at lunch-time, in torch-light at the end of a long summer day.

The Mad House's arrival wasn't entirely conventional. Sitting bow-backed on my window-sill in the Attic, my spine following the curve of the ceiling, I had watched with great interest as a mysterious hut hovered down the track at hedge-height. It was only when it passed a gap that I realised the hut wasn't capable of independent movement - it was, in fact, strapped on the back of a lorry.

Now in place, the close season at its deepest and darkest, the Mad House was soaked in creosote. Resting on a pillow of rhododendron bushes, shutters closed, its white-haired roof gripped in frost, it looked like an old man slumbering soundly, soundlessly.

Inside, garden seats were curled up in a corner. The fishing record book had been taken away to somewhere warm and dry to hibernate - probably in amongst dish towels in one of the Boss's kitchen drawers. The spindly-legged table, where the record book had spent the season, groaned as it dreamed over the colossal weight of some of the fish that had been thrown on the scales at mayfly time, many over four pounds.

The Wild Wood Lodge was in its finishing stages. But I was a door short. A door for the bathroom cupboard.

Funnily, it had been one of the first things I'd got, and therefore was one of the first things to find a home in my sketchy house plan. But from the moment I set eyes on it, it had eluded me at every turn, all summer long. And now, in deepest winter, with the work almost completed, it had vanished. One thing I'd learnt was that somehow, at some time or other, it would materialize - from somewhere. Just like it had done that March when I had found it.

To escape the cramped attic, the three-by-twos, the two-by-threes and the Five Steves, I'd gone for a weekend to a different river to meet a different kind of fly. A fly I have something in common with: the march brown. We share the same birth-sign. We're both Arians.

I had heard reports that in true Aries spirit, march browns had already blown open the flyfisher's season and were exploding off the River Usk, at Crickhowell. Typically, they were selecting the hottest and most fiery hour of the day at this time of year to do this: mid-day. This was the only time the sun had the strength to part the fast-moving clouds and spread silver across the land.

None of your slow, silky, summer chalkstreams for this rough and tumble guy. He's at his happiest huddled away in some cruel corner of a pounding, acid, rain-fed river, with wind blowing the last drops of winter's phlegm from its lungs.

When I've been on rivers waiting for him to pounce, hatches have lasted an hour or so. A fast and furious hour at that, starting at mid-day and ripping through to lunch-time. Or - for the clocks are put back at this time of year - starting at lunch-time and cracking through to coffee.

Either way, I skip lunch in the hotel to be there. To be by the river. But not just to fish that vital hour, like everyone else. No, I had managed to extend the hatch considerably, pre and post hatch. I'm there fishing an hour before everyone arrives, there for the hatch, and I am still there an hour after everyone has gone. All the time making direct contact with the fat little red and yellow speckled Usk terriers who have shared a winter in the stream with the same food they were now ferociously pulling off the surface - only in a different form. Proof enough that the march brown nymph, although a crawler, is no creep when it comes to survival.

So what about these two hours I'd managed to add to the march brown agenda?

The march brown nymph is built like the sole of a deep-sea diver's boot. Flat and broad, he clamps himself to the bottom like a bathroom plunger, as if his life depended on it - which, in fact, it does. To call him a 'stone-crawler' or a 'creeper' (this is how he's boxed neatly away in books) - is only accurate when he's motionless. When he has to move, the march brown nymph shifts smartly, engaging 4-wheel drive to cross rocks and boulders.

Strangely, for something that first opens its eyes to the world in March and April and therefore is born under the sign of the Ram, the march brown is not in too much of a hurry to butt his head through the surface.

When it comes to launching, the nymph fidgets nervously around mid-water, pushing off stones and returning back to them for another trial run. Finally he leaps off the rock with the highest peak, and swings upwards with the flow towards the surface, wasting not the slightest second.

Although impetuous to begin with, when he reaches the surface the march brown is cautious. Our Arian is an Ephemeropteran after all, doing what all good Ephemeropoterans do. As such he conforms to the correct procedures prior to take-off, with all due care and attention. All the time avoiding the attention of any trout who cares to be in the vicinity.

My catch totals indicate that this period of intense um-ing and ah-ing and routine checks, starts approximately an hour before the actual hatch. This conclusion isn't the result of diving with wet-suit and goggles. It's when I start to get bangs on my hatching march brown imitation.

This pattern is designed to imitate one of these march browns. It's called, after great thought, the Two-Minds Nymph. It incorporates only two tying materials. Or is it three? I can never

make up my mind about this. Anyway, whichever of these
materials accounts for its effectiveness - well, you make your
mind up.

To address the trout, I position myself at the end of a fast
run where the water pounds off the rocks and dives deep down to
boulders. On the point of my leader, I put a large, furry nymph
containing lots of lead so that it plummets to the bottom. The
pattern doesn't matter; it's unimportant. This pattern is simply a
ledger wearing a fur coat. On a dropper, about four foot up and
about the same distance from the reel line, I tie a Two-Minds
Nymph.

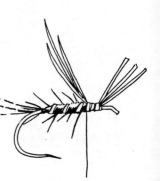

Don't clip!

Now when it comes to fishing the Two-Minds Nymph, the
flyfisher can be in as many minds as he likes about the depth it
has to swim. I investigate them all, with one cast. Not from top to
bottom, from bottom to top.

I cast the rig directly upstream and let it sink. By the time
it is opposite me it has sunk as much as it is able, allowing for
the depth of river and flow rate. As it passes me, I lift the rod and
let it slowly rise so that by the time it is directly below me the
river pace has forced it to the surface.

When the fish start to take the adult I change to a March
Brown dun pattern and fish the top. This I do until the hatch
finishes.

When the hatch is over, I still have an hour to go. I take a
walk and go out looking for stillborns - march browns that
haven't managed to brave the elements and escape the river.
They can be found crumpled up in eddies, under banks in slow
pools and trapped in the sides of glides.

You may not find as many fish out in search of these washed
up tragedies, but often the ones you find are the biggest fish.
Once you've done this, the afternoon and the hills are yours, for
there's not much more fishing to be done.

Deciding to take a long-cut back to the hotel, I walked up a
track to the road. As I climbed the hillside, I saw a derelict
building on the slope and went to take a closer look and poke my
nose about a bit.

The door was open. The floor was covered with straw where

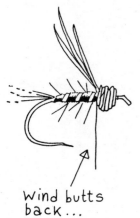

wind butts
back...

... fold
points over
...

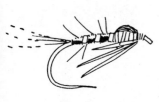

... secure
under

sheep had wintered. Then my eyes fell on what I'd been looking for. Off its hinges, hanging at an angle was my bathroom cupboard door.

To this day, I still don't think I was stealing. It looked abandoned, I don't think anyone wanted it, and I don't think it would have done anything other than rot away slowly if I hadn't recognised its full potential and, well, stolen it. Post-rationalisation apart, how can you steal something that's yours?

I managed to get most of this withered pine door in the back of the car with the hatch open and the seats down. Happy to know that it was loved again, it hung out of the back of the car whistling all the way back to the Wild Wood Lodge building site. Here it was propped up in the Secret Garden, a small walled garden on the river side of the property, ready to be stripped, polished, and hung.

———

Toilet seats, baths, window frames, a bird's nest in the insulation foam. With so many things in desperate need of attention that Spring, I confess I forgot all about my door. Then one morning in June, I got an S.O.S from the river. The River God, the most authoritative and respected rod on The Hollow, had driven his Mercedes into the Nursery Stream that runs alongside the orchard at the bottom of the Boss's garden.

Renowned for its difficult trout, there are really only two places in the Nursery Stream where you can fish for the contents of this tricky little carrier, barely four-foot wide and six inches deep. One of these spots is a large pool under an ash tree. It's possible to take the occasional trout out of this bucket, but only if you're a scholar of Hiawatha. The other prime spot is right in front of the Boss's parking area where the trout get so used to people, they wave a fin at you as you pass. I pretend not to notice.

Because no-one fishes so close to the Boss's home, respecting his privacy rather than for any other reason, by and large (and some of them are very large indeed) these trout know they're safe. That particular day the River God had adopted a new tactic, an entirely unorthodox approach: Why fish for trout when you can run them over?

The River God had been up to see the Boss at his cottage and offered to give him a lift back down the track to the Mad House. Now, as I knew on my very first encounter with him, whatever short-comings the Boss might have, they lengthened considerably when it came to finding something to say. A keeper in love with his river, it filled him to the brim with stories, and he narrated them on a loop; again, again - and again.

Stories like the morning he woke up and found a pelican fishing the pool outside his cottage. A woman from the local Royal Society for the Protection of Birds office came to take it back to the safari park. A woman dressed in an evening dress and stilettoes. A woman with a beard; a man, in fact.

This may have been the story the Boss was narrating and that had disastrously distracted the River God in a hurry to either get to the Mad House and get his rod up and get fishing, or get out of earshot. We'll never know. Whatever the story, just past the ash tree, tipped at a comfortable forty-five degree tilt, front wheel snuggled deep into the marl was the River God's white Mercedes. He'd driven it off the road, across the bank and straight into the stream.

Help was near at hand. But an hour later, Ron Darlington, his brother Roy, Gordon Mackie, all from Skues's beloved Abbots Barton beat on the River Itchen and guests on the river that day - and myself - still hadn't managed to shift it. Work was not speeded up by the waves of giggles from the River God who contributed little, other than chuckling to himself and saying 'Oh dear', over and over.

We tried stones, but we needed something level. We tried planks, but we needed something broader. We tried gate posts, but we needed something flatter. A surface was what was required.

Five minutes later I was driving back down the track with the answer. Sticking out the back of my car again, this time whistling the tune the seven dwarves sing when off to work they go, was my door. Placing it under the front wheels and pushing like elephants, Roy, Ron, Gordon and myself had the ghostly Mercedes slipping up the bank and out. The Boss offering to clear up, we all went back down to the Mad House for lunch.

At the bottom of the beat above the Old Iron Bridge is the Back of Beyond. If the Marshes is the South Pole, the Back of Beyond is the North Pole. It's as far away from the Wild Wood Lodge as you can hope to get in a day, without having to pack your passport. Even for me, to set out there is like going for a holiday. I always take a flask. Sometimes a change of underwear.

On arrival, three areas tout for my business. All totally different, all performing better at different times of the day - and in particular, at different times of the season. Diverse in character as they undoubtedly are, these individual flyfishing dream-makers all have one thing in common: solitude.

Crossing over a stile below the ford, you leave the classic elegance of the main river behind. Nipping at your heels like a terrier, the Red Gate Shallows rush you into an abandoned fishing wasteland. At the head of some shallows, the river digs its toes into the gravel scoops behind the footbridge supports, using them as starting blocks. For two hundred yards it races you down rapids, over trout the size of small canoes, between hawthorn, alder and sloe. The pace is breathless, and more than adequately oxygenated. Overdosed on soluble oxygen, in the Spring, olives take off down this frothy freeway travelling at high speeds regardless of the wild trout patrols waiting in lay-bys to pick them up.

Within yards, the river is a completely different place. At the end of the Red Gate Shallows, it hits an island head-on. Its force divided - a firework extinguished - a fizzled-out flow drops off the back of both sides of the island at funeral procession pace. Burned out, but still smoking, it shunts its way down to the Old Iron Bridge.

Explored, but not yet fully discovered, this wide water is a paradise for a different kind of adventurer. An adventurer who doesn't want to go anywhere. For this is where you park yourself at the mayfly time of year. Sometimes for days. Sometimes for days of the ultimate in absolutely nothing at all. But sometimes, and this has only happened to me once in a decade, a solitary fish appears; a fish to keep fishy dreams three dimensional for ten years or more. For this reason, I go back for more.

Moor Reach trickles down out of the woods and keeps a strong flow all the summer, even though it hands half its width over to watercress beds. Here you can spend an afternoon sitting on a tussock watching trout tails slice water to the sound of shrimp backs cracking.

A lesser drain, the Sheep Dip, throbs between the main river and Moor Reach. Early in the season, big fish travel up there from Moor Reach to spawn. There are holes waiting there for them to hide in - at this time of year, at least.

I had spent the morning with the snipe in this lonely part of the world. This was the stream I had decided to follow. The weed hadn't started to clog this delicate carrier yet. For the time being it was still gurgling out of the poplar plantation in the Wetlands that it cut through, like blood out of a clean wound. In a few week's time, sunlight would suck out what little oxygen there was left in the flow and the stream would scab over, lime green weed covering it like a poultice over gangrene.

Half way up, I spotted a fish take a fly under a little bridge that hadn't been there last season - but that was a long time ago. A difficult trout, by all accounts, tucked well under.

The first cast fell short. The fly was inspected by a grayling I hadn't noticed. The second cast was a little wild, but I managed to get the fly under the bridge. For fear of scaring the trout, I let it drift down. It hadn't touched the line made by the bridge's shadow, dividing light and dark, when the surface tilted slightly and the trout's nose sniffed the fly under.

The nose, with a trout close behind, ran off up to the other side of the small bridge; but I held him back. The fish leapt in the air on my side of the bridge and dived deep into a weed clump before tearing back upstream again, building up the necessary momentum for a second missile launch, this time sea to air.

Hurtling out of the river, the fish stood vertically on its tail. Here its luck changed. It had either misjudged where it was, or miscalculated the proportions of the pocket-sized stage on which it was performing. Either way, the confused trout's head hit the underside of the little bridge with the sound of a wet towel bashed on a rock.

The count-down began. A boxer on the ropes, the trout slumped back on the current and let himself be carried down into my hand waiting in the water to receive him.

The fight over, I decided to cross the small bridge and take a look up river. With one foot on the bridge, I overbalanced and landed on my back in a thick mattress of soft, sweet-smelling mud that looked like tar out of a sailor's pipe. The splat aroused an immediate chorus from the pheasants in the Wetlands.

'Who is that bridge?' they seemed to be asking.

Still at mud level, I crawled over to introduce myself, but this wasn't necessary - we'd already met. The bridge was my door. Lifting it up, I dragged it across to the Game Hut to be collected. If that is, I remembered.

By now, it had a name: the Magic Door. It kept vanishing and reappearing.

In the summer, at sunrise, clouds of rooks gossip their way over the Wild Wood Lodge heading South from one side of the river valley to the other. In the evening, as the sun goes down, they come back the same way. Cemetery is on the same flight path.

A deep, narrow cut at the top end of The Hollow, Cemetery runs down from the Marshes with woods on one side and, on the bend at the bottom, a withy bed of sedge as high as an elephant's eye. It finishes up in a thundering hatch pool that it shares with the Broadwater.

A little rustic wicket-gate at the dog's leg at the top of the stream is really the only feature of any interest on this carrier. Except, perhaps, for a mysterious stone that stands in the meadow. But no-one talks about this stone much. Tipped to one side, it looks like an old cow, sick and grey, lying motionless in the grass. Little is known about it, but there have been theories. One thing we know is that it shouldn't be there. Geologically, it's a misfit. And because it couldn't have arrived by any other means, someone, at some time in history, must have put it there.

I was once told a story about this part of the river by an old man, long dead, who had fished The Hollow for many years.

Late one summer evening, he was making his way from the Marshes down Cemetery when he saw a man in a trench coat and a boy all tackled up standing looking into the big hatch at the bottom. He passed them, wished them 'Good evening', crossed over and carried on down the Meadow Stream, meeting the riverkeeper on the Nursery Stream, whoever he was in those long-gone, pre-Boss days. The old man told the keeper that he had come across the man and the boy.

There hadn't been any guests that day. Straightaway, with poachers in mind, the keeper ran up to the hatch where he met a rod also on his way back from Cemetery. This angler hadn't seen them.

The keeper met another rod up at the Church Pool, at the top of the beat. Again, no sign of the man and boy. The keeper went on to check every corner, for that mysterious pair, who could have found no escape other than past the angler at the top of the stream - or directly over the Marshes, as wide open as a window. With no mist he could see for miles.

The old man told me the keeper was not the superstitious type. But could only come up with one conclusion. Many years ago, there had been an accident on the river. The keeper's son had fallen in the Meadow Stream hatch and had drowned. Shortly after, the following February, the keeper was killed in a shooting accident.

The old man had seen the keeper and his son.

But this was a long time ago. I had walked past the Meadow Stream hatch many, many times since; in rain, sun, wind, snow, night and day. On one particular late summer evening, it had been a different world up on the Marshes. Not a breath of wind, you could hear every dog bark, every door close, every plate clink in the kitchen sinks in the village across the meadow.

At this time of year there is little point in going up to the Marshes before ten o'clock, before the first few sedges start staggering back from the pub in search of sex when they start rolling off the grass under the bank of the river. That evening I watched them in a rising moon, bouncing home on the silvery stream as if on a trampoline.

Walking back, bats in my hair, mauve-tipped grass soaking my knees, I saw a rise. A platinum ring spread out towards me from a corner of Cemetery. I launched a sedge into the night. It was welcomed with open mouth and I spent the next ten minutes in the dark, a blind man battling a monster.

I managed to draw the fish onto a sheet of moonlight so I could stretch my hand down and scoop it out. The trout was big and dark. But just as I slid my hand underneath its thickset belly, it flicked a tail and slid back into the night.

Still on my knees, I leant forward to clean my hands in the grass. It was then that I became aware of someone watching me. Someone leaning up against the tree by the hatch. Someone in a large square trench coat. Remembering the old man's story, my knees malfunctioned.

I got up slowly. The coat by the hatch didn't move. Poacher or pal, I decided to act normally. Walking towards him, I wished him 'Good evening'. I got no reply. He made no movement. He just leaned into the darkness. A square shape, eyeing me.

As I got closer. I tried to say 'Good evening' again, but with my tongue spot-welded to the roof of my mouth, this was difficult.

I got to within two yards before I recognised who it was. It wasn't the keeper, or his son. It wasn't another rod sitting over a rising fish, entranced. It wasn't a poacher. It was something I knew. It was my door, leaning up against a tree by the hatch.

If you're on the river most days, you get to know every tree, bush, fence, gate - every post, every rail. If someone leaves a door behind, you tend to notice it. Water had been running out of the hatch into the woods and the door was to be a temporary barrier while the Boss repaired the camp-sheathing.

Next day, I got him to help me throw it in the back of the Land Rover, on top of a couple of rabbits he'd shot that morning, and take it back down to the hut. I'd pick it up the following day. If I remembered.

Someone once said that when insects take over the world, he hoped they would remember with gratitude how we took them along on our picnics.

One Saturday evening in August, after a week of balmy nights - mosquitoes burned off by the midday sun - an impromptu barbecue by the river had been organised for families of the rods who lived nearby.

I'd been lying on my stomach all day under the branches of a willow tree, keeping out of the sun. I'd been watching trout deep down in the blue cool beneath Sticklepath Bridge hoovering the brick-work, snacking on olive spinners egg-laying in the shadows. From this position, I had noticed crayfish staggering across the gravels, claws revolving like tanks threatened on all sides. They gave me an idea. I decided to try for some to add to the barbecue, and I walked up the track to get my crayfish tackle so I could set a trap before the party arrived.

My equipment is sophistication personified, incorporating all the very latest technological advances in this highly specialised area. It consisted of a perished wader with a rock pushed into the toe. Attached to the buckle at the top of the boot is a long piece of cord with a stake at one end. Inside, from the ankle downwards, I stuff any old fish bits I may have handy: guts, heads, fins, tails, pancreas - no matter. Finally, to make it hum melodiously in the hungry ears of any crayfish in the surrounding area, I top the culinary sock with bits of liver. I then toss this green, rubber-skinned haggis in the river, letting it sink under the bridge and drift into the murkiest of shadows. Anchored to the bank, it is left well alone. This is the secret - for the longer you leave it, the more effective it has proved to be.

With buttered crayfish popping and sizzling on the red-hot coals of my mind, I stood back and waited for the party to arrive.

Families began to show up at eight o'clock. Immense interest was taken in my boot. But I told everyone that silence was the name of this game and that they should keep clear of the river. This was difficult because, for many, my crayfish boat represented the only form of fishing that evening. Rods, lines, fly boxes - flyfishing tackle of any sort-was not allowed.

Wine flowed. It got dark. Not being able to contain the excitement, I grouped the menfolk around in a circle and briefed them on the plan. When it came to hoisting the trap, everyone had a part to play. But everyone must coordinate, otherwise the crayfish would escape. Speed - and discipline - was of the essence.

One man had to take a torch and shine it at the neck of the boot to hold the crayfish in. Another had to untie the rope and hold it. Another - and I recommended the youngest in the party - had to hold the rope and tie it round his wrist ready to pull the boot up out of the water and onto the bank when ordered, as quickly as damned-well possible.

Lastly, a time was set. Ten o'clock, dead.

The barbecue was a furnace. Steaks spat, wine continued to flow. As did blood in neck veins, with anticipation. Thoughts of crayfish had infested hungry senses and stolen the show.

At five minutes to ten, the menfolk took positions. The rest of the party gathered round in a tight bunch. You could power a small town off the excitement they generated. There was a fight to hold the torch. The youngest in the party, conscious of the huge responsibility, wound the rope tightly round his wrist in carefully calculated, close fitting turns.

Ten o'clock. The man shining the torch shone it. The man giving the order gave it. With one enormous yank, the boot was on the bank. The light beam focused on the mouth of the boot. The crowd closed in. Had we enough for everyone?

'Quick!' I screamed, 'Tip up the boot! Pour them out!'

The boy obeyed. With a flick of the wrist he turned the boot on end. A huge red claw appeared. Close behind, hissing and spluttering, a monstrous shiny crustacean, almost two foot in

length, slithered in the torch beam. The assembled crowd leapt
back into the woods. Women screamed. Men choked. The boy fell
back staring at a crimson claw inches from his jugular - and
giggled.

When I set the trap, I had put a large plastic lobster in the
leg of the boot, the sort they hang up on nets on the walls of
Italian restaurants, along with papier-mâché fish, seashells and
dried seaweed.

As the party returned back from the woods, offering one
another words of sympathy and handkerchiefs, I laid the fearsome
crustacean on the make-shift table on a plate of watercress where
the crayfish were going to be. If you'd lifted up the linen cloth
and looked underneath the table, you would have seen it was the
Magic Door lying across two logs.

The door's wandering days have come to a close. It's now
hanging in the bathroom of the Wild Wood Lodge covered in
brilliant white high-gloss paint. But not as brilliantly white as the
blood-drawn faces that sweated in the pale flickerings of a dying
barbecue on its last night on The Hollow.

In January, the mind flares with fires of a different sort, a more
warming kind. When I got back from my New Year's walk to the
village and pike-bait tank inspection, I was happy to find the Boss
was parked on the track outside the Big House talking to Lady
McFarlane. There was a distinct tang of wood smoke on the crisp,
late afternoon air. A cock pheasant, puffed up on the frosty lawn
in front of the house, spontaneously combusted as a flash of
golden winter sun ignited the countryside.

It was colder in the cab of the Boss's Land Rover than the
temperature outside. The back of his pick-up was open to the sky,
like it is all year round. My log supply was at danger point level,
so I looked in to to see if he had any more logs for me. The back
was sprinkled with blood-spattered frost. The two pike he'd
snatched out of Cakewood the week before and tossed in the
back were still lying there side by side, like a lovers' suicide pact.

The week before, they'd made many trips to town Christmas shopping.

I ordered another load, and it started to snow. It snowed all evening. Heavy falls. Before I went to bed I crossed the yard through the lemon light from the windows of the Big House. I'd gone to get a log from the sugar-powdered pile outside my stable block. I took one up to the bedroom to show my wife how much snow had fallen. A bump under a bed blanket, she rolled over wrapped in warm dreams of palm trees and coral beaches.

To get to sleep that night, I counted cold-eyed, aligator-faced female pike on their way up under the Old Iron Bridge.

February

THE DRY FLY, RE-INVENTED

The Ice Man cameth. The Snow Man wenteth. Now the Slush Man, the Sleet Man - and the Rain Man soaketh us. If a month is a colour, February is grey. Grey - with streaks of silver.

From the kitchen window I get a clear idea of the state of the nation. Three ponds had appeared in the pasture between the garden wall and the river. In the field next to the Fly Lane, a tungsten flash in a woodpigeon-coloured sky lit up a tangle of shiny new slivers of waterways. In the distance, a wave of sun swept across the ridges of burnished ploughed land like a floodlight, highlighting a dozen rooks with tin-foil backs, hedgerow-hopping.

This is water the river needs. Vital winter water - the most

important water of the year. Water that soaks into the land, before summer-parched roots soak it up. Water that will seep back and freshen streams in three or four months time. But now it just lies around in places, gleaming in abundance, disrupting the general flow of things. Below Horse Bridge, the fat river had re-routed and joined up with a group of part-time lakes gathered there. In other places, streams overflowed into other streams. Carriers that hadn't existed for ten years joined hands with forgotten drains to form rivers; rivers with islands.

At the weekend, this new seascape confused the Hare Shoot party. Paddling between puddles on the open land, and tip-toeing through spongy woodland like egrets in a mangrove, the hunters would have looked more at home with silver-tipped harpoon-guns, rather than double-barrelled shotguns. Home was on everyone's mind that day.

Back home, the first snowdrops hung their heads in sheltered corners of the garden. Daffodils cowering under the hedge, normally the first to flower up at the Big House, blew out green cheeks ready to burst.

If January had been spent getting my house and home together by the river, February was about getting myself and my tackle together ready for the river.

Living on the banks of a river does more than just change your life. Before too long it makes you want to re-examine other things. Things you thought didn't need changing. Like the way you fly-fish it, and the patterns you've been told to use. As you discover 'river-life' in 3-D for yourself with Wind-in-the-Willows eyes, you start wondering at it all. The thin February sun sitting on the water-meadows, straining through the kitchen window. The sound of water tumbling over the weir when you open a window for a brief moment to let the lemon warmth in. Tap water from your own spring, the same one that surfaces by the Ashes to quench the middle river - pure, bountiful, never failing. Brilliant white swans flying through the trees like ghosts as you pull the bedroom curtains on the grey of a late afternoon mist. And moorhens - what do they get up to down there at nights to make such a racket? (And how do you make them stop?) In no time at all, you begin to question everyday happenings.

Then one day you realise you know the score. You've grown accustomed to the pace, the regularity, the form, the changing pattern of the days as they stretch out to greet the new season, still a long way in the distance. They no longer hold any mysteries. You've got into the flow of things. You've fallen into the rhythm of the river.

As a flyfisherman, very soon you start to wonder in a different way. You start to wonder if things couldn't be better. The river is no longer a place you escape to for a day. It's now your home, not just your escape. If an Englishman's home is his castle, the river is now your own, personal moat. And if you're to fish it, you'll have no second-hand ideas - no matter how good they are. Nothing borrowed. You want to make your mark on it. You want to be master.

You set out to investigate every stalk of weed, every twist and turn, every run, riffle, rivulet, runnel, reflux, reach, race, rush and ripple. No stone, pebble, gravel is left unturned. Above or below, everything in the river is under suspicion. Everything is up for a second look. Everything is guilty until proved innocent. Everything that creeps, crawls, swims, dives, flies or flaps has you (and a magnifying glass) doing the same thing in steamy-hot, excited, scientific pursuit.

Eccentric as all this might sound, I wasn't alone in my approach here. If you check out the weekend addresses of flyfishermen who turned rivers upside-down and inside-out and whose discoveries resulted in similar things happening to fly pattern designs and tactics, you'll notice one thing. Nearly all of them, to a man, either lived - or, at worst, squatted with intent - on the banks of their chosen beat. They weren't day-trippers, they were totally committed. Like me, they decided that just a casual affair wasn't enough. You and the river had to live together. And they went through all the stages I've outlined above.

On chalkstreams it was Frank Sawyer and Oliver Kite, on the Officers' Association Water on the Avon. Back a bit further in time, it was Harry Plunkett-Green at Hurstbourne Tarrant, on the River Bourne. Although he didn't invent any particular single fly, he did more for the Iron Blue than any other angler has done for any one fly pattern, before or since. Back further still, it was G.E.M. Skues on the Itchen, at Abbots Barton. Finally, the daddy-long-legs of them all, Frederic Halford who regularly legged it the long way down to fish his beat at Stockbridge, on the Houghton Club water, on the Test.

Halford, the inventor of the dry fly rule still in operation today, lived a double life and was therefore perhaps the most schizophrenic. For when he wasn't at Houghton Mill on the banks of his river, he was up in London at his house in Notting Hill Gate, in Pembridge Place. I've visited it. Even by Victorian standards, it's grand. It's now a hotel. Palatial rooms with soaring ceilings, make it the the sort of place that required carpeting with wall to wall butlers, footmen and maids - if only to stop the echoes of emptiness deafening you. I don't have a floor-plan, neither do I know the dimensions of his rooms at the Mill which he rented as his weekend retreat, but one thing is for certain, he didn't go Test-bound alone. He invited a set of cronies along with him to help him with his dry fly experiments. One of those people was George Selwyn Marryat.

Now few things in the history of flyfishing baffle me more than why George Selwyn Marryat's name doesn't appear alongside that of Frederic Halford on the cover of *Floating Flies and How to Dress Them* (1886) - the culmination of all the hours, days, weeks, and months they put in.

If you dig into the credits, Halford wasn't slow in showing his appreciation to other friends for aiding and abetting him in his plan to systematically wipe out Test chalkstream trout by 'fair' means, rather than by the 'foul' wet fly. Martin Moseley, for example, top man at the Entomological Department of the Natural History Museum, got more than his fair due of appreciation. Indeed in the introduction of Moseley's book entitled *A Dry Fly Fisherman's Entomology* (1921), Halford allowed Moseley to print a letter Halford once sent to him begging Moseley to write the book. By all accounts, Halford was embarrassed at having relied so much on Moseley's entomological brain when he was writing his own books on the subject. In Halford's letter to Moseley, Halford portrays himself as the oily rag - the wide-eyed apprentice - rather than the Great High Priest of The Dry Fly Code. But he went further.

Swapping his tweeds for sackcloth, Halford, with grovelling respect, goes on to demean himself even more. He presented Moseley with a copy of his arch-enemy G.E.M. Skues's latest book: *The Way of a Trout With a Fly* (1921). As the protagonist of fishing nymphs - 'damp' rather than 'dry' patterns ('foul' rather than 'fair' means) - Skues's thinking couldn't be further from that of the High Priest of dry fly purism's way with a fly. I hold the evidence. This volume, signed by Halford and dedicated to Moseley, sits on a shelf amongst the other books in the kitchen. It should be in the Chamber of Horrors.

Skues wasn't so generous when it came to demonstrating his gratitude to Moseley. For a start, he didn't give him a copy of Halford's book. He gave him a copy of one of his own back-stabbing volumes, *Nymph Fishing for Chalk Stream Trout* (1939). When this literary torpedo was first launched, it hit Halford's starch collared theories broadside, seriously holing, but not entirely sinking, his high and dry code.

I have Skues's *Nymph Fishing* too, signed by the author, and dedicated to Moseley. Not only did Skues sign and dedicate the edition to Moseley, he also signed the title page, just to underline what a privileged fellow he was.

So what about the poor, humble Marryat - apparently an equally free-thinking angler of the day, but one who lacked any urge to put pen to paper?

Well, for a man who spent six years of his life in and out of Halford's room at Houghton Mill, and who was frequently up at five in the morning to help his struggling friend with his dry fly experiments, Marryat seems super-humanly shy of being credited for the hours he put in. Even Halford, if you read between the lines, appears a little embarrassed by the omission.

Was it really Marryat's modesty and lowliness that resulted in his name not being associated with the book? Or was it something else? Did he back off?

Personally, if I had been Marryat, I'd have kept my name well clear of Halford's book. To my mind, the flies described there are so riddled with design faults I'm amazed they were ever wetted. The success of *Floating Flies* was, in my opinion, due entirely to the uniqueness of Halford's dry fly theory and his cataloguing skills, rather than the ingenuity of the design of the floating flies he prescribed.

Marryat kept his views very close to his chest. He certainly never sat down and wrote them out on paper. But he is quoted as having once said the following: 'It's not the fly, it's the drive', which confused everyone who read it in the years ahead and understandably got forgotten, primarily because no-one could work out exactly what he meant. But as mysterious as his words might sound in this day and age, in Halford's day, they had a real meaning which suggests, first that Marryat had a point of view, second, he had a sense of humour and, third, when pushed, he could use words with the same skill as he used to cast a fly.

In his late Victorian day, 'fly' had another meaning apart from 'insect'. It was the name given to a certain horse-drawn carriage. Translated into late twentieth century parlance therefore, what Marryat said was 'It's not the car, it's the driver' - 'It's not the song, it's the singer'. In other words, the model or pattern of fly, whatever that might be, takes second place to the raw skill of the angler at the other end of the rod. This suggests to me that not only was he unimpressed with the cloud of new patterns rolling off the bench at Halford's weekend mill, he had also become disillusioned with the artificial fly technology of his day. More than that, I can only speculate.

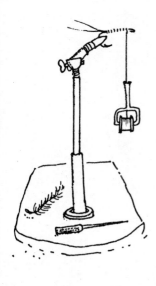

Certainly, over the years, anglers have slowly begun to accept that the Great High Priest's flies weren't exactly heaven-sent. They had their failings. It soon became apparent, for example, that Halford's manic desire to reproduce photocopies of the flies he picked off the river limited his patterns' effectiveness. Indeed, they didn't really make much sense at all when looked at from the trout's point of view.

But remarkably, despite all the tinkerings to the 'look' of the dry fly over the last hundred years, the fundamental question of whether or not Halford's method of dressing a floating fly

makes any better sense has hardly been raised.

Granted, dry flies based on the dressing principles he advocated in the late 1880s still catch trout today. But this doesn't detract from the fact that, as a simple piece of design, the conventional dry fly barely fulfils what we as dry fly fishermen should demand of it.

To start with, the method of tying relies on a quality of cock hackle that was on the way out even in Halford's day. Cock-fighting as a sport had been abolished nearly forty years before *Floating Flies*, at a time when Halford was too young to play in the garden on his own, let alone go fishing by the river. Nowadays, these hackles are about as hard to track down as a decent day's coelacanth fishing. And when you do actually stumble upon such a cape, it requires a second mortgage to own it.

While we're still on the subject of hackles, if we accept that a hackle's main function, apart from representing legs and feet, is to support the weight of the fly in conjunction with the tail, then the way it is tied on the hook actually encourages the fly to sink. By tying it at right-angles to the hook shank, the weight rests on the prickly, film-piercing tippy-toes of the hackle, offering up the minimum of flat area to the surface. This conventional right-angle positioning of the hackle is as logical as designing a ship that sails on its bows. It reduces the fly's floatability; it doesn't increase it.

Only one fly to my knowledge makes any attempt to imitate the correct silhouette of the upwing river fly as seen in the trout's window. This is Oliver Kite's Imperial. Kite, in his wisdom, incorporated a heron herl hump, or thick neck, behind the hackle, to imitate the insect's thorax. This is a distinctive feature of the natural dun and more importantly, since it lies flush with the surface, the spinner.

The trouble is, Kite put his thorax in the one place a trout couldn't see it: on top of the fly. But I don't think this is why the thorax is almost invariably missing from shop-bought Imperials. I suspect the reason thoraxes make such rare appearances on dry flies is primarily to do with convenience, rather than neglect. The conventional positioning of the wing and hackle make the procedure of tying on a correctly positioned thorax too much like hard work even for the most ambitious amateur. Quite simply, the design doesn't allow for it.

Lastly, for over a century now, the dry fly has been chugging its way down-river the wrong way up, virtually unquestioned, exposing the hook and the angler's motives in the most gloriously graphic and three-dimensional way imaginable. They land with the hook the trout-side of the fly. If, as it's very likely to do when supported by a flimsy hackle mounted at right angles to the hook, the whole primitive contraption starts to sink, the hook is the first thing to go under - and therefore the first thing the trout will see, whether or not the fly is inside, or outside, his window.

This design feature, the fact that a dry fly lands hook-down, is a fundamental contradiction of all that is sane on this earth. It's a nonsense that flyfishers have learned to accept. If only I could be sure trout do the same with such astounding regularity. Personally, if I arrived from outer space and somebody tried to sell me a dry fly that lands the way it does, I'd write to the nearest Consumer Complaints Department.

Although you may have been taking all these dry fly deficiencies lying down, I wasn't. My river laboratory in place (somewhere amongst the paint cans, brushes and bottles of turps), my building works complete (but nothing a lick of undercoat couldn't transform dramatically), my scratching-on-scraps-of-paper days gone, and the season not quite a trillion light years away, I had to direct my mind on to something to stop madness creeping in. I screwed a flytying vice to my redundant Black & Decker Workmate, changed my answer phone message to 'We're sorry we can't come to the phone right now, we're tying flies', and started work - a century late, I admit - designing the dry fly the way it should have been designed in the first place. The dry fly that complements Halford's doctrines better than *his* floating flies ever did. A dry fly called the Funneldun for reasons which I will now reveal.

To be historical, the Funneldun started life as a tribute to the mail order tackle trade. A sort of 'thanks for your unswerving commitment in sending me capes of such consistently poor quality that even the moths reject them'. I guess I just wasn't prepared to spend more than a few pounds on a neck of feathers. Was that unreasonable? But more to the point, was it at all possible to make quality dry flies out of capes fit only for streamers? It wouldn't cost me anything to investigate.

I asked myself 'What makes a cheap cape unsuitable for dry fly work?' Answer: the small hackles used to tie conventional dry flies - those found in-between the eyes of the bird - are very noticeably absent from cheap capes. Those few hackles that you are able to find dangling off the skin tend to be the poorest coloured and worst marked feathers on the neck. The small hackles of a Badger, Greenwell or Furnace, for instance, are either the smoky colour of the centres of the hackles higher up in the ranks of the cape, or else they have no markings at all.

Another common characteristic of 'dry fly' hackles on cheap capes is their high fluff content. Once you've stripped them, they're only good for a couple of limp turns. If you think of a low quality hackle as a bottle of milk, there isn't much cream on the top of these hackles - the cream being the precious few stiff, shiny fibres found all the way down the stalk of a quality hackle. This is what you pay the extra for.

Another thing you get for your money with a quality neck are long, thin hackles, short in the flue. On a cheap cape, the reverse is the case. It's the small hackles that are short and stubby, and the fibres long, splaying out to twice the length you expected them to be when you turn them on the hook.

To conclude, if your cape is a cheapie, don't get upset to discover that there aren't many small hackles suitable for dry flies.

It was because of this scarcity of small hackles that I ruled out my first idea of using two of these small hackles per fly, giving me the necessary number of turns to support the hook. By doubling up my demand for small hackles, I'd be drastically increasing my consumption of cheap capes and the more sense it would make to buy an expensive one. And, if you remember, this was the last thing I could afford to do if I was to be able to pay for a season's fishing sometime, somewhere through the mist at the bottom of my garden.

Continuing my search, I decided to re-examine my capes in a more non-specific, forgiving manner, hunting to see if there was a part (any part) of the neck that came anywhere near offering the quality of a more expensive cape. And such a part exists.

These are the hackles capable of tying a respectable dry fly - just as long as you like your itsy-bitsy Pale Wateries tied on #8 hooks. You'll find these hackles in the area above the small hackle zone, a territory rarely ventured into by dry fly dressers unless you're a beginner, or you've been kidding yourself.

The flues of these hackles are much too long, certainly. But on the positive side, you can get at least four, even five turns out of the cream of the hackle. Enough at least to float a fully dressed #14 or #16 hook. But on the positive side, even the worst capes I have inspected have a good crop of these hackles.

Apart from the flue length, these hackles did have one other disadvantage. Although the fibres were of competitive quality, the bases tended to be weak and woolly, rather negating the hackle's spiky merits when tied onto the hook in the conventional way. However, like it or not, these hackles were the best my cheap capes could offer.

So recognising their strengths and noting their weaknesses, on nights when all was quiet except for the baritone hum of kitchen equipment and the ancient freezer in the Decontamination Room, I took them to my vice where I spent a week of long February nights in experimentation.

The solution I emerged with was well worth the midnight fly-oil. For not only did it provide me with a method of transforming Grade Z capes into Grade A dry flies, it also solved several other dry fly failings I had noted in my little black book.

At first I had considered tying in the longer flued hackle and clipping the fibres to size. Aesthetically this has always appalled me - and anyway it wouldn't solve the woolly base problem.

What I ended up doing was starting the fly by tying in the

hackle behind the eye. With this complete, I pulled the fibres forward over the eye of the hook using the thumb and forefingers of my right hand. With my left hand, I built up turns of silk behind the hackle and over the roots to hold the fibres sloping forward. The fly ends up looking like an umbrella blown out by the wind.

By positioning the hackle so the fibres sloped forward in a 'funnel' shape, the fibre tips ended up in roughly the same position as if I'd tied a smaller hackle in at the head. And by tying silk over the base of the hackle to hold it in a 'funnelled' position, I effectively covered up the woolly base so that the fly was supported on the stiff fibre tips.

This simple operation, this 'funnelling' of the longer-flued hackles, allowed me to make superb dry flies out of flabby feathers from capes that would have dropped off the end of even the most shameless of grading scales. Indeed, my Funneldun floated as high and as proud - and as elegantly - as any Hoffman or Metz dry fly. And (this is the bit I like) at a fraction of the price.

As I mentioned earlier, the Funneldun made sense in several other ways. In fact, possibilities reached out and grabbed me by the lapels at the rate of one a minute.

By sloping the hackle forward, the fibres were no longer at the traditional right angles to the hook shank. The right-angles method of tying a hackle to make a fly float suggests to me that Halford may well have gone to help design the Titanic.

The funnel-shaped hackle meant that at last the weight of the dry fly rested on a broad, flat base, eliminating the risk of the hackle tips piercing the surface film. If a physics O-level qualifies me to say so, this greatly increases the chances of the fly staying afloat longer, and greatly reduces the chances of it tipping over, tail in the air - a common fault of flies dressed with their hackles positioned at the conventional right-angles to the hook. Quite simply, as I was soon to discover when the season opened, you have to throw stones at a Funneldun to sink it.

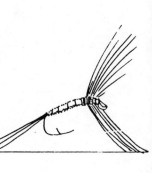

One thing I'd always wanted to throw at a trout was a dry fly dressed with a good thorax. Before the birth of the Funneldun,

this operation was tricky. In fact, I'd go as far as saying it was an impossibility because the thorax, if you're going to be a stickler about it, should be tied at the head of the fly - in front of the hackle and wings - with a small bump behind to complete the correct silhouette.

In the case of the Funneldun, to incorporate this, instead of tying in the hackle directly behind the eye, first of all you dub on a small pinch of light-weight fur and tie in a small thorax 'head' at the eye. Now you tie in the hackle behind this thorax, using it as a 'stop' and support. This way, it becomes intrinsic to the design of the fly. For this thorax, I use hare ear or rabbit fur, depending on the pattern I'm tying.

This thorax has another vocation in life. Apart from giving the fly a more convincing outline, it supports the forward-sloping hackle, stopping it from sloping forward more than you'd like.

As far as the smaller thorax behind the hackle is concerned, you build this up unwittingly when you wind the silk behind the hackle to push it forward. I dub a turn of fur over this silk thorax to give it a little more prominence. By winding your thorax round the hook - not folding it backwards and forwards over the top as prescribed by Mr O. Kite - it can be seen from every angle. Top, sides, and from below.

The design of the Funneldun also allowed me to tie a large fly on a small hook. The significance of this is that if you can tie a #14 fly on a #16 hook (or a #16 on a #18, etc.) there are obvious weight advantages. And the less hook, the less you give the trout to be jittery about, because it reduces the chance of it being seen.

All you need do to tie a large size fly on a small size hook, is tie the long-flued hackle nearer the head of the hook, behind the thorax. When you have 'funnelled' the hackle forward in front of the eye, the illusion is that of a considerably longer, and therefore larger fly. And the fly's floatability is dramatically increased. And once again, because you're using a smaller hook, the chances of the trout seeing it diminishes dramatically.

Now, I hear you saying, I thought you said it was insane that the hook, be it large or small, should be in a position where the trout can see it in the first place?

Before we go on, let's go back. To 1886, the year Halford's *Floating Flies* first fluttered off the press. Quite a year for mechanics all round - for that same year, Gottleib Daimler proudly pulled the wraps off the Daimler Motor Carriage, the first horse carriage to be powered by a gasoline engine. What's the connection between these two events?

There isn't any. It's just interesting to note that between then and now, Daimler's nine mph dinosaur has been developed into something that moves faster than the speed of sound. What about Halford's water babies?

Well, for the dry fly, it has been a century of fiddlings. The basic design and function remain virtually unchanged. Fly dressing, in an effort to do new things, continues to rocket out of the realms of practicality, leaving the happily average fly dresser, like myself, hopelessly confused, finger-knotted and feeling unfairly inadequate.

Although I'm on the side of progress, I don't think the use of moose earlobe fur instead of wool picked off a barbed-wire fence, or introducing violently complex tying techniques to reach tiny ends, is the way flytying should progress. Today, very few creative flytyers are minimising movements, or seeking out more basic tying solutions to offer the everyday fly dresser. Rather than attracting more non-flytying flyfishers into the ranks, they're being scared off.

To top it all, dry flies don't float as well as they might, whether they float the right, or the wrong way up.

In short, I'm really not that sure why flyfishers still merrily knot on a design of fly that best introduces the trout to the hook, especially when they've had nearly a century to sort out this little illogicality. If the Funneldun was to be everything I wanted it to be, it literally had to turn the whole dry fly world 'upside-down'.

Some fine minds have fished the dry fly through its history. Someone even went to the trouble of importing a Scandinavian hook specialist to design an upside-down hook to compensate for our inability - as the nation that first popularised the dry fly - to make proper sense of it. *The Trout & the Fly* goes into the sense of it all in great detail. Nothing new here; credit where credit is due. It took my good friends Goddard and Clarke two years to codify, experiment, research and finally prove the logic of upside-down flies. It took Goddard many hours at the bench. Both the book and the U.S.D. Paradun patterns are works of art.

But as much as I applaud the Paradun's ingenuity - its undisputed ability to pull off all the stunts it promises and lastly, its sheer beauty and realism - nevertheless, the tying procedure has me looking around for extra fingers. But then, it was never designed for everyday usage. It's a special occasion pattern, for use on super-tricky trout.

So here comes my first public warning: If you can whip up half a dozen Paraduns in a sitting, and there are mortals who can, this chapter is not for you. But for ham-fisters everywhere, heads down. Read on - because turning the dry fly hook up in the air needn't demand any greater fly dressing skills than are called on to tie a bread-and-butter hackled fly.

Indeed, my method of inverting a dry fly using standard hooks is so stunningly simple, I can't possibly pretend that it was the result of forty inspired days and forty blood-shot-eyed nights experimenting at the vice. No, the best flytying is about the obvious, and the truth is I stumbled upon the answer by accident.

One feature that always intrigued me about the Funneldun was its love of rolling over on tail and hackle tips, rather than tipping over when blown across a flat surface. I'm no Einstein, but I could only imagine this had something to do with the hackles being funnel-shaped, since conventionally-tied flies didn't perform the same trick with nearly the same nimbleness. This roll-ability is one half of the secret of inverting the dry fly. How you position the tail at the bend is the other.

If you can tie a Funneldun as instructed, then it's easy to turn the fly over so it always lands hook up. All you do is tie in the tail whisks so that instead of them being a continuation of the hook shank, they follow the bend of the hook slightly.

Three things are crucial here. First, that you use a good bunch of stiff hackle-fibres for the tail. Secondly, that you tie a turn of silk underneath the hackle fibres to splay them out. And thirdly, that you find the exact position on the hook bend so that the tails are far enough round to topple the fly. But not too far round to make the end of the body touch the surface.

The body should be held off the water on hackle and tail. This position on the hook bend differs from hook design to hook design, but finding it is simple. One fly should tell you where you should position your tail on the next.

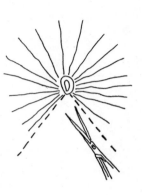

Once you've tied in the tails and 'funnelled' the hackle, cut out a small 'V' from the underside of the hackle. Your fly will now land hook in the air every cast.

Tied in slightly round the bend, the tail acts as a lever and pushes the fly on its back, the funnel-shaped hackle acting as a wheel that rolls with the weight of the hook. Physics, not fluke, insists that Funnelduns always keel over, hook up. It would be against all the laws of nature and gravity for them to do otherwise.

Naturally, because the secret of turning dry flies upside-down is as ridiculously simple as 'funnelling' your hackle, cutting in the all-important 'V' and winding your tail a little further round the hook bend, it's possible to invert any conventional dry fly pattern you like.

Agreed, in order to 'funnel' your hackle you bind in a small thorax, but for all the reasons I've given, this isn't a bad thing. Agreed, you tie the fly off at the tail and not at the head. Again, so what? A fly with a yellow silk body and a Greenwell hackle is a Greenwell's Glory, no matter how you tie it. Only the design of the Greenwell's has changed, not the pattern. And not before time, either.

So far, I've only discussed hackled Funnelduns, I haven't mentioned wings. There's a good reason for this. I'm no Romeo for wings and winging. This doesn't mean I don't agree with all the arguments for adding wings to dry flies - I do. The Wings Supporters' Club put up some pretty convincing evidence, and I sincerely believe that wings are just as important to the trout to tell him when a dun is approaching outside his window (the area immediately above the trout) as a thorax is to tell him when a spinner is approaching inside his window.

No winging is easy. Winging a Funneldun isn't easy, but it isn't any harder than tying them on a conventional fly. At least not if you use feather fibre as your winging material.

I've been using feather fibre on the few winged patterns I keep in my box for many years now. I get all kinds of comments. People tell me that feather fibre doesn't look like wings, that I should use starling quill because there simply isn't a substitute. I agree. There aren't many substitutes for a winging material that disintegrates on your third cast. People tell me I'm a fool to overlook hackle points for wings. I overlook them because I'm convinced that's just what trout do. I don't deny hackle points look very realistic - when they're dry. Wet them and the fibres fold up like a parasol and glue themselves to the stalk. Cutting them out from lower down in the hackle overcomes this, up to a point. Up until the trout feels the stalks on its lips and spits it out faster than Wyatt Earp pulled a pistol.

Not surprisingly, I still use feather fibre despite the critics. And I'm not alone. Almost every flyfisher I met in New York State on my travels uses feather fibre for wings. I'm afraid, as far as innovation in river fishing goes, the average English chalkstream fisherman is still living in the Middle Ages. As for our chalkstream trout, they're positively house-trained compared to trout sharp enough to survive a summer in a bombed-out American public water.

My favourite winging material is grey mallard breast feather. But I often use widgeon or teal. A bunch of blue dun or grizzle hackles will do as third best. Having tied in a small thorax, I tie the wing material in with two turns of silk behind it so that they slope forward, at a slight angle. I then tie in a hackle, shiny-side down, pointing over the eye. This is tied in behind the wing and 'funnelled' forward in the manner described previously.

Wings make a Funneldun a pretty fly, but I still prefer them without.

As the name suggests, the Funneldun was originally an

imitation of the dun, or sub-imago stage of the upwing river fly.
But at no other stage is it more critical to have the hook in the
air than when imitating the spinner, or imago, stage.

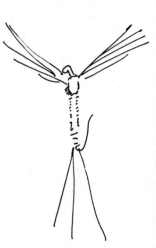

Unlike the dun, the spinner artificial should lie *in* the
surface, rather than on it. Therefore it shouldn't have hackles
holding body and hook clear of the water. For a conventional
spinner to lie in the film the hook has to dangle beneath the
surface, which has to be one of the most effective methods of
alerting the trout to your intentions yet devised by man.

To turn your spinner upside-down, simply over-hackle your
fly with a large blue dun feather. The flues of this hackle should
be the length of the wings lying spent.

Once you've finished the fly, clip the fibres on the top-side
of the hook down to the shank. Instead of the hackles being a full
circle (360 degrees), they should be a semicircle (180 degrees).
You now have a spinner that stubbornly holds the hook high in
the air, clear of the water, the weight of the hook cunningly
pressing wings, thorax and body into the surface where every
good spinner should be.

In the final analysis, apart from its fish-catching qualities, I judge
a fly for it's simplicity. It must be quick to dress and made from
materials that are easy to find, cheap to buy and simple to
manipulate.

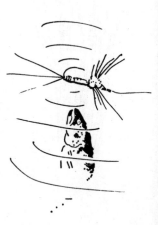

When it comes to weighing up the evidence in favour of the
Funneldun, judge it for its floatability, improved outline and
hook-hiding qualities. These are the reasons why I think it's a
more killing design of fly than the conventional.

The truth is, the Funneldun was never a 'pattern' from the
outset. It's a blueprint for tying dry flies, standard or otherwise,
based on a concept. A concept I call *Volksfliegen*, 'flies for the
people'. These are flies that have been 'designed', not invented.
Flies that answer a particular brief, perform a particular job, pull
off a particular stunt. Flies that are capable of being dressed by
any angler, novice or professional, and used on any day.

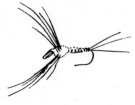

And like all the other patterns included in this book, they have been tested and tried by hundreds of flyfishers, in Britain, in Europe, but more particularly, in the US.

To date, the Funneldun has featured in eight books published in Britain, four published in other parts of Europe, and three published elsewhere. One in New York, another in San Francisco and one printed in Japan. The Norsk Skogbrukmuseum in Norway, the largest museum of its kind in Scandinavia, has just asked for an example to have on permanent display.

Launched in a single article that appeared in a modest bi-monthly angling magazine in September 1979, what swept this little fly to the heady heights of international fame?

In a word, it was powered by simplicity.

Days were flying by now, or rather slipping and sliding on sopping fields. February, the fastest month of the year, ripped through, warming the air with its speed.

As the door to Spring began to open, the skies got more restless and the thin sun thickened. The river stayed leaden and clay-coloured; holding its ground. Blown from the fields like charred chaff at stubble-burning, glossy rooks circled above Robins Wood, gossiping, complaining. Everywhere, the signs that something was about to happen.

The earth was drying out. The snowdrops gone, heavy shoulders with yellow warheads pushed up through the ochre leaves beneath my green-tipped hedge, ready to rise up like a choir and burst through in unison. When they do, I know that very soon I will be on the river.

My river, with my very own Code.

March

SELL THE SIZZLE, NOT THE SAUSAGE

It had been a wild night, and the storm was still prowling around outside the house. Unrelenting, the wind, like blind fists, beat at my windows. My dustbin had spent the night flying round the woods and had landed up in a tree. The Boss found it in the Firs and threw it in the back of his pick-up on top of two grey, hollow-eyed rabbits he'd shot a couple of days (perhaps even a month) ago. He brought the dustbin back to me, along with the news that the Game Hut had been blown over and was lying on its nose by the Ashes.

A sharp, wet wind had spent the week charging down the Bull's Tail at us in snarling gusts. This regimented row of trees, three miles away on the north-facing slope of the Downs, is

clearly visible from the kitchen window. It points a finger due south-west. If the wind blows from this direction, there is nothing between us and whatever it brings with it, which is usually rain. But all week it had been a nervous March wind that could bring anything, at any moment.

The plantation across the river from the Wild Wood was filled with the noise of rasping chain-saws, coming in spurts, as the wind directed. When it howled through the garden, the beech hedge shook. Paper-dry leaves rustled like prayer sheets turning in a packed church.

In the field opposite, a sparrow hawk stood unmoving over the first pile of poplars to arrive up from the top of the Wetlands, just below Horse Bridge. This veteran bridge is a half way mark on the beat. In its day, it must have been the most handsome of the five working bridges on the fishery. Distinct from the twenty-two double plank, single hand-rail footbridges, this solid cart-bridge was constructed to take the weight of a fully-laden horse and cart. Even now, with one of its main support girders rusted and fallen away, it was still able to take the weight of the tractor from the farm and the gamekeeper's Japanese four-wheel drive.

If you look carefully at the two posts at either end of the bridge you will see that at one time it was a patchwork of rustic work. But now the posts are all that remain of the artwork.

Many fish hide underneath this tired old bridge. In summer, during low water, it's just possible to cast a fly at them. The highlight of the season is to find a fish up there feeding on the female olive spinners crawling down the bricking to lay their eggs, and to get an imitation far enough up and under to have it taken by a sinister black nose poxed with grey scabs from grazing on the brickwork.

To ensure the survival of the members of her family, and to make sure that her eggs don't get washed away, the females of the large, medium and small dark olive don't delegate the responsibility of depositing their eggs on the river bed to the vagaries of the current. Instead, the large dark olive gets down and does the job herself. She crawls underwater and lays them out on the site of her dreams. Preferably under a stone, or on a weed stem away from marauding larvae.

These girls favour specific areas of the river for this method of egg-laying: a wood piling or, even better, a concrete bridge support. These are preferred to reeds, sedges or other slippery herbage which don't appear to have quite the same grip, and have too smooth a surface to stick eggs to them.

At Horse Bridge, females land on the cement supports, heads facing skywards, egg-ends turned downwards in the direction of the water, as if testing it. They then turn and begin to inch down the concrete, their wings folded along their bodies. As they push their way through the film using tails as levers, they trap an air bubble beneath their wings. This acts as an oxygen tank as they descend - and a lifebuoy when they release their grip on the cement or the marl on the river bed to make their ascent. This way, they bob up to the surface again like ping-pong balls.

When egg-laying, they face the current and swing their bodies from side to side until a row of eggs is laid in a semi-circle formation. They move slowly forward depositing a row of eggs and forming a flat plate in the shape of an arc with its concave edge facing the current. Depending on the force of the current and difficulties in egg-laying, when they return to the surface their wings either open up like an umbrella and they fly away; or exhausted, they spread them on the surface in the spent position and lie down and die.

The pattern I devised to address these trout under Horse Bridge is called the Sunk Spinner. There are two versions. One imitates the descending female spinner, the second imitates the ascending spinner just as it reaches the underside of the surface film. The two patterns differ in only two respects: the wing position and winging material used, and the amount of weight incorporated in the pattern.

The trout under Horse Bridge are not accustomed to being presented with food parcels dropped on them from above, from under the bridge. The fly needs to be cast well up and under, and over the trout if it is to be taken seriously. If you're skilful enough to achieve this stunt, and your fly is accepted, your problems aren't over, they've only just begun. For, if you're

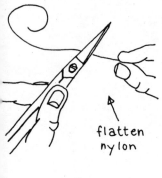

flatten
nylon

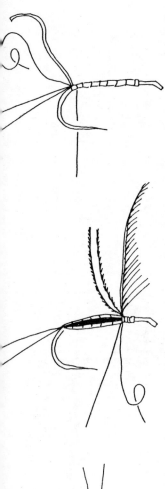

unable to yank your fish from the shadows into the sunlight within seconds, it will dive deep, rubbing your nylon leader along the concrete bridge support foundations, leaving you with a frayed tip, no fish, no fly and only a thin, lukewarm feeling as compensation for at least managing to get a fly to drift down in the direction of the trout before drag whisks it away.

For a quarter of a mile due south of Horse Bridge, in the Wetlands, stately parallel avenues of poplar trees escort you all the way down to the Pheasantry, where the Sheep Dip carrier joins the Moor Reach. When you're on the river bank this plantation shelters you from the prevailing wind from the south-west. The poplars rustle loudly when the weather changes for the worse, and drip like a thousand clocks in a jeweller's when the storm has passed and things look like they've changed for the better. Their erect, military presence brings an order to the tangle of woods and streams that lean in on the river on all sides. But as I was soon to learn, it's wise not to get too accustomed to everyday sights on a river. Much as you would like things to remain as they are, they don't. There are no permanent fittings on a trout stream, no feature is set in stone. Timeless images only exist in photographs, or in paintings. If nature doesn't change nature, man will.

So when a tractor and trailer stacked with freshly felled poplars arrived in the field opposite the Wild Wood Lodge, and they started to unload them by the track leading to Robin Wood, I knew where they had come from and I was out of the back door and down to Horse Bridge as if religion was after me. I wanted to start getting accustomed to the new landscape without delay, without remorse. I wanted no surprises.

To see the first gap in the ranks, the first casualties in the plantation, in a corner where I had so often sheltered from a summer storm with a view across the river to secret trout lies tucked tight under the bank in the shade of the Ashes, made me angry. But I had always known that the poplars hadn't been put there to be a cosy curtain between me and the worst of the weather. They had been planted for a purpose - to be harvested. In the sixteenth century, famous artists painted on poplar board.

Raphael was one of them. But the Boss told me that they had been planted on contract from a safety match company and that, like a field of wheat, one day they would be gone. That day was now long overdue, by some ten years.

Things come, things go. Things change, new things take their place. I had it on good authority that when the area had been cleared - by the autumn was the plan - it would be replanted with alder trees commissioned by a tooling company who make hammer, screwdriver and axe handles. No doubt, in years to come, one of these axes will return to clear the plantation once again. That's the way it is.

Standing on Horse Bridge, I was sad. Squinting my eyes, I tried to imagine the landscape without the poplars. Bending in my direction with the wind behind them, they shook their heads as if to say they couldn't imagine it either. But by April, I'll have shrugged it off; by May, I'll be getting used to the new landscape; by June, I'll have accepted it; by July I'll be beginning to like it; by August, I'll have forgotten the poplars ever existed; by September, I'll resent the fact that regimented ranks of trees had once been planted there in such an unnatural and artificial formation. Like trout, people have short memories. They know what they like and like what they know, for a time at least. And time is all it takes to get used to change, of any sort. Be it a clump of lanky, sweet-sapped trees of minimal commercial value, or the way you tie a dry fly, or present it to a trout.

Anyway, I was out for change. There were to be no fixed ideas, no absolutes in my fishing season, and this was inching closer, dangerously closer, by the day. No single fly pattern, tying style, tactic, or approach could provide the solution to all the trout problems I would be facing in the season ahead.

This would certainly be the case if, on opening day, the weather was to be anything like one of those days in March when the wind rounds up the surface of the unprotected reaches of river and sucks them up into the sky.

My upwing patterns, my Funnelduns, designed for exact-form fishing for trout in a repetitious rhythm of feeding, carefully inspecting every offering before, gently and cautiously, nuzzling it prior to acceptance, would need to be supplemented by some more tactical patterns. Spasmodic hatches and unpredictable weather makes early season flyfishing a smash and grab affair. Not like the sip, suck and see in a sheltered summer bay.

Carried up the track on a gust accelerating off the Bull's Tail, soon I was back in the kitchen behind my vice. Still red-hot with use, it was the warmest place in the house.

Perhaps the most seemingly run-of-the-mill fly of my invention, the Grizzle Mink, can hardly be termed conventional. I'm reminded of this every time I give one away to someone for the first time. They hold it up to the light for a closer inspection, then their immediate reaction is to get down to housework.

Starting with the long body hairs, then moving on to pick out all the loose ends, they have shorn many a Grizzle Mink in seconds of all the qualities that account for its mystical attractiveness to trout.

If you walk to Sticklepath Bridge at this time of year (and you can stop your teeth chattering) you may not be able to hear him, but underneath the grey blanket of winter water, the large dark olive is oiling his springs. Very soon Spring will be the order of the day.

The first fly you can expect to see (and this could happen at any moment) and the first that needs imitating on the first day of the season, is the large dark olive. This is the member of my upwing neighbours who represents the family on opening day. It also gives the trout the first taste of what tit-bits they can expect to find at the surface in the season ahead.

The male dun, with eyes the colour of house-bricks, and his green-eyed sister, both look like they've been moulded out of gun metal. They don't start to load the surface of the river with their flat, dark grey wings until mid-day, or even lunch-time. The large dark olive is happy to poke its head out of the river at the most inclement time of year, temperature and weather-wise. This is unlike some of the other members of the family I was looking forward to meeting later on in the year who cool it out only if the air is dry and calm. It takes the large dark olive longer to dry its huge expanse of wings at this time of year. This affects its behaviour.

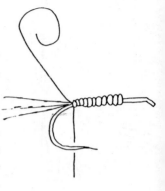

In a month's time, on a day like today, the dun will travel some distance before it is able to part its soggy wings and launch itself to the safety of the dry underside of a branch. During this time, gusts of wind, like the ones that have the branches of my hedge clacking together like a castanet festival, have a greater influence on the dun's journey than the hefty currents of winter water. Instead of a serene, well-composed picture of entomological elegance, the large dark olive can become highly animated, skittering across the surface, tossing and turning on the ripple like tumbleweed on the main street of a windswept Western shanty town.

To a surface-interested trout in these conditions, a static fly is a fraud. But standing lightly on a pair of high-heel cock hackles, hook and body held high on tippy-toes, the Grizzle Mink is capable of 'independent movement', capturing the illusion of a living insect rather than imitating a specific insect. Alerting the trout to its exact whereabouts, not hinting at it. To warm the cockles of the coldest-hearted trout, the Grizzle Mink pattern is made up of a highly volatile cocktail of flytying materials, guaranteeing spontaneous combustion on contact with wind or the sudden rush of conflicting currents. As such, the Grizzle Mink doesn't attempt to imitate anything other than an explosion of 'life' - and lunch.

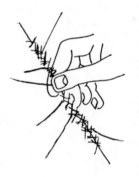

Rather than matching the large dark olive in colour and size, the Grizzle Mink was designed to match its float characteristics and the Wagnerian tendencies of the early season winds off the Downs. I sell the trout the sizzle, not the sausage. Dreamed up on the premise, 'Why wait for a trout to make your fly more effective by pulling it about with its teeth? Do it yourself at the vice!' few flies can claim to be as downright scruffy as the Grizzle Mink. And it's this feature, on a blustery early season day that makes a prim and proper fly take on the appetite appeal of a lump of wood in comparison.

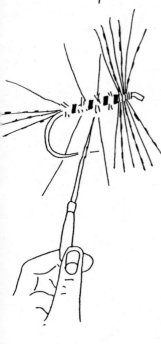

Pick out —
don't clip!

If it has nothing else going for it, a roughly-tied Grizzle Mink does all but crawl off the hook. Twisting and rolling on the surface, and skidding across it on a wind gust, I've seen trout nearly rupture themselves to clamp their teeth around it.

Long before I set up camp on the side of a river, I'd been on a mission to become a Master Flytyer; to achieve unparalleled perfection. Now I was no longer of the same mind. I'd been through the period of making daily trips to the front door in the morning waiting for the latest package of exotic flytying materials from the mail order company; the first to tune my fingers into the latest fiddly manoeuvre, the most anxious to wrap the newest (and weirdest) synthetic material round a hook, the first to kill in order to get my hands on the very latest flytying book.

I'd come in one end and out the other. Flytying was no longer an end in itself, rather it had become the means by which a trout exercising extreme caution could be taken. To this end, any fly that came off my vice had to be designed, not dressed up to look the part. It had to act the part. It had to look like it had flown off my vice, not dropped off it, stiff and lifeless.

What changed my thinking? Simply, trout. Watching them. At close quarters. Noting their reaction to naturals and artificials. On different days, at different times of the day, on different types of water.

One observation remains irrefutable. At times, the more immaculate the fly, the less 'living' it looks, the more hesitant trout are to react positively to it with hungry, teeth-gnashing and confident desire.

I know a fisherman who brings his elderly father to the river for one day's fishing each year.

'I wish I could get him down more often,' he told me when I met him the week after his father had been with him on The Hollow, and had taken the largest fish of the week. I asked him what he'd been using, for it wasn't written in the book.

'A professional flytyer in the States sends him a box of flies every year. He's the son of an old war-time friend of my father's. He doesn't order them. They just arrive. These flies are perfect in every way - and I get to use them first. He never gives me the crumpled ones, he's quite happy to use these himself.'

He went on: 'Mind you, he never lets me keep them, he always asks for them back. But at least I get to use them at their best. That's the sort of big-hearted man my father is.'

I didn't say anything, but he's the son of a cunning old fox.

In the past, I used to think that the great advantage of tying your own flies was that you could control quality. I've never been enchanted with the standard of shop-tied artificials in this country. But today, my thinking has changed.

Store flies are too well tied. Too neat and tidy, displaying a sad lack of understanding of what an insect actually looks like to the trout, when it's heaving itself from the shuck, struggling to the surface, or freeing its trapped wings from a gluey surface film.

The professional flytyer's attention to getting flies looking presentable for sale has me itching to pull them apart when I see them lying like stiffs in the tray in a morgue. An impulse not shared with quite the same enthusiasm by a trout with a few seasons on the clock seeing them parade, lifeless and unconvincing, over his lie.

The more bits hanging off my fly, the more fur flying, hackles ruffling, the more base grubbiness a fly has, the more my fins, like the trout's, bristle. Which is why my favourite flytying materials at the beginning of the season, and beyond, are body furs and hair: stiff and soft, with rogue guard hairs sticking out of the mix.

Before

Quite obviously, the old man was getting his son to knock his flies into shape, getting them in tip-top condition to take on the wilier big boys on the beat. And that day, he took them apart.

A knowledgeable angler matches his fly to the natural insect in colour and size. An assassin matches the behaviour of the fly. He spies on its every move, and notes it. He gets to know its habits and second-guesses them, designing his imitation accordingly. If in the process of imitating these characteristics, colour, or even size, is overridden, this doesn't mean the pattern will be any less successful. Going about the business of

After

understanding the trout's prey in this way, the flyfisherman is also spying on the trout who is doing the same thing - watching every move his next meal makes.

By doing this, he has begun to think like a trout, regardless of whether or not a trout is capable of thinking, or processing thoughts at all. Like all good assassins, he is starting to think instinctively.

For trout are assassins, too.

The Steel Guitar came for lunch. As the finest flytyer of his day in England, as book after book keeps reminding me, he walks past my pile of furs and bursts into uncontrollable laughter.

'What are you up to now, Patterson?'

The Steel Guitar is a big man, at least twice my size. With the same fingers that he uses to tie a split-winged dry fly on a #22, he could hand-land a tarpon.

Once the manager of the best-stocked fishing tackle shop in London, the Steel Guitar packed in the retail trade and now manages a fish farm in Wiltshire. What made him change his tune?

My theory is that he filled the store with so many esoteric bits of flyfishing tackle and flytying materials that the place could no longer accommodate his own massive proportions. One morning he arrived at the shop to find he could no longer get in the door. Something, or someone, had to go.

When the Steel Guitar isn't filling shops, he's filling pubs. He plays in a popular Country & Western band which regularly does the circuit. When it comes to music practice on the fish farm the Steel Guitar can throw open the windows of his house and strum to his heart's content with only a backing group of a few thousand stockies singing for their supper to worry about.

I walked the Steel Guitar to Sticklepath bridge through a drift of daffodils, to the weir at the bottom of the Fly Lane - and away from my vice. This weir has a three foot drop to it. Water pounds over the brim as if poured out of a bucket. This is the

sound I hear from my bedroom window. It's more like a boom at
this time of year. In the summer, it'll be hard to distinguish it
from the wind running fingers through the tops of the firs.

In front of the weir, the river broadens out into wide, flat
shallows. You can wade these in bedroom slippers. High-heeled
bedroom slippers. Deep, narrow channels and pot-holes scatter
across these shallows making them prime trout territory.

That day, the Steel Guitar and I took ourselves there just
before lunch. The river was dusted with early-Spring olives. Large
and medium in size. The sort for which the Grizzle Mink,
although an all-purpose dry fly, is such a deadly dead ringer. The
flats above the weir were transformed into an elaborately woven
carpet of speckled trout, threading, plaiting and weaving through
one another, in their efforts to gobble down dun, hatcher and
mid-water nymph.

The Steel Guitar and I perched ourselves on shooting sticks
by the weir, our eyes running along the top of the sill, watching
trout, their tails slap up against the lip, fanning their fins in the
back-push of water and tipping occasionally at the passing hatch.
Right in the middle of the shallows, about twenty yards out, a
trout as fat as a dumpling, was hard-pressed to hold its monster
proportions in the flow.

To get a Mink to this fish presented two immediate
problems. Firstly, drag. The line would have to negotiate a
multitude of currents concentrated at the crest of the weir.
Secondly, unless the Mink landed slap on the nose of the big
trout, it would almost certainly be snaffled by one of the smaller
fish and the game would be up. Paralysed by the complexity of
these simple obstacles, I piled out my Grizzle Mink, with
everything there was to cross, crossed. But although I'd snaked
out a sensible amount of slack, the Mink fell hopelessly off target.
From that moment on, my fears began to tumble into reality.

On arrival on the surface, the Mink did everything I wanted
it to do. It performed magnificently. Stumbling from one scruffy
guard hair to another and buzzing on the surface to catch its
balance, it had the same effect on the shallows as a blood droplet
in a piranha tank. The surface visibly lifted as every untethered

trout in the area bow-waved in for the kill.

In a fast-action attempt to retrieve my line and cancel the mission, I faltered, pulling in the little slack I had out in the stream. This sudden tightening caught the Mink unawares. With a full-circle spin, it haunched on its hackles and pirouetted at top speed towards the weir, a tiny soda stream of water hissing from its rear to the delight of the lynch party in full pursuit.

Mesmerised by this gripping re-enactment of the scene in *The Swiss Family Robinson* where the raft is being swept helplessly towards the thundering waterfall, the trout I set out to catch couldn't have been further from my mind.

By now the current on the lip of the fall had snatched the main belly of my line and rushed it over, resulting in panic at my end and confusion at the other. For, inexplicably, the Mink screeched to a skidding halt, teetering teasingly on the brim, the trout piled up on its tail, feverishly back-finning and swerving to avoid shooting over. For a split second, nothing moved. Trout and fly hung anxiously in suspended animation.

It was then, out of the corner of my eye, that I caught sight of a solitary bow-wave heading helter-skelter towards the stunned ensemble. As it got nearer, a head lifted out of the water surfacing a set of dentures that began gnashing at the water as if eating its way through it. With a boil, the careering trout parted the shoal of spectators, reaching the Mink at the precise moment the current claimed it for the pool beyond. With a loud pop, the blurred outline of a trout sizzled horizontally over the top of the weir, teeth snapping at a breathy nothingness.

Out of one element and into another, the flying fario applied full brakes mid-air, fins back-pedalling like windmills. And there it hung, just long enough for me to read a look of mild foolishness curl round its gills before, tipping inelegantly, it nose-dived into the frothing pool below. It had been the fat trout. And I dare say it remains in that pool to this day.

The Steel Guitar and I went on to catch several more trout on the same Mink. By the afternoon, torn to shreds, it finally parted from the hook, trout spanieling around the heels of our waders for furry crumbs.

Due to its popularity up and down the valley and elsewhere during the fifteen years since it was first launched in the angling press, there have been many variations of the Grizzle Mink, its reputation understandably blurring en route. Some models have trimmed mink bodies. Another variation advocates the use of feather herl instead of mink for the body.

Before you leap to the vice, throw all the text books out the window. I cannot stress enough that untidiness and pure scruff are the order of the day and are the keys to successful Grizzle Mink tying.

If, no matter how hard you try, your flies always seem to end up looking like an explosion in a furrier's shop, you're a lucky man. But if you're on a retainer from Art Flick not to flash your box around in front of his friends, I can only suggest one thing. Tie your Minks in boxing gloves.

But don't let on to the Steel Guitar I told you this.

The Rookery Nook was a busy, noisy place. Relatives of its residents with white eyes and black pupils were perched far back on the rumps of the cows in the surrounding fields like rodeo riders, using their beaks as crops to peck at their mounts. Yanking out tufts of hairs, the jackdaws were flying over the garden to line their nests under construction in the chimney pots of the Big House. The cows showed no interest. Like holy men they moved through the field.

The Potter, my arty-craft neighbour who has her pottery across the yard in one of the stable boxes, was on the lawn watching them drop down into the pots. Her soot-speckled dalmatians ran from one end of the lawn to the other barking at them. The jackdaws sneered back from the roof top.

One autumn the Potter had lit her first winter fire and filled her room with black tarry smoke. Now, she was trying to calculate which one of the chimney pots, which nestled like oranges in a box on top of a cluster of large brick chimney stacks, was the one that stretched up from her sitting-room fireplace, flowering out into a sky black with twig-and-cow-hair-carrying jackdaws. Every Spring she has repeated this exercise, for she can never remember *which* chimney is hers. And all the time, the offending jackdaws hopped from pot to pot in baggy trousers, dropping down, appearing and reappearing, displaying much the same state of uncertainty.

Down at the river, black clouds of a different kind were gathering for Opening Day.

April

BLACK DOGS,

BLACK FLIES, BLUE SKIES

Five - Four - Three - Two - One - Knock-knock. Roll Cast was at the back door. It was ten o'clock precisely. The season had begun.

Big Ben is set to Roll Cast's watch, which is why it's always right. A cup of no-milk, no-sugar tea was standing to attention next to a pot of freshly picked Easter beech buds, waiting for Roll Cast to arrive. I'd just stepped out of a bath. An opening day ritual, to the musical accompaniment of my very own song thrush perched on the roof outside my window. Water as hot as I can stand. Until my skin begins to pop. Two squeaky-clean legs the colour of chillis slipped into waders. I was ready and waiting for him. All set for the season.

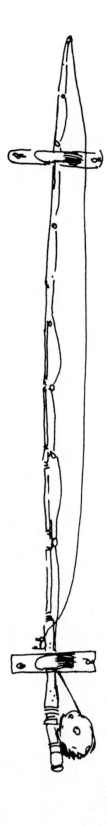

A new year, a new home - and a new rod. 'The Carrot' was on display outside the back door lying across two pine oar racks I'd put up in the terrace. It was undergoing immense scrutiny.

'I'll give it until...' Roll Cast stared up at the orange pole, paused for a moment, calculating it's life-span, '... lunch.'

Roll Cast is my very best fishing companion. Flyrods in hand, we've travelled the world together. From bear-stiff Alaskan tundra after char, to shark-infested flats in the Gulf of Mexico after tarpon. Thoughtful and sensitive, Roll Cast's ability to analyse a flyfishing problem and isolate the fundamentals means that a day on a river is not half as much fun unless it's strewn with tricky fish in impossible positions. For this reason, when you set out down the bank with Roll Cast at your side, fish or no fish, you always return a better angler, with a new insight into a sport you thought you'd grasped.

Roll Cast is one of the softest, most gentle casters you could ever have the joyful privilege to watch. Yet, if need be, he could administer the most powerful cast to get to a fish out of reach of the average angler. His rod was craftsmanship at its most basic. A nine foot reservoir pole, with a fast #5 tip and matt grey varnish, it was known as 'The Silver Stick'. If it wasn't the rod that enabled him to cast as he did, what was it?

In the back of a taxi, the late Lionel Sweet of Usk explained it to me. Protégé of Charles Ritz, unbeaten European Casting Champion for twenty years, Mr Sweet's secret of successful casting wasn't strength, but stealth. He used two images to explain two approaches. One was chopping a log with a double-handed sword, the other was slicing a silk scarf in two with a sabre using the gentlest flick of a wrist. Roll Cast was from the 'silky' casting school.

Needless to say, Roll Cast's fish-catching capabilities were legendary on The Hollow. Even the River God quaked with incredulity on occasions when Roll Cast arrived back with his catch. With the envy he heated up in the colder corners of the more competitive rods on the river, Roll Cast should have all the makings of being the very last person you'd want to share a river with. But the reverse was true, for Roll Cast is totally devoid of the earnest, wide-eyed trout-and-tackle talk that has the toes of my waders curl up and perish. Of all the things I've learned in the time I've spent with the Master, the most valuable thing was that a river is people, not just fish.

I'd met him outside the Mad House; my second season, his first. Until then I'd had the river to myself. Quite frankly, I was happy to see another face. The river was wilder then. Walking down the bank to Horse Bridge was an eerie experience. You set off with a heightened sense of living. Go any further, to the Ashes and beyond, and you waved the world good-bye. It was at around this time I wrote my first will.

Below the Wetlands, there were places that you stumbled upon wearing the same unsure, brow-furrowed expression as Humphrey Bogart in *African Queen*. The banks broken in many places, the side-sedge with expansionist policies, the river seeping into the woods forming a sea of squelchy marshes, you weren't a fisherman, you were an explorer. For this reason, I always let the Boss know I would be on the water, and in which direction I was heading - just in case. This wasn't my idea; it was his. Something about insurance. Public & Employers Liability Insurance. Whatever it was I wasn't covered - although this oversight was more than made up for by the fact that when it came to nature, you were covered in the most comprehensive way imaginable. All over, from all sides, from all angles.

On the bend above the Game Hut, where the Wild Water met the main, a plantation of razor-sharp side-sedge stood well above eye-level, about ten foot high. To get down the bank, you either had to fold your arms over your head and lean your way through the rain forest undergrowth, risking severe facial lacerations, or wade through some sinister scrub with the underfoot consistency of a giant bath sponge. You were lucky to get any fishing done at all. In places you were lucky to find the river, let alone a trout, or a gap to cast a fly through. Finding a useful fishing spot was one thing, finding your way back was another. This was the real challenge.

One morning, on a visit to this unexplored region, I decided to skirt round a thicket of hawthorn bushes. This you tracked

down using sound, rather than sight. The unpleasant location of
an active wasp nest, the bushes hummed like my old freezer. But
they marked the spot where a tiny footbridge straddled the river
in the shakiest of ways, stretching nervously across to where a
small carrier breaks loose from the main river and cuts round a
beech tree. One hundred and fifty foot tall, branches dividing and
sub-dividing as you gaze up at it from underneath, this ancient
tree forms an island of submerged tree roots and sedge more
tightly woven than a tweed jacket. I was quite prepared to find a
tribe of pigmies camping there.

On the far side of the island, I spotted a pod of trout,
refugees from the main flow of the river, cruising under the
overhanging branches of the beech tree, displaying all the
survival instincts of Kamikaze pilots. Flicking (casting was out of
the question) a fly at the trout nearest to me, I got him to follow
my fly to my feet, finally mustering enough courage to lick it off
the toe of my boot at the very last moment. I doubt if it had seen
people before, certainly not this season. I struck purposefully,
took one step back and sank. And kept on sinking. Above my
knees, over the top of my waders. I kept on going down, down,
down into gooey, grey custard. Bowls of it.

One of the tangle of overhanging branches saved my life.
Grabbing it, I pulled it to the ground. In response to this action,
it pulled me up and out, vertically, like being hoisted up by air-sea
rescue.

This was the nearest I'd ever come to death. I was proud of
myself. I hadn't panicked. I'd screamed the woods down, but I
hadn't panicked. I'd lost a wader, a sock and my fish, but I hadn't
lost my nerve. Nor, for that matter, my love of wild places.
Although my fear of wild people remains. Wild people in the
shape of the Boss, when he heard I'd strayed from the beaten
track, against his strictest instructions.

———————

'It's my new rod,' I informed Roll Cast, flicking my Carrot at
imaginary fish on an imaginary stream, 'from America.'

I'd had enough of expensive rods. I'd taken the dimensions of my favourite rod design, a Pezon Michel 8' 10", #4-5, fast tip 'Sawyer Nymph', and phoned them through to Hoagy Carmichael in Bedford, New York State and asked if it was possible to whip me one up in glass fibre. This was the cheapest material I could think of. I was in the garden when a car drew up and out jumped Hoagy grasping a rod tube.

'Take care of it,' he told me, 'It's the only glass rod with my name on it.'

Pupil of Everett Garrison, Hoagy is one of the top cane rod makers across the Pond. You might be able to afford to buy a new car, but chances are you won't be able to afford to buy a cane rod from him. Glass fibre, perhaps - but to this day, he never let me find out its price. It was a gift. Hewn out of a blank the colour of the sun setting in Tunisia, it was love at first sight - long before I'd even got the Carrot to the river. For me, it was to become my very best companion - when Roll Cast wasn't on the river. For Hoagy, the Carrot was to guarantee he had a bed for the night on a river of his dreams, whenever he came my way. For life; or at least as long as I lived there.

'If anybody asks, don't tell 'em I made it,' my favourite cane rod assembler boomed across the garden, as the sun caught the glass of the rod in my hand, light flashing off it like a spray of zest from a tangerine.

But although I love my rods intensely, I have a nerve to defend them against criticism with the aggression that I do. When it comes to rods, I'm a Philistine. I have no idea what makes a good or a bad one. I select them for all the wrong reasons, because I don't know what all the right ones are. If you were to present me with a Garrison in one hand and a bamboo shoot whipped up by a monkey in the other, I'd take the ape pole, on the technically charged premise that it looks 'more fun to fish with'. However, what I don't know about rods is more than compensated by my staggering knowledge of how to abuse them. This seems to come naturally to me.

I was recently reminded of this when, opening the door to the larder where I store my tackle, I noticed that there were more empty rod bags than full ones hanging there. And that the contents of the latter contained 'bits' rather than pieces.

The empty bag next to the freezer remains as a memorial in canvas to why I will never hang another rod on that hook in the future. In an attempt to lift a can of peas off one shelf, a jar of capers off another and remove a leg of lamb from the freezer all in one skilfully choreographed movement, I failed to rehearse the part my feet should play in the performance. Kicking the freezer door shut with pack-horse delicacy, I left a severed chunk of rod inside where the leg of lamb had been.

This was no great loss. A cane rod of eight foot or so, of no fixed manufacturer, I had fallen in love with it at a tackle bazaar. The appeal hadn't been its design or functional possibilities, but its colour. This was a delicious honey yellow, the hue of a well-smoked Meerschaum. Its hopelessly second-hand appearance oozed tales of scores of fish caught, a tradition I jealously wanted it to continue: with me at the cork end. What I hadn't immediately appreciated was that these creels of fish it had monotonously bent into during its career hadn't been the ten ounce Tamar wildies of my imagination. On the contrary, it would be fair to assume that it had spent its days stuck out the back of some Caribbean fishing smack trolling for tuna to which it had attached itself on a regular basis. Held out parallel to the lawn, the tip dipped over and stroked my toes under the weight of a rod length of floating line, the cane reduced to the consistency of cardboard in the rain.

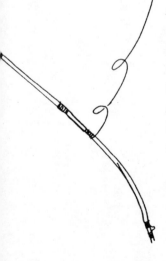

The next hook along held the only rod to survive my childhood. There had been two. The first was long stamped into an early grave when a bull planted the pieces in a Welsh field as I howled tears from the safety of my uncle's car. The survivor in question, a glass fibre Milbro, had started life as a nine-footer. Even in my awkward hands, its perfect balance was unarguable. After two seasons, it was well on the way to making rod design history as one of the earliest examples of parabolic structure, by accident.

Barely an outing went by without two or three inches snapping off the tip. By the time it finally departed, it had become of massive interest to curio-corner tackle collectors. Whittled down to a poky six footer, it had a top section all of fifteen inches. Also several unique features had been added. The most controversial being a length of 15mm copper plumbing pipe replacing a broken ferrule. This contributed greatly to the strength of the rod but at the same time gave it the unmistakable profile of a snake that had half-digested a small deer. I like to think that the thug who stole my friend's van in Ireland that summer in 1980 did so blinded by an unquenchable lust to possess my Milbro inside. But I rather suspect that a Pentax camera took priority.

In the Attic Age, the first season on The Hollow cost me every penny I had. To stay alive between fishing trips I was eating everything I could catch. If I didn't catch, I didn't eat. I filled my pockets with watercress, dandelion leaves, mushrooms and anything else that was edible down there on the river. But more damaging to my health than poisonous toadstools was my tackle. Not having the resources to kit myself out with a suitable rod, I had to make do with a 9-foot, 3-piece cane Sharpe's seatrout rod given to me by my uncle out of the kindness of his heart - and on the advice of his doctor.

My uncle, a strapping giant of six and a half foot, had a favourite party-trick of picking up my two cousins and tucking one under each arm. This would have been impressive enough, but both my cousins had children of their own who liked to be picked up too. These he perched on his shoulders forming a wriggling family tree spanning three generations. You begin to get an idea of the weight and casting action of my rod when I tell you that after two hour's fishing with it, my uncle was ready for early retirement.

I lugged this fourteen ounce tree trunk round with me for two seasons. I have a two inch groove in my shoulder to prove it. Quite clearly, given time, this rod would have destroyed me - a feeling, I suspect, not shared in reverse. At the end of our first season together, it became apparent that I was fishing with tackle that would survive nuclear fall-out. Or so it seemed.

On one of my last trips to a West-country lake, in a

nostalgic frame of mind, I took it out with me on a boat. Opening up the bag and remembering all the fun times we had had together, I placed the middle section down next to me, forgetting that I was sitting side-on in the boat. It plummeted to the bottom of the lake with minimum grace or flow, registering on the Richter Scale on its arrival.

Having gone through almost all possible variations of immobilising rods, I entered into an entirely new, though less imaginative, phase. I started to make rods disappear into thin air. An 8-foot custom-built lake rod was placed on a luggage rack on a train bound for London, never to be seen again. I got to the tube station before realising that the hand that once held it was empty. By the time I got back to the station the train was gone, my rod with it.

During an indecisive period on lakes, I could never work out whether I wanted to fish a sink-tip, a sinker, or a floater. This left me scampering round ponds like a porcupine, rods bristling from all sides. I never quite got used to this way of fishing and ached for the return to simpler days when I could handle any depth with a floater and a leader of various lengths.

I quickly returned to this single rod system when I leaned Rod No 2 - a Richard Walker reservoir rod - up against a tree in a wood and forgot which wood. To this day I still think the wood moved off to another hillside when my back was turned. I was certain it was right behind me when I was fishing; maybe it was me that moved.

By now you're probably thinking that it's as well that I've escaped the desire to own a rod glued together and whipped up by a craftsman from the finest Korean tonkin. Well, I do possess a rare collectors' item. A nine-foot Pezon Michel dating back to the 1950s. Most people would have this in a glass case. I'm too busy sending it to the menders to pay it such reverence. I still have the rod in two pieces. But it's been in many more bits in the past. Referred to as the 'Alder Larvae Rod' by those who go with me to early season stillwaters, it's the only stick I know that can propel a nymph the weight of a small person the sort of distance I require it to travel. It rivals my uncle's long-scuppered Sharpe's for weight, but if I can jam the butt down the sleeve of my jacket I can just bend it two degrees from the straight if I don't mind visiting an osteopath the day after.

On a Yorkshire lake, I had the combination of jacket sleeve and backbone working in symphonic harmony. I was hurling out church roofs disguised as alder larvae with somnambulistic ease. False-casting these nymphs made a magnificent whirring noise. Like a squadron of helicopters landing in a football stadium. In the late afternoon, at maximum velocity during one of these casting work-outs, everything suddenly went limp. At first I thought my jacket sleeve had split at the seams. But looking up I caught sight of my top section snapped off at the ferrule shooting down my line like a ski-lift out of control heading down the bank towards the angler next to me. A direct hit would have put me in the dock for manslaughter. Instead I was guilty of murdering yet another rod.

The repair cost me three inches off the length, but gained me ten yards the next time I cast a line with it. Somehow the loss in length improved the brute-force ratio of its action almost beyond belief.

That year it became clear that all my rods were doomed from the outset. In whoever's hands they were. I lent a seven-foot six-inch Farlow Sharpe rod to a friend to test cast. It had, so I was told by the people who know such things, a 'truly rare action'. Perhaps, because of this, I couldn't get on with it and it was up for sale. That evening it was returned to me with a 'truly rare action' even I could recognise. With the top section split from top ring to third one down, it waggled from side to side making clacking noises like a Cuban folk group. My friend took it to the menders leaving me to collect. It's still there. I daren't pick it up in case I catch it in the door on my way out.

I finally admitted to myself that I could no longer afford to fish with cane. Even when I wasn't fishing with a rod I was still abusing it. Living by a river, once a rod is up, it's up for the season. Sometimes, for life. My little Cliff Constable cane rod put together especially for me by the Steel Guitar, and initialled, will never travel again - unless the sun-roof is open. Left on oar racks

in the open air for a season, the ferrules have rusted together with the effectiveness of Loctite. My Pezon Michel 'Sawyer Nymph' that spent the winter lying across two shelf brackets emerged this Spring with a curve in the tip that can only be fully appreciated by lovers of art nouveau.

Now all my rods are glass fibre. They need to be. Glass fibre is the nearest to disposable rod material I can get.

At 'Au Coin de Pêche' in Paris, the highly sensitive rod craftsman, Serge Pestel, at one time made glass rods that felt like cane. After a demonstration casting session down Rue Wagram outside the shop, I bought two. One at nine foot, the other at eight and a half foot. Almost unique for rods this length, they both took #4 lines and had the speed in the tip to slam a nymph into a trout's mouth as if it had been shot from a cross-bow.

On my return from the bottom of the river, I found one of the Five Steves on my doorstep. He'd been passing and wanted to check the roof was still on. Forgetting to empty the car, I asked him in for a drink, or two. At midnight, having lost the use of both his legs, I pushed him across the lawn in a wheelbarrow to my car to take him home. My car door normally clunks shut. That night, it crunched. There were too many bits of my eight and a half foot rod to count.

By now, I'm uninsurable. I've worn out the Lutine bell. And things don't get better.

Roll Cast arrived - on time again - to pick me up for a day on a local lake he'd discovered nearby. I am late getting up. I fly downstairs and lean my 'Alder Larvae' rod and what remained of my nine-foot French rod against his car while I get my boots. I come back and find the car reversed in the yard to pick me up. Roll Cast is staring at the ground. A 4-cylinder Daimler doesn't step over rods, rather it blends them into the cobbles. We had to chip the pieces out. As well as two rods, the car ground two Hardy Princess reels into two Cortland lines.

The nine-footer was terminal. The 'Alder Larvae' rod went back to the repair shop. Now a further three inches shorter, it casts even better than before.

A few years back, I was tempted into buying a Hardy

'Smuggler', a poacher's rod. It comes in many pieces (which is a good start for me) and folds away into nothing. Nothing to break, I think to myself. I take it with me to the British Virgin Islands on a business trip and I blood it on parrot fish, horse-eye jacks and yellow-tail snappers from the coral reefs on mayfly nymphs. On the second leg of the tour, I visited Bermuda where I met up with a business colleague from France who I knew to be gay. With a couple of hours to spare, I invited him to share the costs of a skiff off Mangrove Bay Wharf. Out on the reef, we shared the rod, flicking Polystickles and black lures off the back of a skiff into a sea drunk with foul-smelling chum. Whereas I managed to hook two small tuna, when it came to his turn, my colleague went on to catch a whole paint-box of frilly-finned, brightly coloured fish, including a Rock Hind that resembled a pair of polka-dot boxer shorts, and a Spotlight Parrot fish that matched his skimpy turquoise shorts. At the end of the day, I grouped his catch together in the record book, referring to them as a 'an excellent bag of lingerie fish'

During my ten-day stay, the rod and I had become inseparable - until we got on the plane back. At Puerto Rico, I changed flights. My rod didn't. At the PanAm desk, I was told that it was on its way to Mexico City. Thanks to my 'Smuggler', I found out that my insurance company still has enough funds invested to keep my business.

Back in Paris, Serge Pestel has received the news about the two rods I bought from him. He's insulted - and highly sensitive. Vincent, my friend in Paris, persuades him to make me a new top for my eight and a half foot if I bring in the pieces next time I'm over.

I'm ecstatic, and finding myself in Paris, I crawl into his store on bended knees. I plead apologies and promise that it will never happen again; that I'll treasure the rod with my life. He asks to see the rod. What rod? I can't remember having one in the Metro with me? I try and explain, but I find it hard it difficult to talk. Mainly because my tongue had spot-welded itself to the roof of my mouth. I'd left the rod in a café on my way to his shop.

You'll appreciate by now that my ability to abuse rods is

bordering on the supernatural. In this advanced state I am even able to transmit my destructive powers to other fishermen, just by fishing with them.

Roll Cast and I went fishing the Usk. Even before I had my rod up, Roll Cast was taking his to pieces. The beauty of a six-foot six-inch tooth-pick is that you can fit it inside a car without having to take it up and down. This was one of the reasons why he had one made up for himself from Cliff Constable cane. The ugly side of a six-foot six-inch rod is that if you catch the fly on the upholstery of the car as you're pulling it out, the tip snaps off making a sound like a pellet leaving an airgun. A noise that, in the memory, scrapes your eardrums like a fork on china.

Unfortunately, he had brought a spare. A rod made for him by the rod-assembly genius, the late Geoffrey Rivaz, from a Pezon Michel blank. Later that afternoon, on our way back to the hotel for tea, we were feeling our way along a steep bank, the river lapping at our feet. To get a grip and to climb higher up the slope, I stood on one end of a fallen tree trunk. Roll Cast was at the other end and between us, we set the log rolling. I jumped clear, but the log bowled Roll Cast over, pinning him to the edge of a small cliff hanging over the river. Amid flying arms and legs, his rod, reel and line arched majestically through the air, silently cartwheeling into the heart of the salmon pool below, the deepest on the beat.

Vincent joined me for a fishing weekend in Wales. We shared a hotel room and as a bedtime story I told him the story I'm recounting now. He's not a man to panic and he assured me that he had brought over with him an old Hardy Jet glass rod #7. A rod that had seen many years' service and would be able to foil all my mystical powers of devastation.

I should have known that it didn't stand a chance which, of course, it didn't. Fourth cast into the hatch, the whippings mysteriously unwound like a bobbin of wire and the joint shattered from ferrule to first ring.

I'd like to think that there's a moral to these tales, but there isn't. Only that it seems to me that the more intent am I *not* to break rods, the faster they seem to break. Or else they simply vanish.

I expect one day, I'll relax and take a rod with me to the grave. But until then, I must live with the fact that if I break a rod on the bank-side, there's no longer quite the same stampede of fishing friends offering to lend me their spare.

If, that is, they have a spare left to offer me.

'Do aircraft land here frequently?' I asked the Boss as he bicycled past Roll Cast and me standing watching a fish, close in, below Sticklepath Bridge. The banks had been laundered, steam ironed - with a crisp crease of trimmed side-sedge, no higher than your knee, no lower than the top of your shin.

Even though I must have walked down the track to the Mad House and back a thousand times since Christmas, the walk to the river on the first day of the season is a different journey, with a special kind of magic. A journey from the past into the present, where everything is new. The first days of other seasons try to come to mind, but are squashed by the excitement and expectancy of the first day of the new season. My mind is too excited to reminisce. To escape London and come to the Wild Wood Lodge is one sort of release. To leave it behind you up the track and venture down to the river to fish is another escape entirely. An escape from an escape, and it's this that puts a different skip in your step, as if it's the very first time the gate has been thrown open to you, allowing you access to a place you've always dreamed of going, but have never been allowed or invited. A place where your happiness lives.

In my hand, my rod felt new, unfamiliar, awkward. I tucked it under my arm out of the way. I was self-conscious about it. I tried to reduce my pace to a gentle stroll - I was going at a gallop. But even though I managed to slow down quite considerably to a cleverly concealed trot, my mind was still at a sprint arriving at the river long before I did. By the time I reached Sticklepath Bridge to gaze over, I was on such a high my ears were popping. I tipped a generous libation of Laphroaig from

a small hip-flask into the dark, swirling depths.

It had been a night of 70mph gales and the wind was still roaring high up in the tree tops. It was too dangerous for me to walk the Square Dance through Cakewood. The banks were strewn with logs and sticks and fallen branches. I poked my head inside the Mad House and walked in to check the new fishing record book, a large format diary. The first day of the season was indicated by a Biro slipped in between the crisp pages. I had been careful to walk across the mats on the floor, rather than the lino, with wet boots. I didn't want to leave any footprints. I would have hated the next man in after me to discover that he hadn't been the first visitor of the season. My first job was to make casts at imaginary trout holds, whether there was a fish there or not - just to check and see if I could still get a fly through the trees behind me in certain woody areas, leafless or not. I also wanted to see the Boss's new benches.

The river was swollen and sullen after the wettest March for a decade. What's left of the water, after the plants have had their fill, we'll see in late June, maybe July. The river wasn't really fishable, unless a sprinkling of large dark olives broke ranks at lunch-time for a happy hour. It's for this reason that the season on southern chalkstreams normally opens on the first day of May, when the fly is friskier, and the trout fatter. The season on The Hollow had always started on the first day of April. This gives any new rod a chance to have a walk around and acquaint himself with the river before the more generous hatches begin and the mayfly arrives. It also gives him time to get to know the general lay of the land; time to note the position of the top and bottom boundaries; time to cast, if not a fly, at least an eye, over the main river, carriers, drains and ditches that lie between them. Time to mark likely fishing and picnic spots. And, more importantly, time to give the Boss a darned good listening to.

The Doctor doesn't usually travel the distance to come fishing until the first week in May. He certainly doesn't take his rod out of its bag until he's heard the first cuckoo. And this year, the cuckoo was late in arriving. The Boss was getting anxious. His pick-up kept stopping on Sticklepath Bridge, a head would appear out of the window and revolve like a radar sensor.

The problem was quickly solved. One morning, the Doctor phoned the Boss on his car phone to warn him that he was on his way back from a conference in Portsmouth and would be making a flash, midweek visit to the river. The Boss was ready and waiting for him behind a tree at the Mad House where the cuckoo normally makes his first appearance staking claim to his territory - all the woodland and fields, from the Firs down to the Ashes.

The Boss watched the Doctor park his car and get out, waiting until he'd turned the corner into the Square Dance and disappeared into the woods. Cupping his hands, the Boss put them to his mouth and began wafting a haunting, melodic chant. Flapping the flat of his fingers at the base of the cup, the way only Larry Adler knows how, he added a sinister, but super-lifelike vibrato to an award-winning cuckoo call, upsetting pheasants everywhere.

The next morning the Doctor was back on the river with time to spare - and his rod. We could relax. The season had officially opened.

———————

The Fast Shallows below the Red Gate are exactly as the name suggests. They're fast, and they're shallow, zipping down a slight gradient at a wild, bubbling, sparkling rate more akin to a rain-fed stream, rather than a sedate chalkstream. But we don't complain - and neither do the trout lucky enough to live in one of the many gravel-bottomed soup bowls laid out on this fizzing dining-room table, waiting for an insect to drop in at lunch-time.

These shallows are only two hundred yards from the footbridge that marks the end of a length of thick water that flows in front of the end of the lawn at the Doctor's Cottage. As soon as this water has massaged the backs of the resident shoal of grayling on the ford behind the footbridge, it tumbles down the shallows to the only other island on the fishery, stopping for nothing and no one.

From there onwards, the river fans out wide, rolling deep

and mysteriously for the last quarter of a mile, down to the Old Iron Bridge at the end of the fishery, and away. Both sides of the shallows are lined with hawthorn bushes. You can't fish them from the far bank. You can't even see the river through a dense curtain of hawthorn, alder and sloe bushes. On the nearside bank, things aren't much better. There are only two places where it's possible to part the bushes and slide a rod out into the daylight and make contact with this giggly stream that has never grown up.

But even when you've found a window to open, there's only room to cast to fish directly across from you. It's like fishing through a car window. For this reason, at this time of year, I climb into the bottom of the shallows and wade up it. This can take a morning, or more, to fish sensibly. And this is where Roll Cast and I set off to spend the first few hours of the season. Large dark olives will be making their first appearance at lunch-time if text books, like this one, are to be believed. But their show is no more than a quick, short strum on the banjo, as this book must be quick to point out. The hawthorn fly, on the other hand, as this book will reveal, is available to the trout all day long, at a shake of the wind's finger. And if there's no wind, I still have an option. I can always try and persuade Roll Cast to go to the head of the shallows and shake bushes.

To the flyfisherman, the hawthorn is an insect. To the trout on the shallows below the Red Gate, it's manna from heaven.

Hawthorn flies gather in, and over, flowering hawthorn bushes where they spend most of the time sucking at the buds and hovering in their hundreds. A restless, smoky cloud, at the mercy of the merest whim of a breeze. Born under decaying leaves in between the rotting floorboards of Wild Wood and the Ashes, the hawthorn is a land insect, not an aquatic one. But it's thanks to them that the season starts with a crash, a bang and a wallop, for the hawthorn fly is the King of Belly-floppers, bringing trout to the surface for the first time in the season.

On the back of the hand, the hawthorn looks like a large housefly. In the air, it looks like a biker in a black leather jacket trailing a long, black pony-tail. This pony-tail is a pair of hairy legs. One thing is for sure, when the wind drops or changes direction, the airborne hawthorn very speedily becomes waterborne - and trout bound. The hawthorn doesn't shy off giving a lively demonstration of why it has never won a medal at the Olympics. Wallowing around the surface on a big, shiny belly, what it loses in spectators at the Olympic Pool, it gains in crowds of winter-starved trout queuing up on the Red Gate Shallows to pounce on it.

I poked my head through a gap in the bushes. Roll Cast pointed to a thin-waisted male hawthorn head-butting my phoney artificial which is trailing on the end of my line in the wind. In one quarter, at least, my artificial has met with approval. For a hawthorn fly with only a couple of weeks to get it all together, this was no casual affair. A hawthorn can't be too fussy. Trout, however, can.

The hawthorn is perhaps the only fly I know that can put the fear of God into a trout when it first appears. I've often wondered why this should be. Maybe it's because the hawthorn is one of the first flies to bring trout to the surface and away from his sub-surface supermarket. I think this has something to do with it. Unlike the large dark olive dun which the trout 'follows' to the surface in nymphal form, the hawthorn is delivered to him from above. Crunch, just like that. With the large dark olive, as with every other water-born insect, the introduction is a great deal more formal and above (or rather below) board. In its nymphal, or pupal form, the trout can investigate the potential food item's credentials as it tracks it in ascent. The trout finally makes its move when its prey is at its most vulnerable, when it is hatching out, trapped at the surface between stages of metamorphosis. When it is 'between insects'.

There's a school of thought that says that trout wouldn't feed on the surface if nymphs hadn't brought their stomachs up there to begin with.

Even so, hawthorns are fearsome creatures. There have been days when I have walked the river bank wishing I had been wearing a crash-helmet. A dense hatch of mayfly can give you the uneasy feeling that they're crawling all over you (which they probably are), but their soft buttery bodies and gauzy wings prevent you from thinking for one moment that you're at risk of injury. A female hawthorn on the rampage falling wide of her mate, however, can fracture your skull.

This early on in the season the hawthorns don't usually appear until there is a blink of sun. For the past three days, this hadn't been happening until near midday but I was still hopeful.

One of the Two Scarlets, a pair of identical twins who share a weekday rod, but exactly which one I have no idea, had been out yesterday fishing the upper Bywater near the Boss's cottage. Early on in the season, big fish make their way up in this direction from the Wetlands. High up in the smell valves of their nebs they carry the walnutty scent of escapee calf pellets from the stew ponds. There had been a gale the night before, and hawthorns had poured out of the bushes onto the river like Licorice Allsorts out of a split bag.

Neither of the Two Scarlets are big men, and the One Scarlet in question certainly wasn't any bigger than the other One Scarlet, which isn't surprising since both the Two Scarlets were exactly the same size. In fact, if there's a high wind on the river, we tighten the guide ropes of whichever of the Two Scarlets is on the river that day, and make sure the pegs are well hammered into the ground.

He'd seen a fish rising close under the far bank, in some dark corner. He'd covered it with a Hawthorn and the fish had taken it without hesitation. After a long fight, the One Scarlet in question managed to get it within reach. A cock fish, it was a monster for the river weighing not that much more than the One Scarlet; five pounds, perhaps more. The fish was not happy. The story goes that when the One Scarlet got it on the bank, it leapt out of his arms, got up and started to slap him round the face with its tail.

To adopt the pinned-down hawthorn's inelegant posture, the artificial needs to lie with its body rubbing into the film. This is impossible to achieve without the hook hanging under the water - if you use normal tying methods. For this reason, along with my more conventional pattern, I always carry with me a version tied

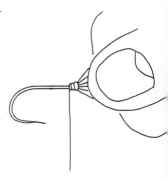

in the Funneldun tying-style. The trick I use to make sure my hawthorns land belly down, hook up on the surface is as simple as tying a normal Funneldun. I always carry a Hawthorn tied this way, for the day I don't will be the day I find a trout that has seen everything, has probably been hooked by everything, and still lives to tell the tale. And it's usually the biggest on the beat.

But sometimes the problem of getting a trout to take your fly has nothing to do with the pattern, upside down, inside out, Mini Mouse or King Kong. Instead, it has everything to do with being able to get the fly to the trout in the first place.

On a well-kept chalkstream - a chalkstream where the bank-side vegetation is left well alone - the fish have places where they can lie unreachable, unmolested. Here, the fishing has an edge. Such enclaves where a trout can dig himself in, are available on the Red Gate Shallows, in spades.

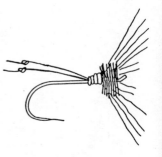

But even if you climb in and wade, flyfishing these furiously fast shallows is no easier than if you stayed at home and fished in your bedroom. Hawthorn bushes hang on all sides like the screen round a four-poster bed. If you're a trout considering moving into the area, take my advice, stay clear if you suffer from claustrophobia. This is not a problem in the mind of one particular self-assured, round-shouldered specimen squeezed into a corner of a black run behind a submerged boulder where wisps of creamy fast water fizzed like soda. This was the position he held as we watched him lift to hawthorns showering down on top of him from a small area just above a sloe tree. Here a large group of hawthorns was attempting to bob on the spot, a high proportion of them ending up in the river and coming down the current at full-speed, as if riding an avalanche.

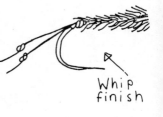

Whip finish

Every one of my fool-hardy attempts at casting at him had thrown my fly into the arms of the bushes, where any self-preserving natural should have stayed cowering to begin with. But the greatest problem wasn't the bushes in front of me, it was the impenetrable wall of grasping branches directly to my rear.

It was my partner's turn at the fish. I poked my head round a bush to watch him in action, perhaps even sneer. But with Roll Cast this was not to be, and I knew it. With a flick of the wrist,

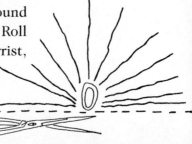

rod pointing in the direction of an area just above the trout, a length of line was thrown forward, Roll Cast's finger holding the line up against the cork handle, terminating slack. I heard someone putting the lid back on a plastic dustbin. It was the trout tipping the surface, crunching his way through hawthorns as if they were macademia nut brittle ice cream.

The rod tilting to the side, Roll Cast raised the tip just as the fly moved down past the trout - on a line parallel to it, but ten foot short of it. As soon as the fly levelled with the trout's tail, Roll Cast raised the tip again smartly, the rod still tilting to the side. As the line and the fly slid towards us, his wrist began to brake slightly as the tip passed the vertical position.

As it moved back slowly, the bushes stretched out to claim the rod tip - but it had reached its most rearward position, and there it stopped. And with it, the line. The rod swung into a vertical position. With thumb on top of the rod handle, Roll Cast applied pressure to pull against the line lying idle in the water in front of him. With the thumb squeezing down into the cork and pointing at an area above the trout, he brought the rod tip forward swiftly, bending into the line. As the rod tip lowered, the line unrolled across the shallows. The fly continued, programmed to strike the black run. Held tight against the cork, the line straightened out and the leader stepped forward, ditching the hawthorn three feet up from the boulder.

The trout didn't wait for the Hawthorn to come; the trout came to the Hawthorn. It sucked the fly in through its mouth along with a creamy mixture of air and frothy water which it blew it out through its gills, making sure the chewy Hawthorn remained to be crunched and swallowed without ceremony. But it never came to this.

Roll Cast tightened. The trout turned to the fast run of shallows for help, this was granted and the fish disappeared down river, not stopping until it was past the island and into open water, the Old Iron Bridge and freedom in sight.

Now you know how Roll Cast got his name.

I recognised the face in the bakery. Not a village face, a river face. It took me a while to place it. It belonged to a guest of one of the rods, from way back. I reintroduced myself to him, avoiding having to mention his name. I hadn't a clue what it was.

I quickly learned that he was down from Scotland visiting his friend, now too old to lift a rod, let alone wave it nimbly across a river blotched with the first sprinkle of olives, like on that Spring day early one April when we met.

Why should the memory of this flyfisherman stick in my mind? What made him unforgettable? The way he caught fish? No, the way he landed them. A dyed-in-the-wool salmon fisherman, his trip to the south of England to fish a chalkstream had been a new experience - and it showed. All his salmon fishing life, trout had been considered second-rate citizens, small fry. When one was found to have attached itself to the end of his line while working a salmon fly, it was whisked out as speedily and as unceremoniously as possible in order that normal service might resume, and real fishing continue.

Leaning with my arms folded on the rod rack outside the Mad House, I watched him make contact with his first fish of the day, his first trout on a trout fly. As soon as it rose to take the little olive, he switched to automatic pilot; or rather, pivot. Turning on his heel, he laid the Greenheart across his chest and placed it over his left shoulder between neck and shoulder blade. Then with his back to the trout, he walked away from the river, horsing the trout up onto the bank behind him.

I was reminded of this unique landing procedure when I received an invitation to fish a stretch immediately below the Hollow beat, where the Boundary Stream dips under the road to join up with Manor Stream. This classic chalkstream beat cuts a deep channel through six hundred yards of open meadow-land before disappearing into a large walled orchard that forms the bottom boundary of my good friend Roddy Doggy's two acre garden. He rents this stretch every year, and keeps it for himself.

Everywhere Roddy Doggy goes, Ghillie goes with him. Ghillie is a big black dog, now silver with old age, yet he still manages to find the will to jump free of an acute arthritic grip

and launch himself horizontally into the flow to mouth-land Roddy's catch flopping on the end of his line. In effect, Roddy Doggy doesn't land fish, he has them fielded. Once his aquatic doggy's jowls have flapped their way across the river like a pair of black rubber flippers, their grip is as sure as death. Roddy Doggy claims that he's only ever lost one fish using this method.

'The fly slipped free and lodged itself in Ghillie's ear,' he explained. 'He can land fish, but could I get him to land himself? And on light tackle?'

Roddy Doggy may have some unconventional ideas about bringing trout ashore, but when it comes to tying flies to catch them, he never strays far from the straight and narrow. During the months of April and May he fishes one fly pattern to the exclusion of all others, and with huge success. A big black brute, the same colour as his dog - and just as fearsome. A fly designed to bite back.

The reason why this killer fly is the same colour as the dog is because it *is* the dog. Bits of it, at least. Roddy Doggy hoped the training might have seeped through into its hair. He wanted a fly that not only caught fish, but landed them. This big black fly was Roddy Doggy's hawthorn pattern.

But Ghillie without Roddy Doggy was like a grenade without a pin. When separated from his master, Ghillie ceased to be the cuddly four-legged flytying kit. In his capacity as guard dog, Ghillie was to be avoided at all costs.

About this time of year, Vincent comes over from Paris. A New Yorker of Irish descent, Vincent married a French girl he met as a student at Syracuse University. After his studies, he moved back with her to Paris, where he now lives and works - and where I met him many years ago when we turned a business meeting into tackle talk. We'd met Roddy Doggy in The Manor pub across the field from his house, and sat talking until closing time. He invited us to fish his beat while he was away visiting his great aunt in Salisbury the next day. A full moon guided us back down the platinum farm track to the cloistered silence of Wild Wood which we fumbled through as fast as our legs could carry us. The Boss was waiting for us outside the back door with a bottle of last year's elderberry wine which, foolishly, I had once commented on favourably. He also had his guitar. He sat in the kitchen singing the blues at us like an old rook well into the early morning.

The next morning, the gutters bubbled. The downpour threw itself up against the window, the panes surged and throbbed. Outside, the daffodils, like two dozen old women shawled in yellow plastic macs rattled under the hedge. We drove to the village, avoiding looking out of the window at the river. We bought newspapers and decided to spend the morning reading and drinking coffee, waiting for the weather to clear. At midday, Vincent suggested we have a local apple brandy each - a Calvados, which he'd brought from his home in Normandy, to pour into the dregs of our coffee. Everyone in his area has an orchard and makes their own distinctive version of this aqua vitae. It's a thriving industry.

Vincent served up two glasses of his apple brandy on a plate, with two lumps of sugar sitting next to it. He likes to dunk sugar lumps in his glass and suck out the whacky apple juice. It's a ritual he turns into a religion. At about two o'clock, the rain and wind dropped, and a powerful sun reflected our minds back to fishing. Putting the bottle into his fishing bag, Vincent slipped the sugar lumps into the top pocket of his shirt, and we set off to Roddy Doggy's by car. Although only five minutes away, we didn't want to waste any time.

We parked by the orchard, and decided to make our way up to Roddy Doggy's house, just in case he'd decided to cancel his trip because of the weather, and to let him know we hadn't cancelled ours. Half way up the track to the house I heard the sound of a motorcycle coming towards us. A motorcycle with teeth that flashed at us when the sun suddenly broke through a cloud. It was Ghillie, puffed out to the size of a small car, as black as night, with a mouth opened up like a ferry ready to load lorries. Airborne, he was heading for us at knee-level.

I was about to turn and run when I noticed that Vincent was frozen to the spot, standing like a Saint, a martyr from the Bible, staring straight at the dog.

I'd heard that the best way to confront a man-eating

anything was not to show fear. The worst thing you could do was turn and run. I planted myself in Roddy Doggy's orchard. But just as the dog was about to reach us, Vincent made a move. He stretched his hand out to the canine apocalypse, as if to offer forgiveness.

Whatever he was doing, it worked. The slavering jaw clunked shut. Dropping back to earth, the dog crumpled up. Lying submissively on his back like a satanic dhurrie, his tongue flopped out. Dewy eyes rolled in the direction of Vincent's outstretched hand, sugar lumps piled there in a life-saving posture.

'I thought the sugar was for the Calvados,' I panted at Vincent, relieved that I hadn't been reduced to the chunky consistency of Pedigree Chum.

'Sometimes,' Vincent told me.

A week of persistent cold winds had held back any hope of a hatch of upwing fly on The Hollow - and it had been the same on the Manor Stream below the road. But the afternoon, like Ghillie, sweetened. In the time it took us to put our rods up, the sky turned blue and bright, although the air stayed clear and sharp. Too sharp to expect any duns, but not stinging enough to discourage the hawthorn fly from coming out of the bushes to meet the tepid sunshine. Away from the shelter of the orchard, in the roadside meadows, a gusty breeze whistling down the Manor Stream, was awaiting them.

It's interesting to watch trout select positions to pounce on hawthorn flies. There are two kinds of trout. One takes up a Hoover position. This is where the river narrows under a bank and where it can suck away at a steady flow of fallen fly. Then there's the mid-field position. Here a trout plonks itself in the middle of the stream and patrols unceasingly. Eyes and mouth wide open. When the first few hawthorn fly arrive, I like to watch trout pluck up the courage to pick them off the surface. Swirls and pirouettes. It's pure ballet, and it could be set to music.

By the look of the fish we saw rising in the orchard, they'd spent all morning at Covent Garden. The afternoon was punctuated with the sound of fridge doors closing as trout stuffed their crops with crispy, hard-backed hawthorns filled with hard luck stories of how they wished they'd taken swimming lessons. I pointed to a trout tucked under a clump of grass in a Hoover position and gave Vincent my last Hawthorn pattern so he could get to work. I set about tying another for myself.

Where Roddy Doggy has a portable flytying kit forever at his side in the shape of the fur-ball Ghillie, I keep a small leather collar box in the boot of the car. This contains the minimum of flytying tools and materials so that no matter where I might land, if fish in the area take fly, I can always cook something up. A hand-vice is fun to use, if you're stumped for entertainment. But I always pack a small vice the American flytyer and author, Darrel Martin, gave me one day when he dropped by and fished with me a few years back. You don't clamp it to the table, you screw it into a log. To tie up another one of my Hawthorns, I stuck it in one of Roddy Doggy's orchard trees.

On completion, I went up river towards the road, away from the orchard and into the meadow filled with knock-kneed lambs, to fish in the wave. I took four trout before the clouds got darker, blacker than the clouds of hawthorn that had now dissolved away with the sunlight. The first fish was as long as my forearm, but as thin as my forefinger. A wild trout that had over-wintered it's last winter. Roddy Doggy doesn't stock his water. He has an even better system. He just doesn't fish any more - and he doesn't let anyone fish it, either. We were lucky that day.

I kept the larger of the fish at just over a pound. Rolling it in a large wild rhubarb leaf, I pushed it head-first down the inside of my boot to give to Roddy Doggy. And just in case he decided to take a rod down with him the next time he went to pick apples, I tied him up a Hawthorn before removing my vice from his sap-filled orchard.

May

MAY IT DRIZZLE

Mid-week, when the water-meadows call you, the fastest way you can get to them from Covent Garden is by bike. A glance at your watch to check your plan isn't too outrageous, an eye around the floor to make sure your boss is in a meeting, a muttered excuse about something you had for lunch, down to the basement to the place where your bicycle is stored away ready for such emergencies - and then the most scary part of the whole operation: The Invisible Man Act.

Knapsack strapped to your back, wheeling a muddy bike up the stairs, you pretend nobody can see or hear you. The only clue is the dubious trail of dried earth cakes you leave behind you. Now you have to get through reception and out of the door. But

your boss's meeting - it finished early! There he is! Striding in through the door just as you are cycling out!

There are daydreams - and there are nightmares you have during the day. This is one of the latter. But if you make it out alive, it's a precious handful of stolen hours, guaranteed, by the river.

All this is a long way off yet. Two, maybe three hours away. Still, it's well worth the conspiracy - and the consequences. And the quicker you pedal, the faster you and your fears magic away into the wide blue yonder.

The station is on the other side of town. The travel services collapse twice a day at rush hour, and the evening rush-hour begins after lunch. A bike, I found, is quicker than a taxi. Fearlessly, I slalom down Oxford Street, swooping in and out between buses, taxis and cars, at extreme angles. I should have been a fighter-plane pilot. But today, I'm a trapeze artist, catching every green light just as it swings my way. If I miss one, I don't notice. My eye is on cars coming at me from either side, not the lights up ahead. I often mount the pavement. In my mind, I'm already on the river bank. If the police stopped me, I'd plead guilty to wearing waders in a built-up area.

At Marble Arch the traffic is static and doubled up right back to Selfridges. Time to flap. My hands leave the handlebars, and I start paddling in between stationary cars, pushing off their roofs, knees ready to deflect vehicles on both sides, feet pedalling ten to the dozen. Now, skimming across the tops of ticking taxis and throbbing cars, I don't cycle to Hyde Park, I swim.

Early May, and the temperature is already into the top seventies. At the traffic lights on the last straight, windows are rolled down. After an unusually hot weekend, bare pink elbows stick out, impatient finger-tips drum on tight metal-skinned roofs. Over the rattle of engines, bits of radio. Snatches of jingles, news reports, jazz, opera, rock - junk. On arrival at the platform, I empty my ears, and load my bike into the luggage van of the waiting train. A two-stop train. If I miss this, the next train is the Orient Express. Stopping at every station, it's murder.

When I had a statutory two-day weekend rod, things were

more straightforward. But now, since the Doctor decided to give me a seven-day, fish-when-you-like rod for the price of two days, my life has become tortuously complicated.

The Doctor, who has the lease of the fishing rights on The Hollow, lives three hours away from the river, with a down wind. From where I live, I can crawl on my hands and knees and be there in three minutes, with time to dust off my trousers. Understandably, he'd come to the conclusion that if I chose to fish outside my allotted span, what was there to stop me? The Boss, for a start, was there to stop me. But Boss, or no Boss, the Doctor proceeded with his super-generous reasoning unabated. All I did was stand there at the end of the phone nodding and agreeing that when he sent unaccompanied guests down - his bank manager, a medical colleague, his wife's brother, a fly-fishing patient, whoever - I would have a box of my very best flies ready and waiting for them on the table in the Mad House.

Delighted as I was with this deal at first, what I hadn't accounted for was the turmoil it was to throw my life into as a result of the freedom and temptation put my way. For now, rather than two-timing the Doctor, which I never had any intention of doing in the first place, I found myself two-timing my work place, which I never had any intention of doing in the second place - even though it was the last place I wanted to be at times. Naturally, I kept my daylight moonlighting to a minimum, working overtime to balance up. But right now, with Spring in the air, a call of nature in a meeting meant that when I asked to be excused, this would be the last anyone would see of me for the rest of the day.

Walking to the top of the platform, I begin my customary search for the loneliest seat on the train, away from chess-playing commuters, and smokers. Nestled like a sofa cushion into a corner of the train compartment next to a window, I stare out at the sky trying to imagine if it is the same sky hanging over The Hollow. It darkens. By the first stop, the blue has blackened quite significantly. It starts to rain. By the time I arrive at my station, the weather has changed once again. Like a thumb and finger squeezed down at the tip of a garden hose, the rain has turned to a spray of gauzy drizzle.

I arrive back in the country in time for peace. A soft sun breaks through, dazzling off the bonnet of my Morris Minor Traveller waiting for me in the station car park - the only car I know to be condemned at the MOT for dry rot.

These were the conditions I had been waiting for. If it's like this tomorrow, the best day's fishing of my life is assured.

———————

Half way up the Meadow Stream, the water flickers down over an ankle-high weir. A strip of highly-polished sunlight broke through the showers and flashed a mosaic of hypnotic iridescent light patterns against a lime-green wall of hawthorn, alder and elder.

This skinny backbone of undergrowth is all that separates the Meadow Stream from the Nursery Stream running parallel to it, eight feet away on the other side. No two streams of identical width - a flick of a cast-distance each - and similar depth could look so different, flow at such contradictory paces, house trout with such distinct feeding characteristics, and contain insects with such contrasting behaviour. The difference is their relationship with light.

The Nursery Stream lies in the heavy shade of trees either side. The Meadow Stream has one bank wide open to a sun-drenched water-meadow. Either way, both streams hold trout that are equally content with their lot, but at their happiest at different times of the year.

Whereas the shady, heron-sheltered Nursery Stream is where trout steal onto the gravels to cut redds in October, at this time of year, on the Meadow Stream side they are invited to the surface to cut their teeth on some of the heaviest early hatches of upwing fly on any two-hundred-yard stretch of river that I know. For this is all this prime trout water measures.

I once made an estimation of the trout population of the stream based on trout I could actually see. With a trout visible every three paces - and where it wasn't, this deficiency was compensated in other places with a trout displayed at every step -

I counted over one hundred takeable trout on offer to a man with eyes in his head and a fly rod in his hand.

'Are you sure you didn't dream up this calculation?' the Greek Bust asked me when I bumped into him standing on the bricking at the bottom of the stream, arms folded on the wooden hand-rail. I paused before answering.

The gentlest man you could ever hope to meet, the Greek Bust, a retired professor of Ancient History, was never short of a witty remark directed at himself or someone else, but more often than not, at himself. As a volunteer casting-instructor in the summer at his son's school somewhere in north London, he was never short on casting tips if he found you in trouble on the river, the wind transforming your efforts at reaching a fish into an Arran sweater.

One thing that he was desperately short of, however, was insulation up top. In hat or cap form, or imitation of the natural. If ever a location screamed 'Hat!', it was the upper regions of the Greek Bust's anatomy. With a marble head sculpted in the classic manner, forever exposed to the elements, the Greek Bust shared the river bank with dreams of distant days. He may have lost all of his hair, but he wasn't going to let go of memories of happier, hairier days when a comb was a comb, a shampoo was a shampoo and if all else was lost, he could always tie a fly out of part of himself.

'I like to feel the wind through my hair,' was the reasoning he gave for walking hatlessly bald, in all weathers.

He was leaning head-first into a silky-soft drizzle, gazing upstream through willow branches, planning his attack, drips slithering down the back of his neck. I waited a while before answering his question about my fish calculation, watching the sun flash off his silver-plated head as it nodded in time to the multitude of fish rising in the stream stretching out in front of him, beneath house-martins breasting the river surface as far as the eye could see. As the soberly outrigged duns drifted down, their wings pressed together like a presbyterian congregation in prayer, they lifted off at the last moment, inches from the bricking, where the air was thickening to the density of bonfire smoke, such was the multitude of fly. I began to wonder if it would take an acetylene torch to cut us out before we both choked to death. In the end, he decided to reply to his own question.

'You're right. You didn't dream it. But pinch me anyway.'

There is something about a day of soft rain that river flies adore. Maybe it's the temperature, maybe it's the increased levels of oxygen in the water. I've studied river insects, their likes and dislikes, but I still don't know why members of the olive family are always there bang on cue, ready to punch through the surface film and, wet-winged, surrender to the foulest of skies the moment a little drizzle arrives.

'What do I do?' the Greek Bust asked me, trembling like a brave man about to go into battle knowing he is hopelessly outnumbered.

'You tell yourself that you're not the only fisherman on the stream today that feels the balance is heavily weighed against him,' I advised. 'For every fly these trout take off the surface, twenty other flies pass over them to take off elsewhere.'

Using the sleeve of my jersey to wipe the mist from my polaroids, I stooped to tiger-height and began creeping up the stream through waist-level sedge conveniently lowered in places by the chewing of friesian cows, the Greek Bust at my side. We dropped to our knees every three paces to size-up a trout in a feeding position. The largest trout we spotted in the first few yards was positioned exactly where a big trout should be.

'I told you this was a classic stream,' I said, nodding in the trout's direction.

Twenty feet above our box seat position, the gradient of the stream slopes sharply, thickening the flow and thinning the water level. A busy rush of white water scrubs the river bed forming a mattress of steely flints that catch the light like a thousand tiny mirrors.

Immediately below this, the stream slides down into a gravel scoop where a clump of ranunculus swayed gently in time like the bow arm of a violinist. Squeezed into a corner of the drop-off on the far bank was an eddy no bigger than a football, an asylum for weary water, confused by the pace of the stream.

The architect of the eddy was a small tree stump a few feet higher up. This was all that remained of a hawthorn that had once stood permanently at a precarious angle over the stream. It had looked ready to topple at a moment's notice for as long as I could remember. But in the end, it didn't fall, it was pushed. A night of fierce, barn-roof-lifting gales last autumn put a stop to its dithering, and the Boss's chainsaw finally put it out of its misery.

A twisted stump now broke the flow, diverting the push of water away from the far bank, down and across to our position on the nearside bank. This took the pressure away from the eddy and the large dark backwater that circled, dizzily, under a viridian cloak of low-slung branches and leaves, the property of a thick limbed willow.

From this point on, it is deep backwater all the way down to the bottom of the beat, where instead of the stream continuing on its natural course and joining up with the main river, it slams into a wall of bricking, turns a ninety degree angle, is redirected down a large underground pipe, shunted under the Nursery Stream, to reappear twenty yards away on the other side of the road leading up to the Keeper's Cottage. Here it bursts out into the morning light at the edge of an ancient wood, breathless and gasping for air.

The willow at the bottom of the Meadow Stream would have been pollarded years ago if not for this subterranean trout shelter. The possibility that one day its leafy shade might tempt an unidentified monster from the cobwebby darkness of the tunnel to take up residence in the stream had given the tree a stay of execution. Any plans of a major haircut had been shelved.

Positioned just above the willow branches at the head of the sinister depths, the eddy is the last shady posting-house before this slow-moving backwater transforms itself into a sparkling, amber-coloured soda stream of crystal clarity, open to the sky and the eyes of any watchful flyfisher willing to wait for two strands of ranunculus to part to reveal a trout hanging beneath.

At the back of the eddy, a branch hovered inches from the

water surface. A small medal of dried grass hanging from a twig commemorated active service during last winter's high water.

Like a finger, it pointed into the centre of the eddy. A finger of fate, it marked the spot where our large trout lay.

The immediate fascination of our trout wasn't its awesome size. It was the challenge of being able to get a fly to it at all; the concentration needed, the skill required, the mastery demanded of me, and of the Greek Bust. For on The Hollow, I look for trout I want to catch, rather than trout I can catch. And more and more, the greatest enjoyment I get from fishing a river is fishing for trout in 'interesting' places - size comes a poor second. The ability to do this is something that separates river from stillwater and lake fishing. Only a river can supply this.

Skimming the underside of the surface with its bluey-black shoulders, our trout was inspecting every fly brought to it on a kiss-curl of topside current. This was busily flicking a continuous flow of duns, still wet behind the ears, in the direction of the eddy's occupant. All our large trout had to do was put its lips together, lift a fraction of an inch to the surface, kiss and collect.

The Greek Bust handed me his fly box.

'Which one of these jokers is going to look more attractive to this gourmet than a natural?' he asked.

Here lay the real problem. It wasn't a matter of simply presenting an imitation of the next fly our trout expected to see. It was more than that. It was a matter of presenting the next fly the trout was most likely to want to select, rather than open his mouth and accept. Altogether an entirely different problem.

I sorted through his collection heaped into a foam-lined tobacco tin and picked out a fly with a hackle that looked like it had swum for England. Limp and soggy, it had everything I looked for in a newly-hatched dry fly: vulnerability. It wasn't so much an insect, more an invalid, and it reeked of all the essential ingredients guaranteed to trigger a mouth-watering response from a trout on the feed - hopelessness and helplessness. I held it up to the sky to squint at it.

'I've been meaning to throw that one out,' the Greek Bust said, apologising for its sorry state.

'Now's your chance. Get ready to throw it out - to a fish!'

When it comes to making a selection from a mass of options, the instincts of a trout are no different to those of a lioness sizing up a herd of wildebeest. And this should also be the thinking flyfisher's approach when it comes to choice of fly pattern. I always put my trust in a pattern that looks, and behaves, crushed and crumpled. These are crucial characteristics instantly recognised by a discerning, tummy-rumbling trout with predatory instincts bristling.

'But tie this one on first,' I said handing him a fly from the sheepskin patch safety-pinned to my chest. 'And just use a little grease from the side of your nose as floatant. Enough to make it legal.'

A lightly-dressed, mohair-bodied, hackle fly with two healthy turns of a soft moorhen wing feather at the head, the Water Chicken is the embodiment of my belief that whatever fly I tie, no matter what pattern, my prime objective is to remove as much as possible between me and the trout. Whatever else it was, it certainly wasn't what Halford had in mind when he set about designing his robustly-constructed ballerina patterns, with the stamina to pirouette on hackle tips for long, turbulent distances on days like today when damp-winged duns clung to the surface in long floats. Not many duns were clearing the stream before reaching the swirling backwater in front of the bricking where we were standing.

The Greek Bust popped it in his tin.

'Don't laugh. It's got the backing of professionals,' I said. 'An entire nation of them,' I added, trying not to hard-sell.

Until 1961 when a law banned it, there existed professional fishermen in France whose daily bread depended on going out and extracting wild trout from rivers for re-sale. The interesting part is that, up against fierce commercial pressure, the professionals opted to use fly above all other methods. Not because it was the most sporting, as we might imagine this side of the Channel. No, fly was employed as it was the most killing. These men had families to feed.

The French flyfishers' 'Succeed or Starve' approach to flyfishing gave their sport an edge, a 'piquant' - an urgency that is quite frightening when it comes to effectiveness.

One feature that drifted out of all the patterns they used was that they were all very lightly dressed. They had a feathery-lightness, a breathiness, an almost puritanical economy which is characteristic of French flytying.

The other feature is that these fish-catchers always went for a pattern with the lowest of profiles. One that represented the insect they were imitating at the 'moment of eclosion', the stage when it is finally freeing itself from the nymphal shuck in the surface film. This, these French assassins concluded, was the time when the insect was at its most defenceless, and therefore at its most interesting, to the trout - and to themselves. For on days when catching trout was business, it promised them higher returns. And that meant every day.

Economy of tying materials was key. These professionals didn't give the trout anything to question. They wrapped as little as possible round the hook to question. As a result, their soft, sparse, easily collapsible flies were engulfed - involuntarily.

'Shall I try for him?' the Greek Bust whispered in my ear, his head resting on my shoulder.

'Not until you can set his rhythm to a metronome.'

The Greek Bust sank to his knees. 'Now?' he murmured anxiously, thirty seconds later.

I told him that I would wait a while longer until I felt in tune with the trout. The Greek Bust dropped onto the back of his legs.

'I should have kept up those piano lessons at school.'

At a time of a steady hatch of fly, the rise is like a heartbeat and each individual trout has its own pulse rate that needs checking. The timing of casting a fly to a consistently rising fish isn't a mathematical calculation, it's an understanding of the trout's own unique feeding pattern. It's the silent meeting of two unconnected minds, like that of an attentive waiter and a diner in a restaurant. Rush the menu between courses and he'll ask for the bill, and go.

Counting to the beat, the Greek Bust began to pull the desired length of line from his reel. Even if you possessed the rhythm sense of a jazz drummer, it wasn't an easy cast. A low-hanging branch was inches from the tail of the trout, like a fickle finger of fate it looked poised to scoop up any object that came anywhere near it. Furthermore, the sparkling rush of water in-between the Greek Bust and the eddy it helped create seemed likely to destroy any attempts at getting a fly to sit dead drift on the kiss curl. I explained the mechanics of the 'puddle', or 'parachute' cast.

'I just needed reminding,' the Greek Bust said, finishing his own demonstration to himself. Lowering his rod tip to drop slack, and allowing his line to ride the flow, he let his fly slide gently into the eddy a foot above the trout, teetering temptingly on the edge of the food-bearing curl in line with the trout's nose. It was a masterful cast. The timing was right. The trout was all set to inspect the next offering in line.

Standing proudly on a fine pair of mixed hackles, a tapered body leaning back on a bunch of matching hackle fibres, at this stage in the drift, at least, the fly appeared to be giving a highly convincing interpretation of the light patterns made by a natural insect's feet denting the surface on the underside of the surface. Seconds later, as it entered into its window, our large trout moved to make the final inspection. But it kept on inspecting until it shook its head in the direction of his lie and returned to it. Courtship interruptus.

'You didn't try the fly I gave you,' I said as the Greek Bust reeled in, the trout having refused his trusty, heavily hackled fly for a third time.

'Your fly needs to see a doctor.'

'It needs to see a fish,' I thought to myself, settling down to another five minutes of trout-watch, picking a single marsh marigold and pushing the stalk into the little hole on the zip fastener of my oilskin. At this time of year, my wife fills a large porcelain basin with them, roots, soil and all and keeps them on the marble washstand in the bathroom.

Our large fish was acting strangely. It was lifting to every dun that skidded off the flow onto the sticky surface current of the eddy. But it was only taking the occasional unlucky few. As we crouched watching, a rogue dun pulled our large trout out of his hole to the centre of the stream - for no reason the Greek Bust or I could understand.

'A grayling would never have done that,' I told him. 'But at least he's willing to break routine. If he's given the correct stimulation.'

Even though you present a perfectly-timed fly and all but conduct the trout into rising up to accept your offering, you can never be certain that it will sing in tune and take it. I decided to address our trout by continuing to use the most elementary appreciation of animal behaviour I could muster. We had tried the 'rhythm method', now we were going to go for another of the trout's more basic instincts - the ability of it to be *stimulated*. If, that is, there's a chance of a meal at the end of it. The delivery of the artificial would neither be timed to coincide with the arrival of the next natural, nor would it come trundling down the familiar track leading to the trout waiting on its station.

By taking this approach, I was not just breaking the rhythm of the trout's rise, I was breaking the standard dry fly code of practice - that of placing a carefully-constructed pattern outside his window, three or four feet up from a trout.

It wasn't this well-trodden procedure that bothered me. It was the reasoning of always wanting to present a fly outside the window first, to stimulate investigation, and thus allow your duplicity to be questioned much earlier than necessary. If the SAS were to ever run flyfishing schools, they wouldn't include this tactic in their curriculum. By presenting our fly way ahead of a trout, we sound an early warning alert that an unverified object is steaming the trout's way, and as good as invite the trout to give the fly a full once-over when it arrives within nose distance.

It was this 'inspection' more than anything else that I wanted to avoid. I didn't have any time for it. And I didn't want to give the trout any time for it either. I decided that the best way to grab the hungry attention of a trout wasn't to waft my fly elegantly into its line of vision. I wanted my fly to hurl itself through its window - unannounced.

Long ago on chalkstreams, I decided that the best way of presenting a fly to a trout and trigger off an impulse to rise, rather than to reconnoitre as the 'Zone Rangers' will have you do, was to get it in there quickly. As soon as you've located your fish and timed its rhythm, forget about all the complex physics of the trout's rise: what it sees; what it looks for in an approaching fly; how it lines itself up to take it. Dump all that. Just concentrate on getting your fly into a position over the trout where you know it is visible to it - just long enough for it to grab the trout's attention. And, here's the rub, give the trout the minimum amount of time to calculate how it should react to the fly. Go for instinct, not science.

It's a trick I developed with grayling. The grayling rise is much more complex than the trout rise. However the trout's position in the river is more variable in terms of depth and proximity to the river-bed than that of the grayling. A trout can rise almost anywhere - ahead of its position, behind, to either side; even, depending on the depth the trout is lying, at a point seemingly unrelated to his territory, as our large trout had demonstrated.

A traditional, meticulously-planned, carefully-positioned fly - and a long, gentle drift into a trout's rising position, may well seem like the quietest and most genteel way of presenting your fly without upsetting the neighbours. But when medium and small olives are flowing thick and fast, as they so often do at this time of year between midday and mid-afternoon, it often isn't the most effective tactic.

Upside-down or not, get your fly into a position where it is immediately in the view of the trout. Long enough to persuade the trout that your imitation isn't a log or a leaf, that it's something edible, and not a threat - and not a million miles away from what it is happily accepting as food. Long enough to command its interest, totally, overwhelmingly, against the competition of the continuous on-coming flow of alternative food items. Long enough to make any specific point you want to make in order to make your fly irresistible. To suggest, in fact, that it may well be better than anything else he's eating at that time. But he'd better make his mind up fast, for it's just about to pass him by.

Long enough for the trout to realise that there's really very little he can argue about - because by placing your fly so near him, so suddenly, it captures his attention completely, commanding an unfair share of the trout's mind, and insists on a reaction to it, without consideration, without caution; with total abandonment.

We watched our large trout go for another dun. Its jaw snapped shut. I checked to see if the Greek Bust had tied my fly on the end of his line this time.

'I bandaged it on,' he told me.

'Right, let him have it. In your time, not his. Don't give him two minutes to think about it - give him two inches to see it only.'

'And if I slam it down on his dorsal and he turns and runs?'

'We look for another fish. No one said is was going to be easy.' But I knew the Greek Bust could get a fly in the window, just as easily as he lined up a fly to drift into it.

To cast a fly directly *at* a trout, rather than *to* it, takes more skill than tossing one into the general swim. It requires teacup accuracy. If you're off target, or you cast wide, you don't get the opportunity to recast and reposition your fly without fear of spooking your fish. Shooting into the window calls for supreme accuracy and more precision than simply blasting the lie shotgun-style.

'That's the reason why flyfishermen present their fly this way. It's easier,' I whispered to the Greek Bust, giving words of encouragement.

On the plus side, with a spaghetti of currents between our position and the trout's, you don't have the same problems with drag tossing a fly directly at the trout. It is usually taken by the trout before the current gets a chance to snatch it.

His fly didn't land where I would have wanted to place it. It landed feet first, barely an inch from the trout's nose, on the far side of it. I would have given it two or three inches more view, but there wasn't time to discuss the matter. The brief moment of drift, certainly no more than a few seconds, gave our large trout just enough time to grab it, denying the fish that crucial fraction of a second for a critical, life-saving, investigation. Our trout lifted up from its position in the stream to the fly, faster than a shaken beer from its container. Just as instantly, as if realising its rashness, it turned one hundred and eighty degrees and headed back, line sizzling, to the tunnel, stopping at the end of the backwater by the bricking where we had been standing.

The Greek Bust ran down after it, dropping his rod-tip to let his line travel unchecked beneath the willow branches. At the bricking, he let the trout swim in circles to calm itself before he led it to the bank and, sticking his hand through the sedge, reached out to grab it. The line had collected a small bunch of weed from under the willow which had worked its way down the line arriving at the trout's nose in a solid clump, blindfolding it. It was this that had tipped the scales in favour of the angler and against the trout, and not just the Greek Bust's unquestionable fishing abilities. Having lost its vision and direction, for our large trout the battle was over.

'You were right about that fly,' the Greek Bust turned and said to me, his hand unable to squeeze round the girth of the fish to lift it out of the water. And large it certainly was. Over three pounds; the biggest fish I'd seen out of water all season.

'What fly?' I said, watching him flick a bunch of feather soldered by slime out of the trout's mouth.

In the end, I'd forgotten which pattern it was that had finally fooled the fussy fish. Sometimes even the most ruthlessly tried and tested imitations are made redundant by the pure inventiveness of the tactic employed by the flyfisherman to put his fly, any fly, in its best light.

———

The last weekend of May. Chaffinches and warblers flopped about in the wet leaves of my hedge. Two messages arrived up from the river. The first, the good news that at last the two cuckoos had got together. I spotted them swoop and stoop across from the Wild Wood to the Firs. The romance of the month had been flamed. The second message came in the beak of another migrant. The first mayfly were starting to blow off the Fly Lane. A house martin nesting in the gables of the Big House dropped a dull-winged dun the size of a cheese spread triangle in front of me on the table in the garden.

To be truthful, the biggest disappointment of the season is when the mayfly arrive. I'd spent the entire past week fishing the tiniest of flies to the biggest of fish that were seining naturals and imitations the size of pin-pricks off the surface. It was the prettiest small flyfishing you could hope for.

In a hot Spring, and it was a hot Spring, you see trout in the weed-beds, grazing like cows in a field of clover. They're vacuuming the weeds for reed smut larvae. Now whether it's the adult of these little devils that go on to form spooky clouds in the sky, or the next insect to hit the river's sticky fly-paper after the hawthorn - its little brother, the black gnat - at this time of year it matters not the tiniest jot. For both are tiny jots, and both are black.

There are several species of black gnat. All are land-born and dark brown with flat, shiny wings. Like the hawthorn, the males are skinny. The females are fat. You can fit two, head touching the rear end of the other, across the nail of your little finger. One species makes an appearance in the Spring, the other in the late summer or early autumn. Like their big brother, the hawthorn, black gnats only appear at the waterside in their adult form to mate, creating large groups in whichever side of the bush or tree is protected from the wind. One false move, one gust of wind and the black gnat is out of the airline and into the fish food business.

Because we're talking small here, at minimum a #18, we go for an imitation of the fat mamma. And what immediately comes to light is just how much simpler it is to tie small size flies using the Funneldun tying-style. Largely because tying in the hackle isn't fiddly. The Funneldun tying-style doesn't require delicate pointed fingers. You clamp your hand round the hackle and bind it down. Finally, you have all the room in the world to whip-finish at the bend. No ophthalmic surgeon techniques needed here to avoid trapping the hackles. Not only is the hook hidden from the trout, but any short-comings you might have when it comes to tying flies or #18 hooks are well and truly concealed, too

Even though the mayfly has been going for a week, I still catch just as many trout on black gnats during mayfly hatches. Mayfly is a state of mind. Before you replace your tin of standard flies with a crate of mayflies, it's good to consider this. It may seem like it, but not all trout are as excited as you are about this buttery bean-feast. Just because you find yourself catching all your fish on mayfly patterns during the mayfly season, doesn't mean this is the only thing they'll take. Not at all. Roll Cast and I spent an entire mayfly season fishing black gnats, Roll Cast taking the biggest fish of a mayfly week. With that particular fish, it made sense to change down. It had seen every mayfly pattern in the book - and many that probably weren't. As is his style when confronted with a tough customer, Roll Cast simply removed as much as he could from his mayfly patterns that might stand between him and the sly old trout. He ended up with a black gnat on a #18.

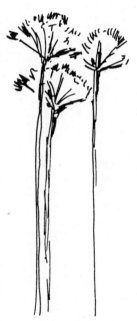

The smell of cow parsley in the hedgerows over the wall from my garden was intoxicating. Supplementing this, my lilac bush was out. Not a time to spend indoors doing anything. This includes flytying. My flytying vice is transportable. It's screwed into an old pine bread-board, so I brought it out into the garden and began tying up a couple of my favourite early mayfly season flies, when fish are gingerly coming up to the surface, distrustful of so many slabs of butter being spread on the river. The fly in question is called the Andelle.

The Andelle is named after a chalkstream in Normandy, a tributary of La Risle. In its original form, it's a hatching mayfly pattern. A damp pattern, rather than a full blown, sails erect, full-steam-ahead, 'One day I'll win the Americas Cup' dun sitting on

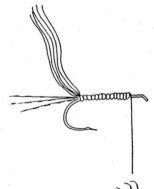

the surface. Not in the surface film, where, as I explained earlier, professional French fly fishermen like to sit their patterns. For this reason it would be classed as a nymph were it to slip beneath the film, and therefore be frowned upon by the Boss. Nymph fishing is not allowed until after the mayfly. Not until the very end of June.

Damp or dry, the design of this murderous pattern is unique, and full of functional surprises. Like those overcoats you can buy that become a raincoat if you turn them inside out, the Andelle can double up as both an emerging nymph, snorkeling; and as a sky-high, dry-as-a-bone Fastnet dun, wind-surfing. Take your pick. But more about this later.

In France, just after the Second World War, rivers - which had been a main source of food - were not surrendering their edible contents with quite the same pre-war ease. Immediately, Andre Ragot and a group of other professional anglers in the Rouen district of Normandy, began work to ensure that at least at mayfly time they could bring home the trout-flavoured bacon. The solution, not surprisingly, was a lightly-dressed pattern representing the mayfly just as it was about to transform itself into a sub-imago, fished in or under the surface film. It consisted of a duck hackle tied in at the head and folded back to cover the body with feather fibres. These hackle tips are then tied off at the hook bend, using turns of yellow silk whip-finished at the bend.

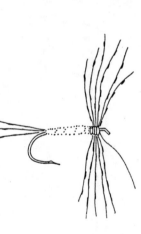

The body was originally wool, any colour of your choice. But I use yellow-coloured polypropylene. With a lower density than water, this body material ensures that my Andelle keeps, if not on the surface, at least in it - to the same extent as the conventional French Partridge Mayfly, and certainly more than a top-heavy Grey Wulff. Both these highly popular patterns are standard and acceptable on chalkstreams in the south of England.

After the War, when only small fish were left in the rivers (and not, I suspect, many of them), built-in resilience was not of great design importance. But in these days of stocked waters, I find that after one or two fish, sporting Gillette teeth, the thread pinning down the hackle tips at the tail of the fly very quickly gets frayed and the hackle opens up. For this reason, I use the thinnest gold thread that I pick out of an epaulette taken off a Royal Navy officer's uniform. This ensures that the hackle remains in place. I complete this operation at the riverside, finishing off the fly independently from the dressing at the vice. By simply folding the hackle over and binding it down at the hook bend using the wire, I can create a hatching nymph imitation, on location. To turn it back into a full-sailed dun pattern, I simply unwind the wire, fold back the hackle and grease it. Without the weight of the wire pulling the tail underwater, it floats as proudly as any other Mayfly pattern. Even though it very soon begins to resemble Mary Poppins's umbrella - after she's been mugged. But as you know, that's how the trout and I like my flies.

———

From the Decontamination Room to the Old Iron Bridge, the area at the bottom of the beat where the river flows into and out of the canal a hundred yards further down, is a twenty-minute walk. If, that is, I avoid the river bank and cut across the fields, through the Hole to Horse Bridge where spire was beginning to shoot up like spears mid-way across the river. I then trek through the poplar stumps, which are bleeding in the Wetlands.

Another way to go is up past the Boss's cottage and along the canal towards Barge Bay. This takes an extra fifteen minutes in all. It's not a route many people take, not even the ever-curious River God. But I often do.

Years back I walked it one mayfly Sunday to the peal of church bells, with the strong scent of buttercups, violets and water mint in my nostrils - in a dance of sun, cloud, thunder, and rain; an endless ballet of weather. I spotted a large wild trout under an overhanging lip of bank on the far side of the canal. It was sipping at mayfly spinner blown high over the tree-tops from a carrier running parallel to it, on the other side of the tow-path. At 4lb 2oz it was my biggest fish of the season, certainly the wildest.

That day on my walk past the Boss's cottage, his daughter

back home from teacher training college told me that I had the river to myself. Only one other car was at the hut and this belonged to the Newspaper Man, a thrusting businessman in his late twenties, with red shoulder-length hair that he wore in a pony tail. He was the owner of a large chain of newspaper and tobacco shops in the Midlands and the West of England. He only comes down three or four times a season - each time accompanied by a girlfriend, each time a different one. I didn't know his name, I'd never met him, he never gave you the chance. He'd unpack his female friend and head for the woods. Very often he'd forget his rod and leave it leaning up against the hut - if he remembered to take it out of the car in the first place.

'An actress, this time,' the Boss's daughter told me, studying her shoes, giggling discreetly at them and waving a hand in a down-river direction, the direction I was heading.

'Cindy something, she said her name was. I've seen her on TV.'

It was early afternoon. The sword-leafed iris flowers had started to unroll. I pounded down the clay canal tow-path at top speed. Cow parsley, rose-bay willow herb and the occasional single mayfly spinner on the wing raced towards me, as I did to them. Still very early days at the start of the mayfly season, the main hatches were starting to appear after lunch when the sun had warmed the water and the air between the bank-side trees and bushes, raising them to the temperature of an airing cupboard where newly-hatched duns could hang their wings up to dry. By the time I arrived, I was mentally prepared for a long wait, for you don't 'fish' for the trout holed up in the Back of Beyond where I was heading. In this wide expanse of featureless sea you lay siege. You sit by this lump of water and wait, watching with your keenest eye open for the first sight of a pair of rubbery, dark-blue lips squeezing through the tarmac-black surface. This action coincides with the silent disappearance of an unfortunate member in a row of mayfly duns coasting underneath the far bank.

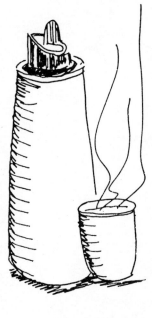

I had taken a flask. If I'm going to be down on the river for more than a morning, I brew up before I leave and slip a small thermos in my jacket pocket to take down with me. I keep the contents to a minimum - tea, and tea only. No milk (the contents stay hotter longer), no sugar - just tea. Black tea, from the province of Fujian in China. Lapsang Souchong tea. Or as my friends call it when the thick, sticky, smoky smell invades their nostrils, 'fish', or 'bacon tea'.

To make Lapsang Souchong, freshly picked tea leaves undergo a long process of transformation. Like wine, black tea is fermented, and demands the same high level of care and attention. First the leaves are softened by a withering process over open fires of pine. This reduces their moisture content and enables them to be rolled without breaking, releasing essential oils. They're placed on mats and sorted according to size and condition. Fermentation is next. The leaves are left to sauna in a highly moist atmosphere. Finally, they're dried in an enormous drying machine.

They say Lapsang is best with salty and spicy dishes, and with cheese. My wife doesn't think it goes well with anything, anywhere. In particular, the sitting-room where she's convinced that the smell of smouldering leaves overwhelms the log fire, and clings in the curtains. In many ways, she's right. Like a bonfire of autumn leaves, Lapsang is the ultimate outdoor experience. Distinctive and unmistakable in its smokiness, the aroma hangs poetically in the trees, wafting lyrically across the river in a sticky black haze. Twisting open a flask by the river has had the gamekeeper running down the bank thinking his woods were ablaze.

The way I speak about my tea you'd think it was a religion. It's true, few smells infiltrate the senses in quite the same way. The sensation is a spiritual one. The tarry smell sticks in the memory with the same adhesive qualities it uses to clamp itself to furniture coverings. To release river-side thoughts, all I need do is brew up - wherever I might be. London, Paris, New York, China. I'm told the smell of tomato soup can play similar games with the angler's mind, but I doubt it somehow.

In the warm sun, my mind was starting to wander. It was hard work trying to keep my concentration from sagging. I was

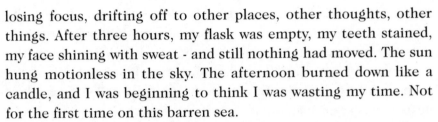

losing focus, drifting off to other places, other thoughts, other things. After three hours, my flask was empty, my teeth stained, my face shining with sweat - and still nothing had moved. The sun hung motionless in the sky. The afternoon burned down like a candle, and I was beginning to think I was wasting my time. Not for the first time on this barren sea.

Then the tarmac blistered. It lifted up slightly, then down again, on the back of an unidentified fish.

There were still no mayfly on the surface. But at least one of the invisible besieged had made a brief appearance on the parapets. It was probably the first time it had felt the warmth of the sun on its broad shoulders that season. But how broad? Trout that live in these parts eat flesh. They have no taste for vegetable fats, the sort contained in the scant sprinkling of surface flies that occasionally find themselves riding over these forbidding depths. Normally, trout in the Back of Beyond are the last to show themselves at this festive time. Normally, they have nothing to lose - just as long as meal times involve the pursuit of a young dace.

But at this time of year, they have everything to lose if they change their ways and rise upwards to accept a gift presented to them, from above. One that demands they leave their element and enter into another to accept it.

The water lifted again. It formed a thick black circle the diameter of a car tyre. I attached my Andelle to the end of the line, and pulling the hackle forward with my thumb and forefinger, I stroked over the ribcage of breast hackle fibres to the tail. Still no mayfly duns. But I was ready for him.

Big fish in big water know what they like, and they like what they know. They are watchful for deceit. More than that, they are aware that they are exposed. They feel it, all around them. They are not following the lead of other fish in the area, because there are no other fish in the area. A rise is an individual, instinctive action, not an involuntary knee-jerk reaction of the sort you witness in stew ponds where, if one fish rises, they all do.

Back of Beyond big trout, when up on the surface, are live wires - coiled springs, forever nervous, forever cautious. For they are vulnerable, from all angles. From above, out of a glaring element, the sky. From below, from attackers within their element. On winter walks to this part of the world, I have seen water swell up and explode as pike launch themselves up and sink their teeth deep into the underbelly of a fish careless enough to lift from the withered weeds on the bottom. In January, this reach surrendered a 32lb pike taken on a sprat. It came up from the depths and swung at the bait, just as the angler lifted it up to his boots. Both the angler and his friend standing next to him leapt three foot back into the fields, their hearts still in their throats long after the sprat and a yard of line had disappeared deep down the the pike's gristly gullet.

As my fish awaited the arrival of his next dose of yellow fats, I calculated the third lift, my forefinger pressing down in the cork on the top of the rod handle. To achieve long distance accuracy, I always cast with my forefinger in this position.

I lined the third lift up against the second, and plotted the fourth. Once again, my fish was on time. Still rising to an invisible food. My Andelle would be next in line. Distance measured, I piled line at my feet and chucked my Andelle immediately - straight into my fish's window. This was to be the first fly both of us would see half in, half out of the surface that afternoon, and I wasn't giving him too much time to quiz which one it was.

Stooped, I watched my fly ride the scum for a short distance to a position just behind the trout. I never saw it disappear. Vacuumed off the surface, it vanished along with the air that surrounded it and my line went slack. A tiny spit of water spurted up like a speech-bubble. It read 'Gone'.

On my way back from the Back of Beyond, as I crossed Snipe Stream, I noticed something moving in the middle of the field, near a small hawthorn bush. It looked like a dog rolling around. As I got closer I saw it was a pert little backside appearing and disappearing out of the meadow grass.

Spinning on my heels, I headed straight back to the river. As soon as I got there, I adopted a studious searching mode, scanning the water furiously, never once letting my eyes stray in the direction of the lone hawthorn. I did, however, catch a glimpse of a jacket hanging from a branch, next to a lady's blouse. It belonged to the Newspaper Man.

Vertically, or horizontally, I didn't see our thrusting young businessman again that season, and the following year he didn't renew his ticket. I never did find out his name, but this didn't matter, either. From that day on, I dropped the tag 'The Newspaper Man', and simply referred to him as 'The Male on Cindy'.

Back at the Mad House, I found a small gathering, and much merriment. My friend Brian Clarke, the angling writer, was celebrating his 39th birthday, and Roll Cast, the River God, and the publisher Timothy Benn, had found a bottle of Southern Comfort hidden in the boot of the River God's Mercedes.

The sun dipped behind the Firs. We talked of many things. But mainly, because the air was thick with them, flies. The story about the week the top river entomologist and photographer from Switzerland, a very dear friend of the River God, came to The Hollow in the search of a specimen of the large spurwing, *centroptilum pennulatum*. He came down mid-week and booked into the Manor. The River God had told him that, as the man on the spot, I would probably know where to find specimens. He was right, I did. The large spurwing is sparse and very localized on The Hollow, but the Swiss entomologist was lucky. I'd seen a handful on Cake Wood. Over the phone, I gave him precise instructions on where to go and how to find them. But deciding that it would be better for me to draw him a little map, the minute I got home on the evening of the day he arrived, I went straight to The Manor. In the pub the barman told me that he was in the ante-room, a small, pine-panelled sitting-room between the bar and the dining-room. But I wasn't to go in.

'Nobody's allowed in there,' he said. 'He's locked himself in.' I thought he must be resting, but the barman was not happy.

'I think he's put a sofa up against the door.' A stormy cloud brewed over the barman's head.

'See those people?,' he asked. I looked across at two silent couples aimlessly stirring cocktails with sleepy cherries on sticks, glancing at their watches. 'They're waiting to get through to their tables.'

'Let me talk to him,' I said.

I walked round to the window and, taking hold of the windowsill, I pulled myself soundlessly up to peer in. I didn't want to wake him.

He was standing on the sofa behind the door. I began to think of nutty Swiss professors.

'Don't open the window!' the nutty Swiss professor shrieked.

'It's me. Neil. How was your trip? Are you alright?' I whispered, trying to normalise the situation.

'...Don't even move!'

'What's the matter?' I asked.

'It's the bottle ...' The River God hadn't mentioned anything about a drink problem.

'... I dropped it, and .... got him!'

He hadn't wasted a second. He'd come straight off the flight, hired a car, driven to Cake Wood and found himself a specimen - exactly where I'd directed him. He'd rushed it back to The Manor to photograph, and dropped the bottle. His sole specimen had spent the last two hours house-hunting on the ceiling.

'Got him, got him, got him! I owe you a drink.'

'At my place,' I insisted with all the local diplomacy I could muster.

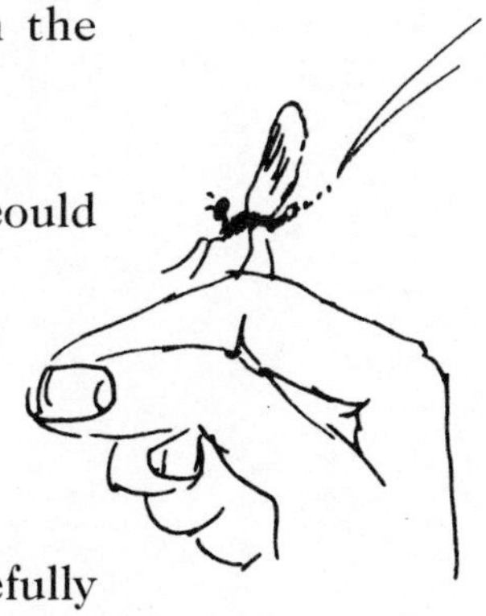

It was dark when the last of the birthday cars staggered carefully across Sticklepath Bridge and silently up the track. Hoping the walk would sober me up, I opted to walk home rather than accept a lift for the sixty-second drive home. On the way I gathered an armful of dried poplar bark scattered on the ground next to the pile of warm-smelling logs in the field. The foresters had been in the Wetlands at six o'clock that morning sawing them down.

Throwing all the windows in the sitting room open, I lit a fire and sat in front of it listening to the flames tell my face and arms how sunburned they were.

June

TORN PANTS, WET VESTS,
WHITE SOCKS

Inside the Wild Wood Lodge, in the main hall, the floor is tiled with paviours. Dark and streaky, the colour of a brindled greyhound, they give off a watery coolness.

The area in the centre of the lodge rises heavenwards, straight up to a cobweb of stripped beams and rafters. A pine cat-walk joins two large bedrooms at either end of the building. With timber walls and ceiling, one of them creaks like a ship's cabin. You don't go to bed, you set sail.

At Christmas I hoist up a twenty-foot Christmas tree in a corner of this hall. Decorations are showered down on it from the cat-walk. From there I poke a fairy into place on the top of the tree, attached to the end of a fishing rod. But at mayfly time, the hall is a different place entirely.

The front door is thrown open to let the hall fill with the smell of honeysuckle, a cacophony of birdsong from the garden, and a thick cloud of insects from the river. If the breeze is in the south, the windows in the hall rattle with mayfly spinners trying to get out again.

For fishermen blown off the river and up the track in my direction, there is always supper. This informal arrangement results in the best sort of parties - surprise gatherings, get-togethers that aren't pre-arranged.

At the first of these impromptu mayfly evenings, well over a dozen uninvited guests filled the hall, almost all of them rods with their guests and a couple of local fishing friends. Laid out on watercress on an ashet on the table in the hall was the best fish of the day. A hen of over four pounds, with three large dark grey polka dot spots on a silver-blue flank and a tail with an edge on it you could use to slice tomatoes. It was taken from a black hole under a sloping alder somewhere in the depths of the woodland stream called Darkest Africa - courtesy of Roll Cast, of course. When it cropped up in conversation, it was referred to as 'The Christ Fish' on account of the fact that it had refused Roll Cast's first two attempts, but on the third cast it rose again, and this time took his fly.

It had been a blistering hot day. The double doors between the hall and the sitting-room were thrown open. But at this time of year temperatures are likely to drop at any moment, so there was a log fire burning in the sitting-room. This had become the focus of attention for the fishing wives present who had had more than enough of fishing for one day, thank you very much. A small group were sitting round the sweet smelling, spitting poplar twigs talking about hugely unpiscatorial matters.

The Actor, a guest of the Academic, was someone I had never met before, although I'd heard a great deal about him. He was from Denmark Listening to him talk on the river bank - and watching wildlife scamper off in all directions and birds rise out of the woods and fly away - I had concluded that he was under an unshakeable impression that everyone in England talked like

characters out of a Shakespeare tragedy, and at the same decibel. From tales I had heard, he was a strong contender for the title of Naughty Dane No I, challenging the holder of this top slot, his fellow patriot, flyfisherman and author, Preben Torp Jacobsen, who had visited the Wild Wood Lodge two weeks earlier and had made substantial in-roads into my schnapps poured straight from the freezer, accompanied by herrings marinated in dill, madeira and curry which I had bought specially for him from the Danish Food Centre in London.

Now what exactly warrants the title of 'Naughty Dane', what you have to do, what you have to endure, what naughtiness you have to get up to, was - and still is - a mystery to everyone. No one seems to know. The only thing we are certain of was that both Preben and the Actor are both admirably capable of getting up to no good at all, at the slightest toss of the hat. That day, without the Actor knowing, I decided to put him to the test in one way or another, whenever the occasion arose, whatever that occasion might be.

It hadn't been the Actor's day. He'd lost his best fish, he'd been late for lunch and missed the wine, and when he tried to climb over a fence, he hooked himself up on barbed wire and ripped his trousers. He needed consoling. I hoped the Academic would bring him up to the house after spinner fall, before darkness fell.

Sure enough, no sooner had I switched on the outside lights than two long shadows shortened on the lawn, walking in the direction of the open door.

The Academic introduced the Actor to the gathering in the hall. Handing him a glass of wine, I took him to the sitting-room with the hope that he'd liven up the female party assembled there. I waited until he was in the centre of the sitting-room and our presence had distracted all the fishing wives and girlfriends from their conversations before introducing our handsome Danish guest to them. Clicking his heel and stooping slightly forward, the Actor paid his respects. It was then that I realised the occasion had arrived. Grabbing the hand that had been discreetly holding up the damage caused that afternoon on the barbed wire fence, I pulled it away. The front of the Actor's trousers flapped forward and dropped to the floor.

The Actor never came back to the Wild Wood Lodge. But shortly after, he sent me a book he had written. A slim, grey-covered volume on Skues, in Danish. It included a Skues nymph pattern, hand-dressed and hooked onto a circle of beige felt attached to the page. Inside the cover is inscribed the following message:

'For Neil Patterson. From a Dane of not so naughty fame.'

It's still a mystery how he arrived at such a deduction, but clearly he felt Preben deserved to retain the title. Actors hate it when the curtains drop.

It's at mayfly time when guests from all the corners of the earth fly in - and not just from Europe. One guest in particular flew in and out again with a tale that was to eventually find its way into a book.

It was prime-time in the mayfly season when American publisher Nick Lyons and his artist wife, Mari, visited us at the Wild Wood Lodge. Now if you don't know Nick, you won't know of the reputation he has. When it comes to falling in, Nick takes this art to new, unexplored depths. For this reason, if you're his host, he needs your total and undivided attention if he's to walk, rather than drip home. Quite understandably, before Mari gave me leave to escort Nick down to the river, I was well briefed. Assurances had to be made.

'Don't bring him back unless he's dry,' she underlined at breakfast. She made me promise.

For two days, all had gone non-swimmingly well. For example, I always made sure that there wasn't too much hot water in the tank when he showered. The most dangerous thing he could do in the bathroom was brush his teeth to death. On the river bank, I never left his side, not for two minutes. Anyway, why should I want to? Nick is a great story-teller. More importantly, the fishing was good, and fishing with a happy fisherman who is catching fish exceeds the pleasure I would have experienced had I been catching the same fish myself. This is what living by a river does to you.

Apart from dropping his Arctic Creel into the river containing his fly box and other essentials, and which we never saw again until it was picked off a weed-rack at the end of the beat several days later, Nick didn't put a foot - or any other part of his anatomy - wrong. The total Lyons unit remained on dry land, and stayed dry. Indeed, I began to think he'd acquired an allergy to anything remotely damp. Even Mari was impressed when he was returned to her in the evening.

Our last day on the river together had been a long one and once again I spent every second of the day with Nick. However, I was anxious that he wouldn't return from his trip feeling hounded. His behaviour had been exemplary, and because I had promised that I would make dinner for everyone that evening, I plonked Nick up on the Marshes, on Cemetery which had been dredged that winter. The bank was high above water level with nothing lying around to trip over. Leaving him in front of the happy gloops of several rising fish, I pointed back across the water-meadows in the direction of the Wild Wood Lodge and told him to meet me there when he'd had his fill.

When I returned, Mari joined me in the kitchen and I reassured her that Nick was as dry as a bone and I'd left him to have the final half hour to himself, well away from the water.

'Sometimes fishing is about being alone,' I told her.

'Sometimes fishing is about being dry,' she told me, 'But not often.' Mari trusted me. At least, she did then.

What exactly happened after I left Nick can only be narrated by one man: Nick. This is how he presented his case to Mari, myself, and later on his return, to the American flyfishing public in his 'Seasonal Angler' column in *Fly Fisherman* magazine:

'Towards evening on my last day, I was fishing an upper reach that had just been dredged. The water was quite deep and a bit discoloured from the soft soil, so I stayed on the high bank and cast comfortably to several rising fish. The two days had been immensely satisfying and without disaster; I'd taken most of the fish I hooked and felt I'd gotten to know the river better. When we walked down to the river from Neil's house, Neil had said that my success was a relief to everyone. It was surely a relief to me.

I'd heard someone's wife, brought to the river with some promise of seeing the American clown perform at this annual carnival, say: "I thought you said funny things happened when this bloke came here. I'm terribly disappointed." Well, you can't please everyone.

'I felt quite content, standing on the rim of that mud mound, casting a little brown sedge to the circles. I looked out over the gentle fields, at the pinkish sky along the horizon line, at the water as it slipped beneath an old wooden bridge, eddied, grew riffles, and spread out into this long flat pool, and then, suddenly, a truly large fish rose. I struck lightly, it thrashed at the surface, and then it bore upstream heavily. It was the largest fish I'd had on in the river, better than four pounds, possibly five. From my height, I had the advantage on it and easily walked upstream and down, several times, to keep it above. In ten minutes it tired and came close to the shore and I was positive it was a full five pounds. But how to net it? I was four or five feet above the surface of the water, no one was around, and I had no net with me.

'I played the fish a bit more, until he turned slowly sideways and quiet; then I lay full length on the soft dredged sod and put the rod on the ground beside me. I grasped the line, leaned as far over as I dared, and came eight or ten inches short of the fish. The 6X leader would scarcely allow me to raise it out of the water. What to do? The evening was growing late and misty and there were ten or twelve circles of rising fish in the pool. I wanted to catch another, perhaps two; I'd waited four years for a night like this. I even thought of breaking the leader off, but it would have been most ungracious to leave my fly in such a fish.

'At last, not knowing how deep the water was, I decided to climb down the bank, digging my feet into the soft mud as I went. A lousy decision. I began to slip down the mud bank, couldn't stop myself, and went into the water, then went on down to the bottom of the river which was six or seven feet deep there.

'I have been dunked a couple of times in my life, once in mud; I knew at once it could be treacherous, even fatal. So I forced myself up against the bank, got my head above water, screamed valiantly for help, and clawed at the mud wall. It didn't hold. No one came. I kept slipping back, gobs of mud in my hands, on my face, my hat off and sailing downstream, the fish gone now, mud dripping down my jacket, into my shirt, filling my hip boots. For a moment or two I was quite sure I was on my way to the Great Chalk Stream in the Sky. Like Everyman, I wasn't ready.

'The water and the mud in my hip boots made them too heavy for me to kick, the mud kept tearing away as I clawed more and more desperately into it with my hands, and I slipped back under the water twice, gurgling and choking.

'The disappointed wife would have got her money's worth. I've often wondered whether the crowd of them would have been too doubled over with laughter to haul me out.

'In the end. I must have levitated up that mud bank, out of fear or desperation, and when I got there, I lay full face on the ground, quietly, spitting out a bit of river now and then, for a full five minutes. Then I checked my rod and headed downstream to tell Neil about all the fish that were still rising.'

In fact, he kept on walking and I found him outside the kitchen, slumped against the wall of the Decontamination Room pulling off his waders.

'What happened?' I asked the dripping Nick, busy constructing the best excuse of his life. It had to be, for Mari had arrived at the top of the steps to the kitchen. She was standing looking down on us.

'Well,' said Nick, lifting his head up slowly, 'one minute I was watching the hatch from my point of view, the next I was watching it from the trout's.'

That night the sitting-room looked like a fully rigged galleon. We dined with Nick's trousers, shirt, vest, jersey and underpants hanging from the mantelpiece, over chairs and anything big enough to hoist them in position in front of the fire. The tiniest breath of draft under the door would have been enough to blow one end of the house away.

Buckets of condensation dripped from the windows, but not quite in the same quantity as the sweat that poured off Nick as he gave Mari a full and detailed account of his ordeal. This story is well documented. It's written on the wall - my bathroom wall. Nick left a 'bum print' where he'd leant up against it to pull off his mud-caked socks.

After he left, I screwed a large glass frame to the wall to commerorate the event. Then I wrote and told him what I'd done. Nick had the last word in his article:

'I didn't please my wife during that last chalk stream idyll, but Neil seems to have gained an historic monument. He shows it to everyone. Lefty Kreh - who never falls in and has been zapping those browns on his doorstep and regaining the honour of the colonies - told me he had been shown that spot with great reverence. It ain't that important to me; just another place where I almost got hung.'

'The Mayfly Hotel' isn't always open. Sometimes I close it down and go out and act the visitor myself. I came to thinking that if everyone has so much fun at my place, I'm owed a good time at someone else's. And do you know something? They're right, it is good fun. And to justify the extravagance of leaving my little, paid-up beat, frothing with mayfly-hungry trout, to go to parts foreign, I think thus: As long as I keep tying my Funnelduns from scrawny Indian cast-off capes, I can afford to nip over to France every mayfly-time and fish some of my favourite streams, with one of my favourite fishing friends.

Vincent lives and works in Paris. On weekday evenings, if he's not playing his piano - an electric practise keyboard that spills his music out onto your feet - he's tying flies in the balcony window of his second-floor apartment that overlooks the tops of the plane trees lining Avenue Trudaine. Perched there amongst hackles and quills, he looks like a bird feathering a nest. At weekends, he fishes. For this reason, I fly in Fridays.

Piling into Vincent's battered Renault, we leave the city early on Saturday morning. The suspension needs repairing and the pot-holes on the road to Normandy have my vertebrae rubbing together like walnuts in a sack. We arrive at his wife's parent's farmhouse in time for lunch and in urgent need of traction.

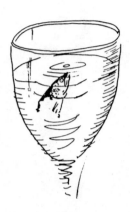

Saturday lunch in Vraiville is always on the lawn. The whole family homes in like pigeons for the occasion. As many as a dozen men, women and children are there, which is perhaps why it's always held outside. There's a lot of talk, and by the time the cheese arrives (cheese with the gift of movement, another reason for making it an outside affair), the nerves of the fishing members of the ensemble - and mine - are jangling like tambourines. We start to see trout rising in our wine glasses.

I'm allowed to leave the table early, with the children. It's my job to tie up flies for everyone for the evening. I slip away to a quiet corner of the garden. I carry a hand-vice and all the materials I need in an old leather collar box. This allows me to whip up emergency flies, on the hoof. I picked up this collar box in a junk shop. To stop me getting collared by the family when I'm away from the house - and therefore supposedly away from fishing - I transformed it into a complete flytying kit containing the barest minimum of materials which I can conceal in a weekend bag next to an eight-sectioned 'Smuggler' rod. The combination visually, or rather invisibly, upholds my claims that there will be absolutely, positively, no fishing done whatsoever, on this holiday. (Flytying is the art of deception. But for the flyfisher, deception - unlike charity - doesn't start at home. It starts on holiday.) This kit brings the children in like wasps round a squashed plum and I'm interrogated like a defected spy.

'Qu'est que c'est?' they ask, pointing at the pile of feathers on the stool next to me.

'Black silk,' I tell them, 'And these are pheasant tail fibres dyed black.' Their little brows do half-hitches.

'This is a large red hackle and this is a smaller black one. And this is silver wire.'

They point at a lump of fur I'm pulling out of my collar box. 'This is white deer hair.' I put my thumbs to my temples and poke my first fingers to the sky to indicate antlers. Their brows do whip-finishes. The Englishman *est fou*!

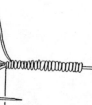

oval
cinsel

This may well be true, but they're smart. They've winkled out one of my best-kept secrets. The ingredients to make a mayfly spinner I call the Deerstalker.

But in those days, it was a pattern known only to a small, trusted group of fishermen lest it should fall into irresponsible hands and empty our rivers of trout!

Smuggled abroad, it was over in France to be tested against the super-wily trout on Vincent's little beat of the Charentonne, a gurgling tributary of the mighty River Risle. A chalkstream similar to those in the south of England, set in countryside much like the fruit-growing regions of Kent.

It's an anxious half-hour further from the farmhouse through the milky Normandy landscape to the stream. The road coils like a snake and Vincent still thinks he's driving in Paris. I don't dare look. I tie up a fly in the back seat and get deer hair in my beard thanks to the suspension; or lack of it.

We turn a corner and the brakes go on hard. The back of the Renault springs up and stays up as if held on a deck chair notch. In front of me is a mill house, crumbling like a giant fruit cake. Sliding through the grass in the orchard is a silvery snail trail: the Charentonne.

A little woman materializes out of the ivy. Sweet and as innocent as she may look, she secretly distils her own Calvados, making her the most charming bootlegger you will ever hope to meet. She rents the beat so there are plenty of smiles and niceties.

We tackle up and I hand Vincent, Claude and 'Le Chef de Cuilliere' - the King of the Spoon - a Mayfly spinner each and tell them it's good medicine. They trust the foreigner. I tell them it's called the Deerstalker and that unless bitten off, it never leaves the end of my line for two weeks of every season. I had only taken it off so I could pack my rod to bring it across the Channel.

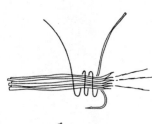

Rib with silk,
then tinsel

Claude takes the mill pool. 'Le Chef de Cuilliere' takes the little stream in the orchard. Vincent takes the slow canal stretch. I take out my leather collar box. I forgot to tie up a Deerstalker for myself.

In ten minutes, I'm next to Claude at the pool. The trout

are all wild on this small beat. As knobbly as footballers's knees. To fish them during the daylight hours is a useless pursuit, even at mayfly time. Vincent's tough little stretch is an evening fishery. The style is small spinners flicked out on breathy casts to slow, circling rises ebbing in the fading light. Rises without centres.

The silence, as I watch the river from my position in the grass, is acute. A bluebottle lands on my cheek. I can hear him rub his hands together.

At five o'clock, I hear another sound, a low-level crackle like paper being crumpled. Hanging over Claude's head is a flimsy cloud of mayfly spinners. I look around: they're everywhere.

I've learned it's a mistake to take this as the first sign of an evening rise. In the past I've seen the sky black with spinners, yet never seen a single one fall on the water, and not a fish surface. Often males will dance for days on end before females join them. For a rise, you must have females.

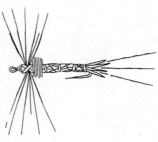

All the same, Claude is itching to cast a fly. I hold him back and he asks me why the wings of the Deerstalker are red and not blue, like the natural. I tell him that many of the most successful evening patterns have red in them somewhere. He pauses and thinks.

'But you've just told me how you took eight trout with eight casts with a Deerstalker on your beat one morning last week?'

Claude had a point, and there was only one answer.

'If fishing was as logical as we'd like it to be, I'd take up tennis.'

By now, he's uncontrollable. He creeps towards the pool on hands and knees. I can't see him in the long grass but I follow his progress by the clouds of spinners he drives up in front of him. I follow on.

The first few circles are just noticeable in the fast water. I scoop three jerking females from the stream as I cross the neck of water that runs from the back of the mill pool. A rise, even on Vincent's temperamental beat, is guaranteed.

Vincent was waist-high in iris at the top of the canal stretch. The water hardly moves here. The trout patrol, sipping spinners

as they go. Although they don't keep positions, they have top and bottom boundaries. Vincent is stalking a big trout, placing his fly where he thinks the trout will rise next - not where he sees them rising. This is precision fishing. It means calculating the trout's pace and rhythm with the accuracy of a high-wire artist. It's advanced stuff. Mayfly isn't duffer's fortnight here.

I arrive in time to see the water bulge and Vincent's Deerstalker sucked down a plug-hole.

'That trout stood four naturals on the end of his nose and refused them all - but he took that Deerstalker without flinching.'

'It's the way it sits,' I tell him.

'Whadya mean? I can't see it on the water.'

'Exactly,' I say.

For reasons I've never quite understood, most spinner patterns have hackles that hold the fly on the surface like a dun. Admittedly, some natural spinners come down on tip-toes, wings erect. But the majority come down noses stuck into the film. Wings, body and tails follow suit; indenting themselves in the film - like falling face first, arms outstretched, into shallow snow.

To imitate a spinner correctly, you shouldn't be able to see the artificial on the surface. Which is why no spinner pattern of mine sports any feature that could possibly prevent it behaving exactly as the trout expects to see it.

With no hackle, keeping a heavy mayfly iron from sinking straight through one side of the film into the other led me to use deer hair as the body material. It's hollow. By winding it on, you trap little bubbles of air. This has much the same effect as strapping lifebelts all along the side.

To give it additional floating capabilities, I let the points of the deer hair fibres poke out the back of the fly like short, stubby tails. This prevents the hook-bend pulling the fly under from the rear.

Vincent's eyes are straining to where (I thought) his Deerstalker lay flush in the flight path of a trout heading up river. The water lifted where I judged his fly to be. He didn't tighten.

'You lost that one,' I muttered softly.

The water immediately bulged in a different place. This time Vincent pulled his rod up hard and the line snapped like a necklace string, beads of shimmering droplets showering in the sunlight.

'Yeah, I lost that one okay.'

Claude had taken a good trout from the pool. A memorable fish. One of only a handful he'd ever caught on the beat. The ground quaked around him. He chattered with excitement.

'Every time that fly hits the water, a fish take it - but I keep missing them.'

'Le Chef de Cuilliere', a reluctant flyfisherman, had gone home. He'd taken ten trout on his Deerstalker, lost it on another, and started dreaming of his box of metal spinners back at Vraiville, banned from the beat and rusting ignominiously in his cellar.

We fished the mill pool until all we could make out in the late evening gloom was the creamy froth slopping around the hatch gate.

On our way home, we stopped at a smoke-filled bar in a farm village. The previous week Vincent was drinking there when the door pushed open and in walked a goat. Without hesitation, it trotted up to the only empty table and ate the table cloth. Turning on the hoof, it slid back through the crack in the door and disappeared. Nobody in the bar looked up from their beers.

The next morning, I was back in the garden filling my jersey with Deerstalkers. I had taken half a dozen trout from the Charentonne yesterday and my Deerstalker, although a little frayed, was still hanging on the end of my line. I manicured it nervously as Vincent shot us to Rouen, the gentle tap of the shock absorbers now a searing clatter of a thousand tin drums.

Our little party split in two to fish the tiny River Crevon, the French twin to the Boundary Stream on my home beat. Claude and I had the top beat. It was choked with trees and it took us all our skill to poke our rods through the bushes, let alone cast. Claude was filled with questions.

'Why do you fish the Deerstalker even though there are duns on the water?'

Near the end of the mayfly time, after a couple of heavy spinner falls, daytime fishing demands intense observation if you're to take the big, difficult trout. Even though there may be a relatively thick hatch of duns and trout rising, the former may not be the cause of the latter. Indeed, in my experience, especially on hard-fished waters where the trout are suspicious enough to escape even the worm-fishermen - as on the Crevon - if it's a choice between dun and spinner, they'll take a spinner; or any other surface food that sits low in the water, or in the skim itself. Any food that's in their element, not out of it.

Because, as explained earlier, these food forms are virtually invisible to the bank-side observer, it's often too easy to assume that it's what you can see on the water that the trout are taking - not what you can't. In the morning, big trout are more likely to accept a spinner with confidence rather than the dun.

That evening, we fished the grander River Andelle, an old stamping ground of Oliver Kite on his Normandy forays. It slithers through a valley filled with orchards and brown cows knee-high in buttercups. I think I overshot my allocated beat and found myself on someone else's. It was much too spectacular a stretch for me ever to have the privilege to fish. To be honest, I really didn't care and fished it up, heart in my mouth. I would only be 'borrowing' their trout anyway.

Close into my bank, I saw a minute dimple followed by a bubble at the side of a log, where slack water circled forming a slow, sucking whirlpool. I crept up to take a closer look. A mayfly spinner trapped in the tiny maelstrom disappeared in another bubble.

A poorly cast Deerstalker fell on the log and I flicked it off, landing it exactly in the path of the whirlpool. No sooner had it arrived than up came the trout, its mouth opening like a great white tropical flower to engulf my Deerstalker in its entirety.

He broke me on the log, but I got a look at him. A trout of at least two pounds; a monster for the Andelle, a fish that must have survived several years of bait and Mepp slinging.

I arrived back home at the Hollow in the evening to find mayfly spinners squatting in my garden. As I unpacked my bag, I could see from the bedroom window cars were still parked at the Mad House. It often happens: the mayfly season stretches over its allotted two weeks. When they enter this third phase, the fish get a great deal fatter, and artificials get a lot less fatal.

The phone rang. It was the Steel Guitar. I had given him a Deerstalker just before I left for France. While I was away, he invited a good friend to join him on his stretch of river.

The Steel Guitar had business to do that afternoon. At midday, he left his friend fishing for a trout tucked under the far bank. At six o'clock, he came back to find his patient pal still fishing the same fish, rising as if on tracks. In frustration, his friend told him to throw at it. First cast with the Deerstalker, the Steel Guitar tightened on a trout and within moments it was sliding into his net.

'Tell me,' his friend asked, 'Why did Neil wait two years before telling you about this fly?'

I don't know what the Steel Guitar answered, but I'd ask this: Why did he wait a whole afternoon before telling his friend about it?

I took my rod out of its tube, put the reel back on and climbed up my rod like a monkey, threading the line as I went. I unpacked my jersey, pulled a Deerstalker out of the wool, tied it on my line and walked down the track to the Mad House just as the sun dipped over the Downs and the first angler to leave switched his car lights on.

On the river, I found nothing that I didn't expect. All round Sticklepath Bridge, all the way up to the Slip on the Marshes, the trout had erected look-out posts and were carrying regulation magnifying glasses. 'Duffer's Fortnight' was over. Once again, the mayfly had taught the trout more than it had taught the flyfisher. But it was tricky conditions like this that had led to the development of the Deerstalker. I felt confident.

My first cast landed in front of a trout vacuuming a black glassy calm in a pool behind the hut. Not a big trout; but larger than the Charentonne average. I went through the motions, but it didn't. It never rose again. The same thing happened with the fish above it, skimming the underside of the surface with his skull, licking every spinner from beneath the surface plate. It dissolved into the evening the moment my Deerstalker landed.

As I headed back, guided by the light from my kitchen windows, I realised that it was time to scrap the stun-gun and go for bear. Collecting an armful of poplar twigs and branches, and leaving the front door and windows open, I lit a small fire in the sitting-room and lay on the rug in the orange glow counting the knots in the timber ceiling and fussing over the challenge of what could possibly outgun the Deerstalker?

If I ever have flytying problems, I fall back on one simple principle. The less you give a trout to find fault with, the more chance you have of it not faulting it. The first step is reducing the size of the hook. The next is reducing the quantity and the number of materials you incorporate in the tying procedure. Hook-wise, the Deerstalker couldn't be smaller without making it smaller than the natural, and therefore unnatural - a typical fault. How then could I make the hook smaller without dramatically altering the body size?

The answer might be to have a detached body, one that flies off the end of a smaller hook keeping the body length, but reducing the hook size. I've never liked this style. The detached body is usually stiff and lifeless, for you can't use soft, buzzy materials without it winding round what little hook there is and losing its natural shape. If a trout is to take anything hard and bristly into its mouth, I'd prefer it to be a hook, rather than body material.

My solution was this: you add heavy things to nymphs to make them sink, why not add buoyant materials to make your fly float? The answer was a thin strip of white polypropylene. Next, I threaded three hairline black horsehairs through the length of the body and secured them with two turns of black floss at the butt, to hold them in position and imitate the last segments of the spinners body. I tie in this combination of body and tail two thirds of the way down a standard #14 dry fly hook. I form a black thorax with a clipped black hackle in the same way I do the

Fold tails in with yarn

... secure with floss

... knot & varnish

... trim yarn butts

... tie in at centre of hook

thorax of the Deerstalker, with two winds of a large iron blue hackle at the head, representing a spidery web of wing veins. Virtually hookless, this light, fluffy pattern blows about on the wind, alighting on the surface of the river like thistledown.

I was well pleased.

May had been a hot, dry month, and I was pleased to see that there was still enough water in our river to float a mayfly on the surface without its belly rubbing on the river bed. The February rain was bubbling through on time, as predicted; as prayed for. I held back going to the river the next day. My first day back, I had things to do. Like go to London, do some work, earn some money, act responsibly. On the train on my way back in the evening, I reviewed the thinking behind the White Sock, the name I had given the Deerstalker's knee-high-to-a-mayfly counterpart. I couldn't wait to give it a first trial. This exaggerated my impatience to arrive.

Confidence oozed out of the train compartment, along the corridor and out onto the Marshes as the train pulled into the station at the end of the beat. The local station, a blip on the network, hardly even a halt for commuters, suddenly became a centre of hurried activity for what must have been seconds. All of three people got off, I stepped onto the platform into a smoke screen of mayfly spinners hanging over the platform, avoiding taking in a deep breath. Even before I'd got home, the river was whispering 'Fish me'.

Anxiety attacks aside, I didn't feel under any pressure to get to the river. In the third week of mayfly, I don't take my rod off the rack until long after supper. As if teasing myself - although I saw it more as therapy - I walked to the centre of the canal bridge and slumped over it like a pair of old corduroys on a coat-hanger. I watched the train chug down the line, clicking slowly out of sight, round a curve, pressing on through a snow storm of mayfly. The level-crossing barrier lifted, animating life suspended on the other side. Car engines shifted into first and second, then faded as they disappeared up the hill into the village and away, leaving silence and the blue mist of diesel and petrol fumes yielding to the smell of damp vegetation. In the water-meadows, a coot brayed like a crazed donkey.

I walked up to the main road and crossed the Marshes. Cows stood motionless, eyeing me. Trapped in thick grass, you could only see their heads. Immediately I got home, I changed out of my suit and loaded the front of my jersey with the White Sock, in triplicate. As I made my dusty way down the track, I manicured each of them individually. On Sticklepath Bridge, the murmurs and vibration of the spinner was so intense, I might have been on the Starship Enterprise.

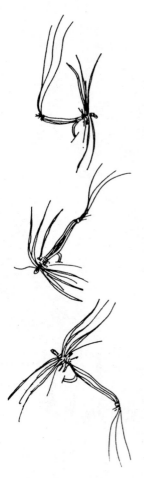

A tight huddle of rods and their guests were sitting behind glasses of wine in front of the Mad House. Men with leather faces, red-armed and red-eyed, tired after their day. The River God was there with his friends. When this group of anglers get together to talk about fishing books, it isn't about ones they've read, it's about ones they've written. All assembled had their name incorporated in one famous fly or another, even if it was only an initial. I could have crossed the field and gone through the Hole to Horse Bridge, but I was going up, not down river. I hurried by. I was longing to cast a fly at two fish who had introduced themselves to me the evening before. I'd marked them down.

They were lying deep under a bank on the Broadwater, tipping up and down at spinners on rocking chairs. I crept towards the spot behind a hatch-pool I only ever visit in mayfly time, or in September with a wire nymph after the chub that skulk around the still, clear waters in the chrome sun, rejecting this, rejecting that, rejecting everything. I don't know why I bother.

As the sun sank down behind the Downs, once again I found myself travelling on hands and knees to where I thought the two trout were lying. A twist, a turn, a circle, a swirl told me where one of the fish was patrolling, just like the trout below the hatch in Normandy. I'd seen it all before. I unhooked the White Sock from my bottom ferrule and let it drift out on the end of a positive cast that cooled the air with its directness. I aimed to have the White Sock parachute down just below the last rise, for this was where I had calculated the trout would turn to find its next meal.

My eyes strained to where, I thought, the White Sock lay flush in the feeding path of the trout. The water lifted where I judged my fly to be. I was just about to strike when the water bulged in a different place. Involuntarily, I pulled my rod up hard and the line snapped like a violin string.

I lost both fish. The one I thought had taken my fly, but had taken something else - and the second fish, the one that had actually taken my fly.

Like I say, in the third week mayfly time ceases to be a fool's fortnight here. Even though you fish exactly the right fly.

The last week of mayfly is the second week of June. I had been away all that week but I managed to get down to the river at midday on Saturday. At Sticklepath Bridge, a solitary, sooty-eyed spinner cut a jet-black dash against a high, steel-rimmed sun, confirming that the party was over for another year.

On the Fly Lane, trout were fast asleep on the river bed. Some had their heads under the blankets of ranunculus; other were tucked under the bank covered with rosebay willow-herb and comfrey. They made no fast moves - in fact no moves at all. The pace had ground to a halt, and once again, with no cars at the lodge, I had the place to myself.

Gazing at a trout wrapped up in a gravel scoop, its mind somewhere else, I realised that all of a sudden the distance between the angler and the trout had widened considerably. The game had changed.

Mayfly is fun, but it makes the angler lazy. It deadens his brain, it dulls his instinct. Day after day of aerializing large floppy flies, slapping them down on a sea of trout-mouth vortexes, delaying reactions to allow trout to mouth, suck in and eventually get their lips round the huge yellow slab of butter floating on the surface - it does something to the angler and his

style. Something negative, something destructive, something damaging to his ability to cope with problems - the sort of teasers that will confront him in the months ahead. It's not surprising that at this time of year, a good many of the rods on The Hollow go away, never to return.

On the other hand, trout fortunate enough to have survived the holocaust are now super-trout. They're slicker, they're smarter, they're the wise guys. The Hollow flyfisher is no longer greeted by a river of carefree, foolhardy fish showing themselves readily, flirting wantonly. All this is gone. Now he's face to fin with the horrible reality that things will never be the same again for the rest of the season. And I too was subject to all this grimness. My riverside cunning and instinct had died on me weeks back. With the eye of a bat, and the ear of a hawk, my basic senses needed drastic realignment. My reactions needed sharpening, honing and polishing if the season wasn't going to grind to a fishless halt. I needed an edge. And the course of treatment devised by Roll Cast and myself for this feeble condition is called the Grand Slam.

Stare into the oily clarity of a deep pool and what you see is a bowl of fish that haven't been worn down or been tampered with. I am reminded that The Hollow is not a monoculture. Spry, sprightly, tireless and dynamic, coarse fish are an invigorating sight on a steaming hot day, when nothing much is likely to happen until the sun dips below the Downs. When it comes to speed of reaction (indeed giving any reaction at all) they offer the greatest challenge. You're looking at the perfect foil for your benumbed brain. The essential players in the Grand Slam contest.

To win the Grand Slam Award you have to catch one specimen of each of the following fish: a dace, a roach, a chub, a perch, a grayling and a trout; in any order, all in one day. Now if this sounds easy, here's the edge. It's sight-fishing only. You must find the fish, position yourself so you can see it (but not it you), present the nymph, and time your strike accordingly. For bait, you're only allowed to use wire wrapped round a hook.

Using wire and hook only is minimal, but it isn't a

limitation. It's an advantage. It allows you to tailor-make your nymph on the spot so you can get it to the exact depth of the fish you have singled out. Without it being too heavy, and therefore too bulky; or too skimpy, and therefore too lightweight. For this reason, on a Grand Slam day, I don't take flies with me, instead I take a small round plastic box with a flip-off lid. Inside is a selection of hooks, from #12 to #18, and three spools of fuse wire in different colours - gold, copper and red - wound round wooden sewing thread spools. Holding the hook between the thumb and forefinger of my left hand, I bind on a thorax just behind the eye using just enough wire to sink the hook to the fish's position, taking into consideration the flow of the current.

Coarse fish, using nymphing tactics, are demanding - to varying degrees. Some are trickier than others. The easiest is the perch, with the grayling coming a close second. The fastest is the dace. The most unpredictable is the roach; the most illusive, the chub. But some general rules apply to the approach to fishing them with a nymph. And because, of all the fish in the stream, the trout comes top in the Easy League, these rules can be applied to nymph fishing for trout as well.

Success depends, first of all, on polaroids - and second, on you being able to present your nymph at the precise depth of the fish you are after, directly in line with its nose, and with enough weight in the nymph to give you total control so that you are able to lift and tweak it horizontally if its course needs resetting. Or vertically, to stroke the fish's nose, if inducement is needed. This is why wire, rather than feather or any other imitative ingredient, is the most important material when tying nymphs and putting them into service, for you will not be asking your fish to buy the look of the fly, you will be selling it the movement of a nymph. Or a small fish, in the case of the perch. With this achieved, now all that is required is a quick eye and a light hand.

At this time of year, when it comes to the take, the fastest in the stream is the dace. It's the first to recover from spawning and is therefore the fittest. A shoal of dace in a gravel-bottomed soda-stream stretch can be a formidable challenge. Clean gravel is not an easy background to have against you when sight-fishing

with wire nymphs that seem to prefer to reflect the surrounding landscape rather than deaden it, they stand out for this reason. Especially when your prey is no more than a shadow in the stream itself.

Of all the coarse fish, the rapid-rising dace requires you to stand over him, wound up like a coiled spring. Dace make headlong attacks, and you can be forgiven for missing his first few bolts at your nymph if you're not totally connected, by mind and body, to the nymph. A close inspection by a dace is a rare event and not to be trusted. It usually means that your dace has already made his mind up and is highly cautious and not likely to accept a nymph of any size, at any depth, on any terms.

The 'anticipation' strike, as I call it, may not be the most accurate solution but it is certainly a method I use when the correct set of circumstances present themselves. To perform this strike, I don't wait to see the dace take the nymph, I lift the tip of my rod the moment a dace arrives in the surrounds of my nymph. This method of striking is often the only way to ensure that the 'strike alert' from my brain transmits to the hand, through the rod tip, in time to reach the nymph still hovering in the water which has been sucked into the dace's mouth for tasting.

A shoal of dace isn't normally a forgiving crowd, but they are a great deal more charitable, and will therefore give your nymph a second viewing if it is whisked away before they reach it for inspection; rather than if it is pulled away *after* inspection, after it has been spat out and the dace is pulling itself away for good. For this reason, unless a dace floats into the swim while I'm fishing for a less speedy member of the Grand Slam set, to get my hand and eye in I always start off with the perch.

The perch, the easiest to catch, is the hardest to locate, giving me a chance to do a general reconnoitre of the water while in pursuit. I usually find my perch after I've marked out the whereabouts of all the other specimens I'm after. The bigger perch frequent the deeper holes, but I normally go looking for the larger shoals of smaller perch. They seem to shoal according to size. But this doesn't mean a Big Bertha won't sometimes steam in, stage right, and grab your nymph without you knowing it was there. These shoals of smaller fish often pull out of the weeds like little motorized submarines, hanging suspended, drifting forward on revolving paddle-boat fins, when you're fishing for other specimens. They are attracted by the commotion and the flashes of various fish hurling themselves suicidally at my nymph as I keep missing them on the strike. Perch are not only greedy, they have a mouth capable of opening up to the size of a car boot to prove it. When it sees your nymph, a perch either goes for it, or sometimes it will follow it for a couple of feet, nose glued to its tail. Give your nymph a flick and the perch will gobble it up.

Although pattern is of no great consequence, flyfishing for perch is probably best described as 'fry-fishing', for that's what they like to eat. A metallic-bodied nymph, the more flash in it the better, is preferred. And the more jerks you give it in the bright midday sun, the less of a jerk you will feel when it's time to check in at the end of a Grand Slam day. At least, in the perch department.

Meanwhile, in the chub department, you're against one of the world's great recluses. Chub shoal, but only in twos and threes. Where the perch puffs up and attacks, and the dace launches itself against a nymph like a Polaris missile, the chub comes and goes, reappears and fades. Perhaps with a blush on its gills, you can't always be sure.

I set out after chub with the most confidence on sizzling summer days. I make for corners in narrow streams where the flow is hardly detectable under overgrown bushes and overhanging side-sedge. I head for still, quiet places where you can't see where the reeds end and their reflections begin - where hidey-holes abound, and where chub are bound to be hidden away.

A chub on the feed, or just on the loose with a friend, patrols. Chub have their boundaries marked out. In this small zone, they have a dining-room area and a coal cellar to escape to when bombarded by wire nymphs. Of all the coarse fish you are likely to chuck a nymph at, the chub is the most wary of hefty objects arriving from above, out of the blue - unlike the dace, which is often intrigued by the disturbance, or the perch which is positively excited by it. For this reason, I usually select the biggest of the patrol and concentrate my total efforts on this individual's downfall.

To do this, I spend a great deal of time watching it police its beat, moving round with the regularity of a minute hand on a

clock face. I work out where best to make my ambush. This is a place where the current is at its slowest, where I can lower a nymph and have it stay on the river bed waiting for the chub to return. Behind a weed-bed on the chub's route, where the flow is slack, the current non-exsistent is a favourite position. As soon as the chub are at the furthest point from this carefully selected spot, I lower my nymph and let it sink to the bottom. The pace of an approaching chub is snail-like. You will not be asked to make any hasty decisions if the chub decides to go for your nymph as you lift it up in his path. Everything about the chub is deliberated, calculated, wilful. Nothing ever happens on the spur of the moment. If he wants to take your wire nymph, he will take it in his own time. But this doesn't mean you stand there waiting, sleepily. Your hand doesn't have to be speedy, but your mind must be processing the chub's every move, calculating the lift and strike. Strike too soon, or too late, and you miss perhaps the biggest fish you are likely to catch that day - game or coarse.

Your strike warrants careful consideration. It must not be too fast. Neither must it be too slow, for a chub can puff out the heaviest wire nymph in milli-seconds and blow it from one end of the pool to the other if it discovers someone's been trying to make a fool out of him. If your doctor ever recommends you need to take it easy for a few days, take a wire nymph out after chub. One day is enough to relax you, two days you'll be fully recovered, three days and you'll probably have slowed down just enough to cure those hooking problems you had on day one.

Of all the coarse fish on the Grand Slam slate, the chub will probably be the biggest you catch. The bigger they are, the more likely they are to take a wire nymph. I've had them up to five pounds. For this reason you would imagine they'd be my favourite coarse fish to take on the wire nymph, but in actual fact, they aren't.

Although my love for trout almost gets me arrested at times, I place the roach as the prettiest fish that swims The Hollow. The real reason I fish for them at all, isn't to put them in a net and weigh them, but to hold them in the light and look at them, from all angles. The fact is, if I couldn't fish for roach, I'd paint them and be just as content.

In the roach department, sometimes the impossible happens. I had a shoal marked down above the Beech Bridge in amongst a forest of weed fronds where Darkest Africa shallows off to meet the main river. Roach shoal up here in great numbers after spawning, to clean off. As the last to return to their pre-spawn glory, they stay in these parts for a good long time. Sometimes for the rest of the game season. Grand Slam day or not, I always throw a wire nymph at the shoal every time I find myself in that darkest part of The Hollow; mainly because there, amongst the quarter and half-pounders, I once spotted a roach three times the size of the average. Amongst the wavy fingers of ribbon weed, the attraction of this fish was hypnotic.

It took about two weeks of making some very serious attempts at this roach to realise that this was one fish that wasn't going to give itself up easily to a primitive wire nymph. Each time

I got my nymph on course, he'd make a move - in the opposite direction. Eventually, increased pressure made him flee the shallows altogether and bury himself away in the black, tarry waters that gave Darkest Africa its name. But I was not bitter. As I waited for it to return I was quite happy to throw various other differently weighted wired hooks to a succession of silver twinkles winking at me from the shadows.

People say that roach can only be taken on the dry fly. I've heard this said a great deal, but it's not true. You just have to make sure you deliver your wire nymph bang on a roach's nose. This means a lot of standing around on the bank tying up tailor-made wire nymphs in order to get the weight right. Roach are very gentle feeders. They remind me of my grandmother. When we used to visit her as children and stay for Sunday lunch, we'd have finished our pudding long before she'd finished chewing her first grapefruit segment. A roach's mouth is as paper-thin as the skin of these grapefruit segments. Gung-ho striking may get the hook to set in time, but it'll zip straight through and out, a wound I wouldn't wish to inflict on any fish, whatever shape or size.

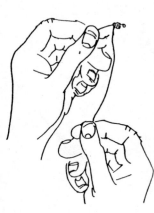

One hot summer day, in search of shade, I crept into the cool of Darkest Africa and watched my shoal drift aimlessly between the weed-beds, like wisps of smoke, in pursuit of whatever they were in pursuit of. In passing, I slung a lightweight wire nymph at one of them. From nowhere, the big roach appeared, and took my nymph in one monstrously silent gulp, before any other member of the shoal had a chance to even consider inspecting it.

Lying in the palm of my hand, supported by the flat edge of my thumb and the inside tip of my little finger, the big roach felt like a thick-cut sirloin steak. I can feel it as I write. It was like no other fish I had hand-landed. Large roach have this ample, dense, mattress-like feel to them. Laying it gently on the grass, its mouth blowing bubbles, I ripped two pieces of sedge from the bank and laid the end of the first stalk on the roach's nose, and marked the other end at its tail. I then chopped the stalk to the exact length using the scissors in my Swiss Army knife. I did the

same with the other stalk, measuring its girth. I then returned the roach, watching it sink out of sight into a part of Darkest Africa where even the strongest sunlight had never managed to penetrate.

That evening, I sent the sedge stalks to the eminent angling expert Peter Stone, in Oxford. Coarse fishing guru, writer and taxidermist (and present when Richard Walker caught his record Redmire carp in 1951), I asked him for his opinion on the size of the happily-released roach. It was two months before he rang back. I remember, I was in a bath. Peter had researched the sedge lengths thoroughly. The fish was two pounds, perhaps a little over. But two pounds was good enough for me. It was the biggest roach I had taken on a wire nymph.

If roach are playing up and difficult to catch, I suggest you postpone the Grand Slam and wait until temperatures rocket. The hotter the weather, the better and bigger the roach. On the day my big roach finally took the wire 'nothing' he'd stubbornly refused so many times before, the sun was white hot in the sky and in Darkest Africa the river ran like treacle. That steamy hot afternoon, my muscles alert, my instincts at snapping point and a wild, quick-silver glint in my eye, another river was running - sweat, down the valley of my spine.

Yes, the hotter the better.

July

THE SHOOTING-STICK PHILOSOPHY

At this time of the season, I wake up in the mornings an old man. With pains in my back, aches in my shoulders, I'm reminded that like all the other rods on The Hollow, I have a nickname, too. My name is 'The Heron', given to me by the River God because when I'm onto a fish I stoop over it, spine arched as if I'm about to stab it with my nose.

There hadn't been a single day in the previous week when I wasn't out on the river. If not in the morning, or in the afternoon, then in the evening. My whole body was creaking like an old gate.

Not in too much of a hurry to get up, I lay in bed looking at the yellow country outside stretching in front of me. I was

thinking of the three cock capes I had nailed on planks to dry in the sun and had forgotten to bring inside, and listening to the birds and sounds of the river through a window wide open to the morning.

The Galloping Major normally arrives at 9.30 on the button, parking his car at Snowdrop Land. If I was an assassin, that's where I'd lie waiting for a pot-shot at him on a Saturday morning. But I'm not, I'm in bed, or at breakfast, or both. But I'll take a bet that no matter what I'm doing, at ten o'clock I'll hear a crunch of gravel. This is the Galloping Major, skidding to a halt at the Mad House. In this short time, he's fished half a mile of main river - in one hour, on the button. A fleeting glance at the record book, a spark from gravel flints rubbed together underfoot, a tiny puff of smoke at the heel and the Galloping Major is on his way upstream. You might meet him again at the Mad House around lunch-time when he tumbles back like a stick from a spent rocket, fizzled out, fishless and fretting.

If the Boss is passing and ricochets off him, he's unlucky. For nothing upsets the Boss more than hearing that his rods aren't catching trout. If he puts his heart and soul into the river he's bound to take this personally, and I don't blame him. So when the Boss stopped on the track and leaned out his Land Rover (the couple of rabbits he'd shot at the end of the mayfly season still in the trailer behind him and now humming in the midday sun like a female backing chorus), and told me that the Galloping Major was moaning about empty baskets, I knew he wasn't angry - he was soul-destroyed. Especially when the story he'd been given went something like this: 'Look, I've walked from one end of this fishery to the other and back again this morning and I've only seen two trout.'

I tried to comfort him. I told him I was amazed the Galloping Major wasn't seeing spots before his eyes at that kind of pace. As a keeper even more seasoned than the contents of his trailer, he shrugged it off, reluctantly. Thrusting the gear stick down the sore throat of his work-horse's gear box, he kangerooed along the track in the direction of the village. I headed off down the track to the river.

I had sympathy for him. Flyfishers on chalkstreams walk too fast when they're astream. I'd go further and say that it's not the speed at which they travel that limits their chances of catching trout, it's the fact that they move at all.

On my way down the track, I stopped to pick bark off the latest batch of warm, sweet-smelling poplars stacked up at the side of the track, baking in the sun like apples. I tore some off and threw it in a pile in the dust to pick up on my way back. It makes good kindling.

There were no cars at Sticklepath Bridge. I had the river to myself, again. The sun was hot and I began to wish I'd come down earlier. There might have been a small hatch of something at this time of year. But right now, there wasn't a fly to be seen, or heard. The air was silent. I was able to detect the tiniest wing beat. The thick, morning water rubbed round the brick bridge supports like lava.

I decided to patrol the Square Dance, a compact area of mixed waters, incorporating a stretch of the main river on one side - and Cake Wood. Carpeted with comfrey and ferns and wallpapered by ancient woodland, this shady stream is tucked away behind the Mad House. Here, the sun never breaks through the trees until late morning.

One of the best anglers I met in my first year on the river always used to disappear into an area of the river with about enough carriers to confuse an Indian scout. He wasn't just a good fisherman, he consistently dragged the biggest fish back to the hut. When I saw him set off, my heart went out to the trout. Yet to see him in action, you'd think nothing worked from the knees down. A solicitor from Kent, he was the text-book chalkstream fisherman. Tweed jacket, cap, tackled-out by Hardy top to toe. He was as straight as straight could be. Straight out of E.A. Barton's *Album of a Chalk-Stream*. No-one, nothing, could be straighter. I called him Curly.

With his Volvo parked at the hut (doors and boot locked), Curly would go straight to one of three spots - often the same one every trip. There Curly would stay. I had enough time to walk round every likely fish-holding position on the river before he even lifted his rod. But at the end of the day, he'd have taken a heavier bag. In those days, this trout enemy No. 1 paid a princely sum each season for his fishing. I calculated he could have bought the amount of bank he actually fished for a couple of quid, freehold.

Why did Curly catch bigger trout than somebody who spent the day stream-walking? And why is it so unusual to come across anglers like the trout-slayer I've just mentioned who fish from a fixed position?

This isn't such an odd question to ask if you think about other forms of angling - coarse, sea, salmon, wet fly, stillwater trouting. This obsession with fishing on the move is unique to chalkstreams. Why?

Maybe chalkstream anglers are loathe to remain standing in one spot on a river because they have no need to exercise territorial instincts on their beat. With restricted access, their solitude is never threatened.

The beat is theirs. No coachload of anglers is likely to spew out a hoard of green umbrella-toting fishermen, hell-bent on making claims to the best swims on the beat. The fact that I had the river to myself again happily confirmed my theory. Exclusivity, the fact that on most chalkstream beats there are relatively few anglers per yard of bank, is the reason. This, linked with the general belief that fish are always better on the other side of the fence; somewhere else, so keep moving

But like most of the good and bad habits connected with chalkstream flyfishing, you can usually trace them back to Mr. Halford. As the prophet of the idea that fishing the water blind is about as sporting as shooting chickens in the yard, he introduced a new concept. Namely, that before you could even start to cast a fly to a trout, you first had to find the fish in question. At least see evidence that it was there and feeding: a rise, or some other movement on the surface. In an historical context, Halford substituted the sense of feel so important to the wet fly fisherman of the time, with the sense of seeing.

To his downstream, lure-dragging contemporaries, who spent long monotonous hours anchored to likely spots praying that an obliging trout might just hang onto their offerings (it's no wonder they packed up fishing after the mayfly), Halford's thinking did more than offer an effective alternative to wet flies. It represented an excuse for fishermen to stretch their seized-up leg muscles. And to this day, the ritual of going out and looking for an opportunity, rather than perhaps waiting for it to come to you, is still as much a part of chalkstream tradition as casting a fly upstream.

At Beech Bridge, I stood and looked across to the trees on the other side of the river. The water runs deep and slow under the branches there and I tried to picture trout that might be tucked under the bank. Big trout, their fat bellies sqeezed in-between the damp, mossy roots.

This is a slow, strange, sipping area. An area of puckered lips, rather than snapping jaws. Lips sucking at microcosms. It has everything a chalkstream angler could ask of a stretch of stream - except for the chalkstream angler's favourite kind of trout. Trout that show themselves. Trout you can see.

I leant back on my hands and clasped the wooden bar connected to the concrete and flint footbridge by three metal supports. They twanged nervously. I held my position.

In my experience, the advantages of seat-of-the-pants fishing outweigh the advantages of sole-of-the-feet fishing. Stream-walkers disagree. They say 'How do I know I'm not sitting over an empty hole?' I have to admit there was a time when I could understand this line of thinking. Every time I stayed still for five minutes I'd find myself asking the same question. But after I'd managed to fidget my way through the initial few minutes and settle down, it was amazing how fast these doubts dissolved with the arrival of a trout mere yards from my feet, or at the sight of a fin beckoning me from the edge of a weed-bed. Flyfishermen who use this 'empty hole' theory to justify their stream-walking can never have travelled up their river on an electro-fishing boat, greeting each scoop of the net with 'Goodness, I'd never have guessed I'd find a trout there.' It's really quite revealing. But having said this, I agree that some places are better fish-holders than others. And some places hold bigger trout than others.

Where are these places? And how can you find them? I was standing looking over one now.

The metal railing twanged like a slack banjo string as I settled in for the duration. Strangely enough, I've yet to read a fishing writer who has been wholly enlightening about stream-craft. By that I mean you can't teach anybody to find fish off a page. Think over the chapters you've read entitled, 'Finding Fish'. What can you remember? Like me, you probably only have memories of shaky maps of imaginary rivers covered with Xs marking the spot, the whole effect being that they were sketched at full gallop. The fact is, trout move around too much during the year to be pinned down in this way. From surface food-bearing lies in the Spring, to nymph-bearing lies in the summer, to give an example. Even in the course of a day, a trout may be found in a totally different area in the evening to where it was that morning. It's too much like musical chairs to be coded and systemized. The fact is, finding fish is to do with understanding fish. This takes experience and more often than not, gut-feeling.

Personally, I go looking for likely fish-holding places with the same enthusiasm as when I was knee-high to a pair of waders. I still rely on the same schoolboy curiosity and ingenuity. I can confidently say that I'm no better a trout scout than when I was twelve.

That mysterious hole under the willow, that dark pool where the weed tresses wave like flags, under that old farm bridge. The chances of a big trout living there are so high, you'd never find me passing these places by in a hurry. As I think back to the big fish I've taken in the past, not one of them came from a place I wouldn't have expected to find them. The places you instinctively *feel* should hold big fish are the places you should head for with your shooting-stick. This is the best and most honest advice anybody can give.

Having said this, you may at first pass a lot of spots that look potentially productive but have never produced trout in the past. I suggest you forget the past. The reason why these places don't produce their fair share of monsters is often to do with a lack of understanding of why big fish get to be so big. They manage this because they stay out of trouble. They don't sit out in the middle of the stream in full view of the casual stream-walker. As a result they are rarely pestered by them. But for the reasons I will now give, these piscatorial Howard Hughes are in mortal danger from the man who sews leather patches on the seat of his breeches and adjusts his eye-sight in the manner I will now describe.

Charles Ritz once said that a fish seen is a fish almost caught. Flyfishermen tend to glide over the big, wild trout because they take this too literally. They look for whole fish, not parts of them. Nymph-fishermen, in particular, miss trout because they don't hone down their observation to look for trout portions, 'extracts of trout'. Tails, fins, snouts poking out of weed-beds, silver patches where scales are missing against gravels, pinky warts. The more exacting flyfisher looks into the river and asks himself 'When is a trout not a trout?' He looks for imaginary trout and takes away the tail, the fins, the gills, the body, the head - hoping something in the tight area he scans holds one or more elements of a trout. Only then can he conclude that a trout is not a trout - when it was never there in the first place.

As I mentioned earlier, trout tend to move about in the course of a typical day. Big trout are perhaps the only exception to this rule. But just because they don't commute from one position to another doesn't mean they don't move at all. From my shooting-stick, I've noticed that big trout tend to move to eat. An inch here, an inch there, drifting slowly back, or pulling to one side to intercept a shrimp passing close by. They also move when disturbed, prompted by the arrival of another fish in the same weed-clump, or at the shadow of a bird flying overhead. These tell-tale signs are often only blink-and-you'll-miss-'em glimpses. The angler not there, not waiting for these opportunities, misses them. But what about the dry fly man watching the surface?

Again, from a sitting position he, too, is able to increase the amount he sees simply by training himself to stop looking for ever-spiralling rise-forms. He must adjust his vision to register changes of light on the surface, inverted dents, shimmers, nervous water. Having done this, the smallest dimple becomes an eruption, and the most gentle, insignificant flicker of the film becomes an opportunity.

This way of seeing is especially relevant to summer on the chalkstreams, when long ago I came to the conclusion that the commonest and most walked-over daytime rise-form isn't really rise-form at all. It's a sound. The muffled sipping of trout, like Victorian middle-class ladies drinking hot soup, delicately sucking at small insects and nymphs glued to the sticky film. To the man who has been sitting quietly studying his stretch, such a rise is as visually and audibly arresting as if somebody had slung a half-brick into the water.

The amount the eye is capable of seeing is in direct relation to the speed at which it is travelling. The faster you walk, the less you will see. The slower you walk, the more you will see. The longer you stay in one spot, the better the chances of you seeing (and hearing) everything you're ever likely to see (or hear).

This is the Shooting-Stick Philosophy.

In effect, by standing still, you automatically improve your vision. And it's being able to see more opportunities that I believe is the main advantage of fishing from a strategically placed stick. The second advantage is something I've already touched on: acquaintance with the environment around you. After twenty minutes, you start to get to know your patch as if you were born and brought up there. Even sub-consciously, you are aware of surface and underwater currents, the pace of the water. All these things add up to better presentation. The current carrying the food to the trout, for example, may not be the current you imagine it to be. It may be one of many different currents on the surface flowing at a different pace, from a different direction. An artificial sailing down one of these other currents may sound the alarm bells to the waiting trout. The natural drift of flies on the water is often more important than matching the hatch.

As a resident in the area, you're also an expert on the most prominent food-types on the menu in the trout's local restaurant. This is unavoidable. By rooting yourself to the spot, you qualify as a bush and a good deal of what is flying around will land on you. This familiarity of the food in your area may seem a small point, but often different flies will be hatching off at different parts of the river.

This detail isn't always appreciated by the stream-walker simply scanning the water looking for trout. His scant interest in the relationship between locality and the trout's life-style and food type is often the reason why the stream-walker's fly, that fooled a fish on one beat, fails to catch a fish on another.

But this telescoping-in on a relatively small area of water scores most on summer evenings when fish up and down the river are selecting different flies in different stages of development. By remaining in one spot you are, in effect, behaving like a trout in a feeding position. Like the trout you will be aware of what fly (and at what stage of its development) is passing by in the most abundance and, therefore, the fly the trout opposite you is most likely to be feeding on. It's this kind of understanding and intimacy with the trout that I believe can only be appreciated over a long period of time. A long period of time rooted to one place.

Finally, this approach has one other advantage on summer evenings. It stops you chasing from one trout to another and finishing the day with a pulse rate of 120 and a trout total of nil. I'm now totally convinced that it's not anglers that trout are allergic to. It's *moving* anglers. By staking out a spot, you have control over how much your area is disturbed, or left undisturbed. The latter is essential if big, shy trout are to come out of hiding.

On the hard-pounded public waters of the Croton River in New York State, where I once fished, the flyfishers stand over their plots with the patience of loyal dogs sitting bent over their dead masters' graves. After ten minutes fishing, you start to understand this logic. With waves of spoon-slingers marauding up and down the bank, it's the only way you can ensure that the fish in your area are not knocked unconscious before they get a chance to see your fly. This kind of ground-hogging may not apply to the etiquette-ridden beats in the south of England, but on some club or regularly-frequented hotel waters, for example, it makes a lot of sense.

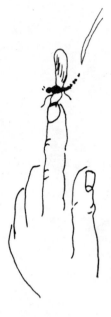

Half an hour had passed. The heat had soldered my hands to the metal rail. As the sun moved over my head, the deep blue shadows intensified under the bushes and a single ring, a ring with no centre, ebbed out into the middle of the river. This was the half-brick I had been waiting for. Evidence of stirrings from one of the many invisible trout in this dark area. Trout paraded like a row of Doric columns, their metallic blue skulls flush with the underside of the skin of the film, as if holding up the surface of the river.

As if built of marble, these weighty trout, one of them at least three pounds, had proved impossible to move - either upwards, out of their element to intercept something on the surface (a nose breaking the surface might break the silence), or downwards, and thus breaking rank (perhaps disturbing a neighbour) to snaffle a nymph. To the angler glued to the spot who by now would have noted and inwardly digested all these details, it was time to draw conclusions - and get to work.

The grey specks in the late morning sunbeams that gave the scene Seurat's pointillist quality to the angler on the move, had more significant implications to the man on a stick trained to notice, rather than simply see all around him. They were midges. Chironomids, just like the ones so familiar to the stillwater flyfisher, only smaller.

As, year on year, the water level of the river drops, the flow slows down, water temperature rises and the river becomes more closely related to the contents of a water butt, midge have become a regular feature. You notice these things when, you're sitting on a stick by the river, or when you're sleeping next-door to it. I had given these changes some thought.

On my walks back up the track to my vice, the river still hot in my blood and the flapping of midge wings still buzzing in my ear (and a good many of their less fortunate companions in my hair), I started a search for the solution. As is my way, first I tried to find out as much as I could about these latest entomological arrivals, and how they behave. Especially since they looked like they were here to stay.

Midges can emerge on rivers at any time of year and at any time of the day, depending on three factors. Firstly, the species. Secondly, the temperature. And thirdly, the length of daylight hours. The longer the daylight hours, the larger the number of midges that hatch, and the more varied the species of midge. Fortunately, before I stopped on Beech Bridge, I had decided it was going to be a long day.

In slack water, for some chironomids, life starts at the top. The adult female lays her eggs gently on the surface in one dollop. There they stay until the little larvae hatch out and plummet to the bottom. On arrival, most of the worm-like larvae either make dug-outs in the silt, and build tubes of bits of gravel which they attach to themselves with a sticky substance. Or they simply spend the day flapping about feverishly using sinuous whip-lash movements.

Colours vary. At the bottom of fast, fizzing water loaded with oxygen, larvae tend to be green or brown. In slow-low oxygen water, they tend to be more reddish and purple. Known as bloodworms, these larvae are full of haemoglobin to help them store oxygen.

The midge pupa looks just like the larva, in many ways. But closer inspection reveals wings and legs tucked away at the thorax, like a parachute. You will also see fluffy, small white breathing filaments at the head and tail. Fully equipped with the most up-to-date means of accumulating oxygen, midge pupae make regular trips from their homes before hatching. They do this to build up their oxygen store so they can break out of their skin stockings and power back up to the top again.

At the surface, they either attach their respiratory tube and hang horizontally in the surface, their thorax piercing the surface, or they rove, wriggling just beneath the surface.

Compared to a hatch of mayfly, a fall of spinner or an explosion of sedge, all this hanging-out beneath the surface may seem decidedly uneventful. Not so. These midge manoeuvres may not be able to move mountains, but they can shift Doric columns - if only slightly. Just far enough for them to suck in these squirming danglers, just far enough to register a thin, single ring on the water surface. To the flyfisher lounging on a stick or leaning on a bridge rail with nothing better to look at, this single ring is a shock wave. It's certainly sufficient to register an opportunity.

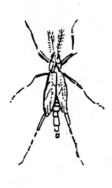

As I stood on Beech Bridge watching, these single rings began to run circles round my mind. Small things began to take on an importance disproportionate to the tiny, yet vital ends they tried to create. How was I to get one of those gaping mouths to close round my hook?

Work began to design a tiny hatching-midge pattern (most of the species on chalkstreams are tiny) that could be cast high above a super-nervous trout so as not to arouse suspicion. A pattern that, having broken the surface, stopped there and sank no further. A pattern I could depend on to ride the distance, not on top of the surface above the trout, but on a plane somewhere just below the film. A midge pattern that would appear trapped in the surface, ready to launch itself.

The search was for an imitation river-midge pupa which, just like its stillwater cousin, would hang from the surface film like a ceiling light. The story of this pattern's development has been catalogued in many articles and books before this, but not by me. All I was responsible for was the original idea and the name of the pattern that resulted from it: the Suspender.

The flytying challenge was to find a way to make a nymph pattern hang from its head as if suspended there, the weight of the hook and the body dangling down like the natural. The method of doing this came to me from the American flytyer, Charles E. Brooks and his pattern called, the Natant Nymph. To imitate the budding thorax of a hatching upwing river fly, he filled a little sack, made from nylon stocking material, with dubbing and attached it to the back of his nymph. Instead of dubbing, I filled my nylon sack with one of the hundreds of little polystyrene balls that fell out of an impact-proof envelope containing an order from Nether Wallop Mill, Dermot Wilson's defunct and now legendary direct-mail tackle shop in Hampshire. To this day I still say it took Dermot's balls to create this pattern.

The next thing I did was to tie it in at the head, sloping *over* the eye. This way the contents of the nylon stocking suspended the fly in exactly the place I wanted, permanently. Giving it a name was the easy part.

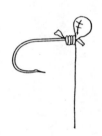

Examining the Suspender that I floated in front of him one evening in a wine glass, the River God took the idea further. He took it away from rivers, to stillwaters, where he rightly saw a wider application for it. He suggested the use of a much better floating material which he used in the manufacture of fly-box divides - Ethafoam. For this I am eternally grateful, for impact-proof bags are made differently now. He also did without the two turns of hackle I wind round the base of the sack. Thoroughly tested and proved on stillwaters though it now is, on small streams, in tiny sizes, that hackle gives me confidence that the outline of the ball is obscured. Call me old-fashioned, but I still recommend my Original Suspender with the hackle ruff, designed to imitate hatching olive nymphs - and now midge pupae - for use on rivers where blue-skulled trout lurk in the shadows.

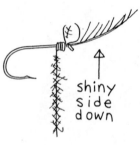

shiny
side
down

To help me locate trout on hot summer days, I cheat a little. As well as my polaroids, I hang a small pair of 8x20 Zeiss binoculars round my neck, measuring four inches long. I put these between my eyes and my polaroids to shield the glare. It works. And it allows me to confirm any vague distant movement, helping me put a shape to a fin, or an approximate size to a fish.

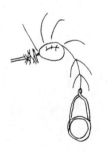

A silver-skinned circle uncoiled and slithered its way across the river. I received the signal as I was still leaning back on the bridge. I knew where the trout was lying, but not where he was positioned, at least not precisely. He could be behind the low overhanging branch, or in front of it. If only to calculate the life-expectancy of the minute Suspender, this mattered.

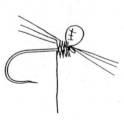

Great care had been taken to secure the tiny Suspender to the two pound test, double-strength tippet. I had threaded the line through the eye, being careful not to trap the highly controversial hackle. Bringing the end of the tippet back on

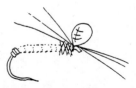

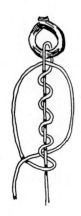

itself, I wound it twice over the line and brought it back through the loop in front of the eye. Until quite recently, I used to stop and pull the knot closed here, but now I go on. I bring the line through the knot loop and securing the hook in one of the rod rings, I wet the knot, hold both ends of the line and pull the knot tight.

This is how the professional guides in Alaska tie flies onto the leaders for their wealthy clients. In the Tundra, there's nothing much to do in the evening. When the guides aren't swapping notes on where they'd spotted big fish that day, they'd be huddled in a tight circle testing knots against all eventualities. Different breaking strains, different brands, different angles of pull, different tensions employed when pulling the knot closed, with and without saliva, etc.

A guide's reputation is wrapped up at the eye of a hook. A trophy rainbow lost with only a curly leader-tip to show for it does the same to a guide's credibility as missing the runway does to an airline pilot. It can wreck a career, overnight. For this reason, guides spend nights checking knots, over and over. In this midnight knot laboratory, reputations are protected, embarrassment saved. The results are authoritative. You ignore their findings at your peril.

At the Beech Bridge, whatever problems lie ahead of you, you don't have any behind you. Just as long as you keep to the centre of the bridge. On the back-cast there's all the room you could ask for. Cake Wood meets the main river here; your back-cast straightens out over open water. This is just as well, for to get a line across to the gladiators limbering up under the bushes opposite means a lengthy cast, a minimum of fifteen yards. A line of that length picks up the gentlest hush of breeze.

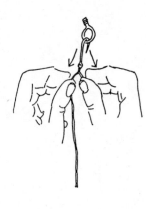

One of the trout tipped the surface again. I heard his stony skull chip the surface of the water and the peck of his beak sucking in a forbidden wisp of air. I hung a long line behind me. Pulling back down with my left hand, I hauled all the aerialized line forward. Lifting my rod tip up smartly just before it alighted on the water, the line dropped with two deep curves set in it to cushion drag.

In the dark I could just make out a tiny white dot. The Ethafoam periscope had surfaced. The course had been set. It was five seconds from its target.

I didn't see the rise. Instead I saw the Suspender down-periscope and dive. This was all the indication I was given telling me that the fish - at least one of the fish - had taken. The periscope reappeared, this time in a cloud of spray, immediately plummeting back down again like a stone. The metallic-skulled submarine was heading for the depths - and the roots.

I had suspected this would be the fish's first, and most dramatic, move. I was ready with my response. As soon as I made connection, I began crab-walking off the bridge and down the bank, letting it feel the weight of my walk. With as tight a line as my eighteen inches of hollow, floating Shockgum allowed, I pulled him decisively into the sunlight and horsed him to my ankles. A wild fish with a bottle-green back splattered with a handful of purple polka-dots, it was one of the last in a long line of a particular strain of fish in the river. A cross between the original river stock and the Loch Levens that were introduced into the water fifteen to twenty years ago.

Catch-and-release in the summer on a south of England chalkstream, is not so much a question of conservation, it's a matter of common-sense. It needs to be practised with great care and a clear understanding that with the best intentions in the world, not every trout you wish to return will survive the rest of the season, or the winter. The slow-moving, nitrate-stained chalkstreams do not contain the same volume of fizzing, oxygen-rich waters as the rain-fed streams of the United States, where the catch-and-release system is the letter of the law. Nevertheless, in Britain, while catch-and-release may not be a legal requirement, it remains sensible practice for all anglers with conservation - both of the trout and the sport as a whole - in mind. Once you understand this, then you will understand the importance of rigorously adhering to the following catch-and-release rules.

First, it is essential that you use barbless hooks, or barbed hooks with the barb snipped off with a pair of pliers and the base of the barb filed off. You cannot return a fish if there is any more than a pin-prick to indicate that he was once hooked.

Second, you must forego the pleasure of fully playing out your fish. In its place, you must develop an even more pleasing experience: that of leaving the water knowing that your fish will live to fight another day, and another season. An exhausted fish stands little chance of surviving under the fierce heat of the rest of the day.

Third, you must never touch a fish with your hands if you intend returning it. Trout are protected by a thin film of mucus that prevents disease from attacking their skin. To the uneducated flyfisher it's a nasty yucky slime. To a trout, it's as essential as a sun-block in the Sahara Desert. If I'm returning a fish, I never touch it at all. In fact, I don't really return it, for it never really leaves. Standing in the water, I bring it to the heel of my boot. Running a pair of blunt-nosed, smooth-sided pliers down the line, I push the hook down and out of the fish's jaw. If I need to touch the trout, to get at a fly that may be in a place I can't reach easily, I slip on a rubber finger-grip, one of those things people in post offices use to hand-count letters. I wet my hand and push down the trout's lower jaw with my thumb so I can get in. This rubber finger-grip has a secondary purpose. It protects me from being shredded by the row of razor-sharp teeth on every trout's lower set.

I never grease the line when I fish my Suspender. Quite the opposite, I do everything I can to ensure it sinks. If I keep a fish, I always run my tippet down the fish's side. Mucus is the best 'sinkant' you can buy. A fly in a fish's window is a normal sight. A crack in the glass is suspicious. For the surface and sub-surface flyfisher, it spells bad luck.

I have a lot to thank luck for with every trout I catch. But at Beech Bridge, fortune played no part in the fact I was there, waiting, when the trout decided to show himself. This was calculated. When I go after big fish on chalkstreams, I arrange a meeting, and hope they keep the appointment. To me, this seems a much more sensible plan than setting out in the hope that I might just accidentally bump into the fish of my dreams. For this

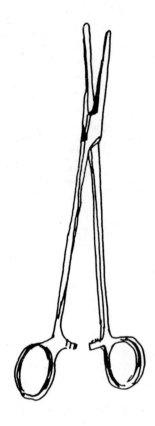

reason, and for all the reasons I've just given, The Shooting-Stick Philosophy has proved to be bad magic for large trout that thought they were safe. In fact, the more above-average trout that I spot using this strategy, the more I come to the conclusion that stream-walking (delightful as it may be if you like rambling in the country) is really nothing more than self-defeating.

The Photographer, one of the rods from way back, remembers Oliver Kite once fishing The Hollow. He has the little bag in which Kite kept his flytying kit. It has 'O.Kite' written on the flap. This bag was originally given to Kite by the River God who, in those days, ran a fishing-tackle factory.

Earlier in the year, we had fished together in the company of Preben Torp Jacobsen, the record-holding 'Naughty Dane', once a great friend of Kite. The Photographer had brought the little bag along to show Preben, who recognised it immediately. Understandably, the Photographer had to give it to him, if only to help him stay afloat as the waves of nostalgia poured in on him. Over lunch, Preben told me that Kite had once told him: 'If you're going for a picnic by the river, leave your rod at home.' What better recommendation of The Shooting Stick Philosophy?

However there will no doubt be some of you interested in the idea who think all this Hawkeye stuff of staring into the water is strictly for the birds for the eagle-eyed. In fact, it's the reverse. One of the rods doesn't wear spectacles, he wears goldfish bowls. He threads his thumbnail half a dozen times before he finally gets the nylon through the eye of his hook. One fine day, I got him to see sense and borrow my shooting stick for a morning.

After an hour he began to wonder why one of of the gravels on the river-bed kept appearing and disappearing. In fact, as he later told me, it was a trout's mouth opening and shutting in the depths. At the Mad House he discovered he'd caught the only trout over three pounds that month.

Perhaps I should tell the Galloping Major about our mutual fishing companion's good fortune.

I would, if I could catch him.

Having spent the last six months with me on The Hollow, you'll have gathered by now that the special association I have with this particular stretch of river rivals some of the most famous and most ardent love stories of all time. Even Lady McFarlane making her way back to the Big House, cast in a deep blue shadow by the dipping sun, sensed my affair was entering a new and more intimate phase as she passed by me one evening. I knew this by the way she looked at her watch and raised an eyebrow at the fresh morning spring in my step when she saw me setting off to the river at eight o'clock in the evening after the usual barbecue in the privacy of the Secret Garden.

But that evening was different from all the other Saturday evenings we'd met crossing the field leading to the Hole - the route I take at this time of year, at this time of the day, to avoid the sight of fishing boots coming off and the sound of car boots slamming the river farewell at the Mad House. For whereas under one arm I'd got my rod as usual, that evening I had a sleeping bag under the other.

The field shook out her yellow hair at me as I passed, but I wasn't interested. Tonight I was sleeping with the river.

At Horse Bridge, I felt I had gate-crashed a reunion party. All the characters in my field guide to river entomology were there. An evening like this astream is tiring work if you've been on the river all day. For this reason, I'd stayed well clear.

I spared a thought for those still down there who hadn't. Finishing off their lunch leftovers for dinner after a hard day in the sun, suddenly it's back to work again. Suddenly it's time to work out which fly the trout are supping. Suddenly it's time to make decisions. Which stage of that fly are they picking on? Which pattern is it best to tune in to? But more importantly, which pattern is tuned in to the trout, as their hungry lips snap at the surface? Which pattern will hit the spot? The clock is running. Seconds, minutes, tick-tock away. Then someone pulls the switch. The sun goes down, the moon comes up and it's time to go. No wonder the best time of the day ends up the most frustrating time of the season.

Oh! I do feel sorry for the man who doesn't live by the

stream. But you'd have thought for one night, for one wild night in a lifetime of fishing days, some would stay on and see what it's like to live by a river, not to have to rush off at this, the best time? Who's to know? Who's to see you? Who's to care? In July, even the dark is not *that* dark, if that's what's putting you off.

But no one ever stays. And here I am, a ten-minute trot away from my bed, the world and the woods to myself, looking for somewhere on the ground to sleep. Somewhere close enough to the river so I can hear the gravels breathing on the river-bed next to me. Somewhere far enough away from my house to make it an adventure. Somewhere out of earshot from my bedroom so that if I should snore, I won't wake my wife.

I decided to sleep with my friends the poplars, in a small clearing next to the last remaining clump before the landscape opens out into water-meadows and the Back of Beyond. I laid out my bag ten yards from the river on a bouncy ground-sheet of dried sedge. From my sleeping bag shelter, I was going to examine an entomological meltdown. And this evening, this was guaranteed. The sky glowed like a warning light. Every fly was poised to explode out of the pages of my book into a sea of picky mouths.

But in particular, I wanted to examine what I believed to be the cause of most of the confusion on nights like this. As you might expect, this is not always your inability to recognise the insects buzzing round your ears. Rather it's an intimate understanding of one river fly in particular. It's this insect I wanted to put under the microscope. And that fly was the blue-winged olive.

Taking a simplistic look at a chalkstream on an evening like the one I was about to sleep in, the blue-winged olive is the most common upwing fly you can expect to see in one guise or another. It's certainly one of the most widespread of the upwing flies, appearing in the early summer through to the late season. But I've spotted them in every month of the year. I've even seen grayling rising to them on Christmas Day.

But rather than what time of the year the blue-winged olive appears, a more interesting thing about the blue-winged olive is the time of day it appears. In the early and late part of the summer, the blue-winged olive is an evening fly, continuing to hatch well after dark.

On the tip of your finger, the blue-winged olive dun is the only olive with three tails. Both the male and female dun have bluey-grey, slate-coloured wings. On the water, you can identify them at a distance. Unlike any other upwing river fly, apart perhaps from the sooty iron-blue dun or the large spurwing (which floats down-river with its gunmetal wings separated forming a 'V'), the blue-winged olive comes down the river as if there's been a fire on board and someone's just put it out. It has a smoky halo. Also the forewing tends to slope back over its arched body. An observation I've yet to see recorded.

While we're on body language, the body is small in comparison to the wing. Once again, another unpublished observation, but then I'm an amateur bug-spotter, not a Fellow of the Royal Entomological Society. From this lowly position I've noted these features. They're recognition points I found well worth remembering just in case I inadvertently yank a member of the tell-tale tail trio off when I swipe a specimen off the water.

The body colour of the female is greengage-olive; the male, rusty orange-brown, with red eyes - from staying up late at nights, I would imagine. The female spinner has been dubbed 'the sherry spinner'. The male's red eyes reinforce the rumour of this alcoholic feature of the female. In actual fact, by the time she has courted, mated and dumped her eggs in the river, the female is more the colour of a freshly boiled lobster. Females carry their eggs around in green Marks & Spencer plastic bags. They curl their tails around them, pressing them hard against up the last two segments of their bodies. They do this with so much pressure, it physically dents the underside of their tail-ends. The eggs - all one thousand of them - are dropped from the air, separating on impact.

The male spinner is smaller. Instead of the female's shopping bag, he sports two fork-pronged claspers. These have a slight bend, suggesting the owner might have spent the night before sitting in the front row of a Uri Geller show. Whereas at this stage the female has a pair of cool greenish eyes, the male's peepers continue to burn, red-hot, late into the night.

I have never concerned myself with the nymph in any great detail for, as night cloaks the woods, I will not be addressing the trout beneath the silver circles with leaded patterns; but perhaps it's worth a few words.

It's a crawler nymph and not a free-swimmer like most of the other olives you're likely to meet on a chalkstream. As the name suggests, the blue-winged olive nymph hugs onto anything with a little grip. This includes the surface when it finally gets there. An interesting observation I have made, since confirmed by angler-entomologists I've shared it with, is that the blue-winged olive nymph seems to keep these clingy tendencies when it reaches the under-surface of the stream. The fact is, the blue-winged olive takes longer to hatch than other insects I've espied on the river, or in my aquarium.

Now whether this characteristic is a unique life-style feature of the *ephemerella*, or a consequence of the fact that when the blue-winged olive nymph hoists itself to the surface to head-bang it's way out, it discovers that it's up against the same resistance as if he'd nose-dived into a pot of strawberry jam, I don't know for sure. And I don't really need to. All I'm interested in is what trout are doing when their skulls are scraping the under-surface of the river and not snapping through it at something sitting in - or on - it. What are they feeding on? What *could* they be feeding on? What should I be putting on?

At this time of year, the surface angler will know that the surface film is at its most gluey. I've often seen trout feeding just underneath the surface skim, taking what I thought were tiny midge pupae, as discovered on Beech Bridge. Instead I took them on a larger version of my Suspender-tying system.

The tail of my original hatching blue-winged olive pattern consists of three bronze mallard breast feather tips, a dirty olive wool body, and a soft, dark brown mink fluff fur thorax. At the head, the suspending mechanism I mentioned earlier. As a collar, I tie in one turn of a small, dark-centred Greenwell hackle. This I wrap round the base of the ball.

Whereas nothing much has been written about the blue-winged olive nymph, from an angling rather than a scientific point of view, the blue-winged olive dun has inspired some of the most imaginative fairy tales ever to flutter off chalkstreams.

I walked up from Snowdrop Land and lay across a footbridge. I had managed to get right behind a trout feeding close into the sedge where the current narrowed and carried on running under my position. I was catching the blue-winged olive duns that this trout didn't have broad enough lips to collect himself. Apart from confirming the fact that trout take flies from the surface, I didn't learn much more than this. As it took the fly and sank beneath the surface, a lot of the received wisdom of flyfishing sank with it.

We're told to watch out for 'kidney-shaped' whorls, the sure sign of trout feeding on blue-winged olives in one form or other. We're warned that trout actually pick on one particular sex to feed on, flaunting the Sex Discrimination Act of 1975. The colour of the blue-winged olives is also a cause of great concern. Pooh-pooh, all of it. Even the last point.

A trout's vision is not dissimilar to ours. At least when it comes to registering colours and shades. It follows that as the light fades in the evening, the trout's eyes, like ours, slowly alter. They see objects in terms of black and white; colour is less discernible. Especially when the fly is right overhead in the window.

During my trips across the Channel to France, I quickly learned that some of the best-known flies developed over there weren't tied by amateur flytyers, they were designed by professional flyfishermen, in the truest sense. What these flyfishermen taught me was that when you're up against a problem on the surface, sink to the lowest depths. The lowest depths of the surface. Don't perch your fly up top, lower its profile. Get it to sit *in* it.

My blue-winged olive pattern is a radical departure from standard practice. Instead of being a blue-winged olive dun as dry as Tombstone Arizona, it sits *in* the surface. For a tail, I use a body material. It floats in the same way as a swimmer floats. It doesn't surf, which is what most dry fly men would like their flies to do.

For the tail I use a tuft of yellow polypropylene yarn. It's got neutral density and is less dense than water. The body is a lime green poly dub. For a support hackle, I tie four turns of a small blue dun. The main hackle is two turns of large (greater wing covert) feather from the outside of a moorhen wing.

I walked up-river. The sun had dropped behind the Downs. The bank was lined with the dark shapes of reeds bent over the side of the river like mourners. Moments from dark, I should have been on my way back up in the direction of Horse Bridge and across the field and home - on automatic pilot, my eyes fixed on the light from my bedroom window like a homeless moth. But instead, I was tuned into a cloud of blue-winged olive spinners. I had followed them up at a trot, against a distant orange glow, joining them mid-journey on their private, single-minded mission. On our journey together, I was reminded why they are one of the most common upwing flies across the country. The nymph may not be very quick off the mark, but the spinner makes up for its nymph's tardiness. To ensure the survival of their species, the spinners of these smoky survivors are full of sharp moves and false clues.

Consider those familiar evenings when they're in the air and trout are rising for all to see, but against all logic, your sherry-spinner imitation is about as popular as Count Dracula in a blood bank. It was only by wading in the river on those evenings that I discovered that the spectacle of spinners dancing in the bushes, or even egg-layers parading upstream as they had been doing that night, does not always mean that spinners will be on the water later on, and that the trout will be feeding on them. Since then I have noticed two things.

Male blue-winged olive spinners will often gather night after night for a week or more before being joined by females, when mating and egg-laying finally takes place. When females fail to arrive, these males do not throw themselves in the river in despair, like heart-broken Romeos; they return to the woods to come back again and again until their patience is rewarded.

But what about females moving up-river carrying with them their little green shopping bags curled under their tails? Surely they have to be on the water later on in the evening? The answer is: yes. But the twist is that neither you, nor the trout on your patch, may ever see them. I have followed a cloud of these egg-layers for a distance of half a mile and more where either I have lost sight of them, or could follow them no further. I assume that they do this to counteract the slow movement of eggs and nymphs downstream from where the eggs were originally dropped. If the female did not deposit her eggs further upstream from where she herself shook off her nymphal shuck, in the upper reaches of the beat, they would slowly get washed from our river. Indeed, in time, they'd get washed from the entire river altogether.

This provided me with a reason why my Sherry Spinner pattern should be snubbed so often when, having studied the bank-side evidence, I had concluded that the trout rising were feeding on spinners I had seen flying past my nose earlier on in the evening. Simply, these spinners were not there.

But on my camp-out night they were. At least, that was what

I thought, for I could hear trout under Horse Bridge. I was well upstream now, mid-way between beds. It was dark and fishing still had not begun.

I have often thought that the best blue-winged olive fishing - not the easiest, but the best - was after dark. One black evening I had been feeling my way back home after a late session on Cemetery. It was dead of night when I got to the stews beside the Boss's cottage and all I could hear was the splish-splash of hungry fish. I thought the Boss had been midnight-feasting his fingerlings just before I had arrived. In fact, they were after blue-winged olive spinners, syphoned off Cemetery, down Nursery Stream and into the stews. The Withy Bed at the bottom of Cemetery is a favourite egg-laying site.

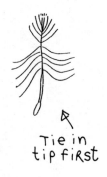

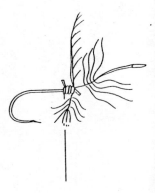

Above Horse Bridge, another prime egg-laying site, the sky and the fields are wide open to the moon. My leader cut silver grooves in the moonlight to mark the spot where my Funnelspinner drifted down. Named after the reddy-orange body material, I always fish a Rusty Funnelspinner on these occasions. Having made all the calculations and deductions, I don't like to throw all my efforts away on account of some technicality, like a trout turning his nose up at my fly thanks to the sight of a hook dangling in the water. The blue-winged olive is a big fly. The bigger the fly, the bigger the hook - and therefore the bigger the reason to keep it out of sight. This I do by using my Funneldun tying style. This allows me to tie a #14 fly on a #16 hook - and then, just to make sure, turn the fly upside down so the fly is in the bat's, rather than the fish's, view.

But my Funnelspinner was snubbed, time and time again. Even though I covered each rise repeatedly (I believe in making my flies work). And I think I know why. On July evenings - or nights, for that matter - things aren't as straightforward as you'd like them to be, no matter how much thought you put into it. There's a certainty of chance, and it helps to know the options. And tonight, options there certainly were, for the blue-winged olive isn't the only fly to appear out of the blue, and out of the dark.

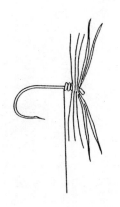

As the name suggests, to spend time with the pale evening

Tie in tip first

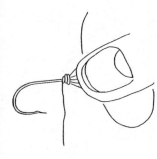

dun, you needn't get up too early in the morning to encounter this straw-coloured fly. Pale in complexion, presumably the result of all those late nights, its prime time is July and August, although the official emergence time is May through to October. It is widely distributed, making its bed in the more sleepy stretches of river, both acid and alkaline. For this reason, it is strange that on slower chalkstreams it appears to be very localized. But where it is in evidence it boasts quite a reputation with those who don't have to dash home at night.

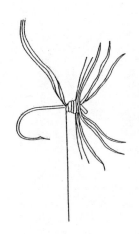

The nymphs of the pale evening dun are agile darters and have one distinct feature worth mentioning in case you want to search around during the day-time doldrums to see if the stream you are fishing has a good head of pale evening duns, making it worth your while to stay on late in the evening. As it is predominantly a river dweller, and there is no need for an auxiliary set of oxygen fans, their gills are single.

The male dun has yellow eyes, pale yellow legs and pale grey wings, with a hint of green at the roots. The body of both sexes is a pale straw with a honey-coloured thorax. The male spinner has lemon-yellow eyes. The female has an ochre thorax, dissolving down to an amber tail-end. She is a very pretty fly. But if in doubt about the dun's identity, check the wings. The pale evening dun has only one set, making it one of the simplest flies to identify confidently on a summer's evening when many different species of similar size and colour are out on the town.

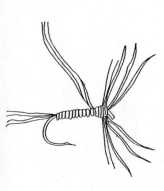

Getting the time of year, the day and the exact location correct are not enough if you want to spot this fly. For a start, instead of polaroids you would be better off wearing ultra-violet spectacles, for the pale evening dun leaves it to the very last moment before poking its head out from under the sheets. Often it waits until all the colour in the sky has bled out before making an appearance (although you may see spinners that have emerged from duns the night before).

More often than not, the mating and egg-laying happens after dark, when most anglers have gone home. This may well explain why, historically, this fly has not been rated as highly as it might. But those eye-witnesses who have not been in a hurry to

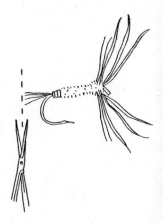

leave the water insist that it commands greater interest than blue-winged olives hatching out at the same time.

I tied a small cream-coloured pattern on my line, sucking the last remaining drops of moonlight out of sky from between the clouds to see. Another steel-rimmed ring reverberated out from just behind the bridge, and once again I ran my eye along the silver wire of my line, indented on the surface. At the fly, it coiled out into large loops - and I struck.

I missed it. Too early, or too soon, I will never know, but it was my last chance of the night and I made my way back to my four-poster poplar position - a tree at each corner of the shallow heap of dried sedge and leaves I'd collected to make a mattress. The temperature suddenly dropped. I could feel it change on my arms. The river bank became a sea of puffy mist. The river began to smoke.

I had camped in a place not too far from the main ride that starts in Snowdrop Land and twists through a cobweb of woodland tracks, eventually ending up at the Boss's Cottage. Often, the Boss cuts back through the woods after a late session at the Manor, rather than take the main road. But the Boss has a problem. He finds it difficult to tell right from left, an essential talent when it comes to picking one's way through the woods if you don't want to end up spending the night in the open with me. To help the Boss with his disability, his brother had worked out an original system. He'd stuck a rubber frog, one of his kid's toys thrown in the back of the Land Rover, on the right hand side of the dash board. On the left, he stuck a threadbare teddy.

Couched in my four-poster sleeping-bag, I gazed up at the stars trying to remember what they all were, my ears were filled with owls and choruses from the same midnight chicken that keeps me awake at night back home. I expected the Boss to come crashing by down the track at any moment, his brother guiding him through the twisting rides with shouts of 'Teddy. Now a frog. Take the next teddy. This frog. Hang a teddy.'

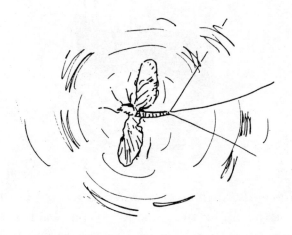

August

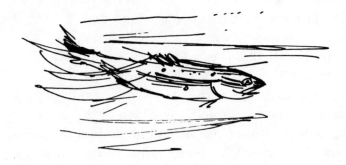

THE MONTH OF THE MOP

When I look back over the seasons, my memories keep telling me the same thing. August can be a bitch for the surface flyfisher. If a trout remaining in the river at this late date hasn't had a sniff at every conceivable fly in the combined boxes of the entire syndicate, then it's either a trout in an impregnable spot that can't be reached, a trout that has yet to be seen; or he's just downright anorexic.

One thing is certain: well-seasoned August trout all seem to behave in the same way. Cast a fly at a contender on the fin and you can often get him to the surface to scrutinise a hook gift-wrapped in fur and feather all bound up in silk. You can even get him to turn and follow it down for some considerable way - after all, it's rude to snatch a present when it's being handed to you. You might even be able to extract the merest hint of a genuine feeling of delight - heavily veiled certainly, but then your fly is yet to be positively accepted. Contact might even be made - you'd swear the trout's nose rubbed along the length of your offering.

But it's usually at this point in the ritual, after a token acceptance, that your trout swings back in the direction of its lie with a 'Thank you' on its lips rather than your fly in its jaw, having ever-so-politely rejected your gift and let it pass by. And not for one moment being the least bit aware that there was the slightest shadow of any deceit afoot. There was just something wrong. Something wasn't quite right. All this leaving you with the distinct impression that if happiness is to prevail, your fly needs to be taken back and changed.

It's occasions like this, when your surface offering appears totally acceptable but isn't totally accepted, that I call 'Marks & Spencer moments'. For if they were able, trout - like so many people after Christmas - would join them in the queue with your fly, along with their jumpers, jackets, skirts and shirts, hoping to change them because they weren't quite right.

Examining these encounters with trout, my reckoning is that more often than not, my gift-wrapped hook isn't returned because the trout didn't like the colour, or for that matter, the shape or style. It was the size that had been wrong. It didn't fit a cautious, late summer trout's expectations. And this, quite simply, is the August problem: How do we get trout to abandon caution?

It's 4.30am. A new month arrived with an old adage. If doctors bury their mistakes, lawyers file them and architects build them, what do dry fly fishermen do with their boo-boos? In the first light of dawn I searched my soul for the answer.

The bedroom window was ajar. I was beginning to hear the effect of a new gamekeeper. He'd taken over a corner of the field opposite my garden in front of the Rookery Nook and ploughed and planted two strips, one with kale, the other with maize. He wasn't having any of his precious birds leave home. As a result, I had a platoon of French partridges staying with me with throats like faulty exhausts, none of them with any plans for going anywhere. For the second morning running they had woken me up early. I was wide awake, thinking; wondering.

The hatches of lazy, lemon-eyed pale wateries had been heavy all week. The cooler temperatures from the north-west had encouraged them to hatch every afternoon at the same time. But winds in the evening had kept them sleeping in the bushes.

The curtains were motionless. For the first time for a long time there wasn't a breath of wind. The spinners would be out stretching their wings on the soft, morning air. Should I go down to Sticklepath Bridge? Or should I stay in bed; thinking, wondering? Would this be a mistake? And if so, what would I do about it?

It may be unforgivable for a flyfisherman living right next to a river not to grab every available opportunity to be out there fishing. But what about the less fortunate? Flyfishermen in general? What do they do with their mistakes?

I turned over into my pillow. The truth is, for over a century, dry fly fishermen have been tying their mistakes onto the end of their lines and casting them at trout.

I lifted up in bed and looked out of the window. A pheasant the size of my pillow sat puffed up on the wall in the dewy half-light. It stuck its neck out at the thin sun, played the bongos with its wings and croaked out some mist. Leaning back too far, it fell backwards onto the lawn.

Pheasants make mistakes, too, I thought. And what do they do with them? They just carry on making them as if nothing had happened. Just like dry fly fishermen. But things had happened. Dry flies had changed, hadn't they?

I thought back. Yes, but not much. Dry flies were still too big. And if I was to get up and go down to the river, the fly on the end of my line would need to be smaller. And go down to the river, I decided, was what I should do. It would be a mistake not to get up - even though the pale watery spinners decided to hold out for another day. On a soft, understanding morning like today, not getting up would be a mistake.

I never once subscribed to the traditional ten o'clock kick-off time on chalkstreams. I used to think it was something to do with gentlemanly behaviour. Like giving an old lady your seat on the bus, or taking your coat off and throwing it over puddles for women in the street, you let the trout have a lie in before you launch yourself from the Mad House to spend the day shuffling around the bank in harrowing, harassing, red-hot pursuit. Not so: this was another mistaken concept. In fact, it is part of a conspiracy to ensure chalkstream flyfishers don't come face-to-face with their fear of small flies - their phobia of the fingersome. For the best dry fly fishing in August relies on being able to handle artificials on a titchy scale.

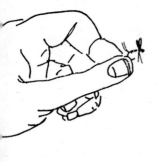

It also depends on something else a lot more ungentlemanly, and a great deal more formidable. This is having to be out on the river bank, rod in hand, mini-fly knotted on the point, raring to go, almost five hours before the first flyfisherman arrives, only to spend the day wondering why all the best trout you spot during the day are lying down on the bottom of the stream looking like they'd throw up if they were to see a fly on the surface. For early morning, as I discovered by accident, is the major surface-feeding time. In fact, very often the only main feeding time until the evening.

And now, the sun barely risen, was that time. The smallest upwing fly on the river was about to rise, and fall, as quietly as snow.

Caenis is chalkstream Semtex. Buried away, it is ready to explode at any moment. The short, stubby *caenis* nymph is a shallow burrower, inching its sinister way around the corner of the river above Sticklepath Bridge where the Nursery Stream slopes into the main river. It's these muddy, oxygenated corners where *caenis* appear to thrive in the vastest concentrations. Corners with just enough silt to cover and conceal its creepy-crawlings.

At no time in the flyfisher's calendar are they more deadly in the hands of a trout assassin than when the sun begins to rise in August, to sit high and hot all day making hatches of anything else unlikely.

The most distinctive feature of both the female and male *caenis* dun and spinner are their short, broad wings (until recently they were known as 'broadwings') and the dull cream stumpy body. The only real distinguishing feature between both the female and the male dun and spinner is that the tail of the spinner is marginally longer.

There are two groups of *caenis*. One hatches in the early morning, and one in the evening. The best hatch of the two is in the morning, for this fly is larger in size. This makes it well worth getting up for. And its my opinion that the *caenis*'s appearance at this god-forsaken time, rather than for any other reason, is what has earned it the name 'The Angler's Curse'.

However, if you are not cursed with having to travel to the river to fish the hatch carefully and thoughtfully, the *caenis* is the Angler's Blessing. For it allows you to enjoy some of the prettiest and exacting dry fly fishing, in the company of the river-side's most private and intimate rustlings and whisperings. And all the while the world you've managed to extract yourself from is wrapped in dreams (or nightmares), in bed, asleep. Now that Man in the south of England no longer needs to go out and hunt to live, surely these dawn pleasures are reason enough to go fishing?

But beware. As I mentioned previously, *caenis* don't hatch out - they blow up in your face. Suddenly, they're there, on your boots, in your hair, up your nose - in their thousands. Not surprisingly, they have the same immediate impact on the trout in that region.

In an equally instant fashion, dun turns into spinner. In minutes, not hours. This happens as soon as the dun comes in contact with an obstacle in the water that it is able to clamber onto. A post, a reed, the wading parts of your anatomy. Transformed, the male and female mate without ceremony, all over your leg.

With this informality completed, the females lie spread-eagled on the surface. Fanned out in this position, they extrude their eggs in a straight stream, to the uncontrollable delight of

every trout who proceeds to hoover up these little flies one after another as if they were soup.

To maximize the opportunity of these sugar granules sprinkled on the river, the early-morning riser needs to hatch a plot, and there's a secret to the approach. Like all the best laid plans, preparation needs to start well in advance; pre-planning is required. For the man who lives on the river, this is executed on the night before the expedition, because the decision to proceed is usually made at the last moment. For this reason, the procedure is simple. It has to be.

On my way from the bathroom to bed, I lay my hip waders on the floor of the Decontamination Room, making sure my quilted 'mattress jacket' is not buried under all the coats on the peg. I fill the pockets of this strategically-placed garment with only the most essential items of tackle. A fly box, floatant, my thumb grip and blunt-nose pliers. I hang my polaroids (for eye protection only, for I will be fishing exclusively to rising fish) and my scissors, dangling on a leather bootlace, onto one of the oar racks that normally supports my rod when I come back from the river. If it's an early start, I push the two pieces of my rod together and put it to bed on the racks outside the back door, new tippet and fly attached, all ready.

Upstairs in the bedroom, I make a 'clothes path' on the floor, marking out the route from the window to my bed with trousers, a shirt, a jersey and socks. This way when it's time to make the return journey in the morning, unconsciously (in the dark), I simply climb out of bed into my socks and dress my way to the window, arriving there mole-eyed and fully clothed. I leave one side of the curtains open. Not that I expect to see light streaking through when the alarm shakes me out of bed at four o'clock. But there's normally enough soaking through the shallow darkness to let me see if the river is asleep under a blanket of mist. Or if it's raining. Most pre-dawn mornings I crawl to the window praying for either, or both, these sights. It's the excuse the blanket-warm flyfisher waits for. Either of these two conditions grants permission to abort his plan, throw off his clothes, climb back into bed, and forget the whole thing ever

happened. Mist and rain murder an early morning hatch of
caenis.

But not this morning. (Or was it still night?)

———————

'I can smell the honeysuckle,' my wife said as I creaked open the
bedroom door in the dusty shafts of sleep-filled light. The
partridges had woken her, too. 'And I can smell the roses.' All
sorts of thick perfumes were wafting up through the window from
the Secret Garden below.

'I can smell the river,' I said as she turned into a second or
third dream.

Downstairs in the Decontamination Room, I threw open the
top hatch of the back door. In the half-light, the pheasant hopped
off the wall and crackled through the dry cow-parsley on the
other side of the flint wall and away. In the Spring, the noise of
the river fills the house. In August, the shallows in the Fly Lane
are insulated. After they've flowered in May, the Boss wades in
below the Sticklepath Bridge with a scythe and cuts the long,
waving, fringe-leaved tresses of ranunculus forming bars across
the river like lengths of dark green loft-insulation unrolled
between roof rafters. The river is silenced.

In fact, there is no sound from anywhere at this time of the
morning. The cows in the field between me and the Mad House
sway like drunk men knee-deep in a thin mist. I set off with
muffled steps noticing that my sun-dried waders are starting to
crack after afternoons of heavy beatings. The tops slap against
my thighs in time with my step. I slow down. Unless you want to
wake the world, this is not a time to cough.

There was still darkness in the west when I arrived on
Sticklepath Bridge. The woods still had their black velvet
curtains pulled. Without this back-drop, it's hard to tell if *caenis*
are there or not without close inspection. Sometimes you see
nothing against the sky through the gap in the trees. But take
one step to the right and you choke for fear of breathing in a
thousand micro maniacs. A summer snowstorm in the woods,

their numbers sugar-frost the black, transforming it to white. I am happy *caenis* don't have engines. The sound would deafen you.

That morning, I didn't need to see them. I knew they were there the moment I put one foot on the bridge. Silver whirlpools on the shallows were sucking the first warm glow of light out of the morning sky. The trout were up before me.

I climbed down the bank and stood by the bricking at the side of Sticklepath Bridge, poking my head round to look under. A fish carried on rising four feet from me. He had a rhythm going that would have got Duke Ellington's feet tapping. Under the bridge more fish were rising to the same rhythm. Two members in the same combo were so close, if I had reached out I could have pulled them out from under the blanket of fly by their ears. Every now and then, a new fish got out of bed and started nodding its head in time to the beat of the hatch. Two or three china moths had also got up early. These moths are aquatic and spend most of their pupal lives underwater. If you ever bump into caterpillars scuba-diving, you now know what they are.

A black rope of rooks flapped in a steady line due south to a corn field they could see directly across the valley from the wood where they roost, in the lee of the opposite hillside. They only move from one hill to another towards things they can see. The same shambolic procession will return in the evening by the same route, back to their cawing tree-top cribs, passing directly over the Wild Wood Lodge, at eight o'clock. At this time of year, you can set your watch by them.

The bleary-eyed flyfisher needs to be on the water early. Not to fish, but to make the correct deductions. To single out fish worth concentrating on. This is your bonus for getting up early, you have every fish in your region at your disposal. The flyfisher can be choosy, and so can the early rising trout. They take the best positions, where flow and fly are thickest and the smallest amount of energy needs to be expended to mop them up. The later risers tend to be more cautious. They are often the largest - and hardest to catch. As a result of their tardiness, they find themselves in places where the fly tap is not twisted on to full, where the hatch is passing over them more slowly, more steadily, in a trundling trickle. These cautious, less energetic fish are the ones that the assassin should set out to assassinate.

The area under the far bank was as dark as a crypt. I still had half an hour left before the thinly-diluted orange colour dissolving in the watery sky finally concentrated, and the sun popped up in the east to expose me.

At first, I didn't see the fish I had marked out. Like so many trout I find at this time of year when you've had a summer to get to know the difference between a duck snapping at nothing and a trout sipping at something, I found it using 'ear sight'. I heard its presence. Early morning heightens all your senses. It is not a time to be 'blind' in one ear.

Focussing in on the sip, I saw that the fish was rising so tightly against the bank, that it looked as if it was out swimming with the cows on the farther side. I began to think it would be easier for me to go back, cross over the bridge and go and pick him up. Instead, I stepped carefully over a shoal of grayling, a cool lick of water seeping through one of the cracks in my waders and slicing my thigh as I made my way across the shallows to an island of watercress. Here, I decided, was as good a place as any to use as base camp for my attack.

I checked that my leader had no grease on it from the day before. I like to make sure my leader sinks, totally, and doesn't crack the trout's window. Like the nose on my face, my 18" Shockgum leader butt is always there; no need to check that. No need to dip my fly in floatant. My yarn-winged *caenis* pattern has all the floating properties a fly of this size requires, built in.

When it comes to *caenis* patterns, I only ever match the spinner. This is because the largest part of the *caenis* hatch is spent planning your moves. By the time a fish has been selected, the rhythm of its rise calculated, the first few duns will have eclosed, transformed and mated. What a busy morning! Anyway, the difference between the dun and the spinner, or between the male and the female - even between the six species of *caenis* (and one *Brachycercus*, another 'curse' to add to the list) is minimal, and they are all indistinguishable from one another - by angler and, I speculate, by trout.

The strategy for fishing the *caenis* is text book. A trout nodding its head and clicking its fins to the beat of a hatch should be approached carefully, but closely. Keep your waders muffled. Make no false moves, but when you make a move 'heron-hop' in the water, lifting your feet up and out off the river one by one, sliding them back in toe-first.

A trout lying in centimetres of water, his head resting in the under-felt of the surface, has the curtains of its dining-room window half closed. Its vision out of this small crack is minimal. This allowed my trout, lying in a bay the depth of a cereal bowl, to see his breakfast glide over, only at the very last moment. Given this considerable blind spot, I decided to glide over alongside the fish and fit myself in as snugly as I could, as closely as I was able. I began to move from the watercress in the direction of my preoccupied prey. If ever there was a reason for designing silencers for waders, then this was it.

Positioning myself as the trout's Siamese twin had immediate advantages. Deep down in those dark shadows of the crypt, I would be able to see exactly what was going on. In fact, when I got there, I discovered that there was nothing deep about it. Bellied out on the gravels, this trout had all but run aground. And because of this, he was making not one, not two, but three simultaneous rises forms. One with his nose pecking at the surface, the second with his dorsal fin waving in the air and the third with the tip of his tail wagging as he tipped back down. In this semi-beached position, it was physically impossible for him to lower his tail to tip his nose to the surface; the water was too shallow. To take a fly from the surface, he had to elevate his entire body, horizontally. It was like watching a hovercraft lift off. If I'd cast to the rise I'd been watching from my position at base camp I would still be there now, casting - to a fin! Always get as close as is sensibly possible to your fish.

Silently installed in position, I wasn't going to stray from text-book tips, or truths I'd arrived at myself. Like always avoid knotless leaders, for they lack an essential stiffness so necessary to deliver a smooth turnover. My simple tapered leader formula,

12" lengths of descending breaking-strains of line following on after an 18" length of Shockgum, finishing with an 18" tippet, has always delivered my fly on target at the end of a leader as rigid and as straight as a poker - even though sometimes the knots may be larger than the fly on the point.

Casts needed to be flicks. Lots of them. Short flicks. Drifts, the same. As I stood there watching the trout lift and drop, lift and drop, doing everything I possibly could to prevent my foot starting to stomp to the rhythm, I noticed something else. Close inspection revealed why I hadn't interested all the trout I'd tried for on other mornings.

Currents react in different ways. They have no permanence; they don't shoot straight. They snake and wind. They shimmy and shally. They Tango, Samba and Hot Potato around the floor like a jumping bean disco. And on the surface the same thing happens. There were two streams of *caenis* spinners (and duns) coming down at my ship-wrecked trout two rod lengths away. I was now so close I could hear his belly squeaking on the gravels like fingers on a balloon, and he was on stream for only one of these current strings. Get my fly onto the wrong stream, the one nearest to me, and I might as well fish to another fish. It was only a matter of inches. A foot, perhaps.

Swinging my hand on a lose wrist like a saxophone player waiting for a break, and mentally clicking in the beat, I flicked my Twenties Loop *caenis* pattern centre stage leading it in easily. Placed directly on stream for the trout, I counted my fly into its solo. All the time, I kept watching. All the time, I kept that rhythm clicking. And all the time I pointed the rod to one side to direct the belly of the line in a downstream direction. All the time I kept the tip held low to maximize the pull of the current on my hook. And all the time the forefinger of my right hand clamped the line down on the cork. By doing all this, all of the time, I was conducting the perfect 'non-strike' - the strike the current does for you.

Snap-Crackle-Pop. The fish had wolfed down my pattern for breakfast - one-two-three beats ago. By pausing for these beats before lifting the rod tip, to let the current, and not my wrist and elbow, set the hook, the river directed the hook to the cutting edge of the trout's mouth - the scissors. Only then, when the pull of the stream heavies your line, is the trout fully alerted. It's then, when the surface erupts, that you can bring the redundant rod into play.

'Not guilty,' the Trout Assassin says, accused of deceiving the trout. 'It was my accomplice who pulled the trigger and set the lethal hook.'

When you fish small flies, the river is your accomplice. Let it do the dirty business. Never forget this. This way, you get off free, every time, unlike the securely-hooked trout.

Back in the river, the moment the current set the hook, my landlubber trout headed directly up river, never once turning into the main current. He only deviated from this single-minded, straight line route once. But not centre river, stage right. Throwing himself clean out of the water, he spun up the stem of an overhanging branch, deep into the arms of a bush. With a wiggle and a waggle, the fish was scale to bark with the trunk, and his pace starting to slow down. With one elegant flick of a tail, the trout left the dance floor, dropping back down through the foliage, leaving my line coiled up, wound round, knotted up, twisted round, wrapped up a branch inches from the river. It takes two to tangle.

I thought I still had the trout on because I didn't see a bow-wave indicating a sharp exit. I waded up and across to find my hook in the wood and the trout a memory.

By now, the sun was peeping over the Downs and I was tired. The gamekeeper had slashed open the gauzy screen that separated me from the waking world. All it took was a blast from the horn of his Japanese 4x4 telling his pheasants in the pens he was on his way and that they should group for feeding. I retraced my footsteps in the dew. The sun had torched Sticklepath Bridge. It glowed orange like a poker. The last half-dozen spinners smouldered in the shadows; wisps of smoke. But there were no trout to extinguish them.

A distant sigh from a lone car passing on the main road brought in a new day, folding me in light. A day that seemed over, before it had begun. A day when I had shared one of the river's best-kept secrets and felt the power of nature's silence.

———————

Tying flies for August trout reminds me of the story I once read in a newspaper about bombing raids that were carried out by the Royal Air Force over Germany during the last war.

To minimize the number of bombers that got shot down, someone came up with the idea of flying gliders over Germany, as decoys. For weeks on end, the Germans merrily shot away at these shams thinking they were the real thing. Then one day they started finding large splinters of balsa wood lying in the fields and put two and two together. Immediately they began to employ radar that could tell the difference between wood and metal.

Realizing their cover was blown, the Brits weren't slow to react. Wasting no time at all, they added metal ribs to the glider's structure. Once again, this proved highly successful until the Germans began noticing that a lot of the planes showing up on the radar didn't have engines. They started using heat-seeking equipment to work out which planes had engines and which ones didn't, and therefore which ones weren't worth the price of a shell to shoot down.

Not to be beaten, the Brits fitted small heat-emitting devices to the gliders. That was until the Germans discovered that some planes didn't make any noise when they flew over, and so the Brits added a heat-emitting devise that made the noise of an aircraft engine. Needless to say, it wasn't long before the Germans worked out a way of telling real noise from fake noise. And so it went on.

In the end, the only way you could fool the Germans into thinking there was a bomber overhead, and not a decoy, was by sending up what was to all intents and purposes a real plane.

The moral of this story? Am I suggesting we pick *caenis* naturals off our waders and thread them onto bare hooks? Not quite. It's simply that, German or trout, after a time the only real sham is the real thing. There's no such thing as a perfect imitation. So, my good flytying friend, why bother trying? Why make life difficult for yourself?

And this is the secret to tying itsy-bitsy flies. Making tying simple. Not trying too hard. And when the jaws of an August trout close in acceptance of your simple new pattern, your own jaw shouldn't drop open with amazement.

The way I see it, the best way to outwit a picky trout is to play him at his own game. In other words, avoid giving him things he can be picky about. Remove as much 'fly' as possible that stands between you and the trout.

It's not hard to get your head round this logic. It's just not quite as easy to get your fingers round the solution. So what is the approach to tying flies tied on hook #20 and smaller? Let's start at the beginning.

I call so-called 'mini' or 'micro' flies 'Twenties'. It doesn't sound so fiddly. The term 'micro' is an exaggeration, put to us by flytyers who want to hype their prowess at the vice. In a quest to offer so little fly, they have a great deal to answer for, as I will explain.

The mistake amateur flytyers make is to buy this hype and believe that tying flies on small sizes, and fishing them, is a problem. Something only an expert can get to grips with.

I could forgive frustration if you were a flytyer fifty years ago when the smallest hook available was a #18. But now hooks descending into the ranks of the invisible (don't go away - I'm not suggesting you need go this small) have been with us for years. But still 'Fear of Flytying' images - of magnifying glasses, Barbie Doll fingers, ophthalmic surgical techniques - still prevail, haunting flytying benches everywhere; by day and by night. To such an extent that any fly pattern demanding to be tied on anything smaller than a #18 is still too much for the average flytying flyfisher to swallow. Even though it is often the only thing that a late season trout will be happy to digest.

Now this shouldn't be the case. The truth of the matter is that no-one's made tying Twenties easy. And this, I believe, is why Twenties dry fly fishing on English chalkstreams is still in its formative years.

To overcome this, as far as patterns for surface insects for cautious trout are concerned, my late season dry flies - Caenis, Spurwing, Pale watery, Smut, Mosquito, you name it - are completely different from the patterns I use to imitate naturals earlier in the year. Not just in size, but in style of dressing. This is because I don't just scale down. It's back to the drawing board. It's a re-design job, involving more (or as you will discover later, less) than just turning your hook upside down. It's much more fundamental. It's about giving the appearance of no hook at all. This is the thinking behind my series of Twenties patterns. The less 'fly' the better.

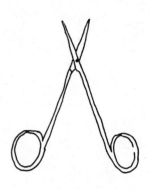

Advanced flytying techniques aren't about knowing the obscure, they're about understanding the simple. Tying one of my Twenties series is about the obvious: minimizing imitation to only the most obvious features from a trout's point of view, and selecting the minimum number of these features. And then using the minimum number of materials, in the minimum quantity, involving the minimum number of tying procedures.

I remember someone once telling me at the local Fly Dressers' Guild that you can always tell a beginner at flytying. You can't see him for materials - and the trout can't see the fly for feather and fur. You can laugh, but this is the most common mistake made when old-timers at the bench start trading down to Twenties. They think it's just a matter of notching down the procedures they've been programmed to use over the years, employing the same old 'front to back to front again' tying style. Here's what I mean:

Tying an artificial Caenis pattern taken at random, using conventional procedures - ones we have been using for over a century - involves the following list of materials: tying thread, whisks for tails, a body material, a rib, wings and a hackle. Six materials, at least. To strap this all down to the hook involves, I calculate, ten procedures.

Thinking small, and putting on a 'Time & Motion' hat, I came up with a pattern that demands just three materials (including tying silk) and an unconventional tying style that involves four tying procedures: including winding the tying silk on, and tying it off again.

Feel that confidence oozing back?

I did this by reviewing every step of tying a conventional fly and asking two questions: Do I need to do this? Can this procedure do two or more things rather than just the one?

Hackles are the prime cause of artificials ending up over-dressed and bulky. All a hackle does is support the hook on the surface and imitate legs, and perhaps upright wings. Unless you're specifically imitating the hatched-out dun that uses its legs to keep its bulk high and dry, there's really no other reason for hackles to be there. Anyway, I concluded, if your hook is small and light, it shouldn't need more than picked-out fur to keep it buoyant. And picked-out fur, to my eyes, imitates legs more convincingly and realistically than two or three turns of hackle.

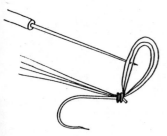

For spinners that spread out their wings to collapse on, and land-born drop-outs that crash-land on the sticky surface film before they have time to lower their landing gear, hackles can also be abandoned altogether. Dun, spinner, drop-out; a fussy trout is much more likely to accept an artificial of any or all of these sitting in, or half-ways in, its element. Rather than one perched outside it, a principle I have advocated on more than one occasion in this book.

This left me with three important recognition points - or 'outline' guides - that need to be incorporated into the tying stages: wings, body and tail. Wings? Here, we've decided, can be our main support. Body? Certainly. But do we need to dub, then rib it? Tail? Yes, but only if the natural has one.

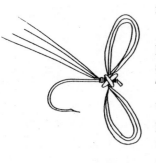

Regarding tying style, I began by dispensing with any procedure that seemed fingersome. Not many flydressers subscribe to this principle in print. Their egos won't allow it. They like to make tying small flies appear difficult. They add unnecessary elements and tying stages. It makes them look more professional. It doesn't catch them, or you (or me) any more trout. It just scares the pants off you and puts you off wanting to tie small flies for life.

Tackle shops are no better. They're wary about stocking them because they're bad for business. A tiny strand of wool, which is really just about all that my little flies are, wrapped round a hook, doesn't justify the premium price they want to ask for it. A fair price might reflect adversely on the price of the more complex tying procedures of the flies in the boxes next to them.

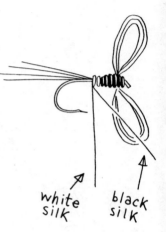

white silk   black silk

And this is the only problem I can find with the style of tying my Twenties that I developed and named the Twenties Loop Series: they have no commercial value. They make tying small flies look too easy. For this reason, they're worthless. But as a foil against an August trout, with a mop for a mouth, they're priceless. For the beauty of a small fly, with no features that a trout can find to criticize, is that when taken, the fly is sipped in with astounding confidence. So much so, it makes you wonder why you don't use the same pattern in the Spring.

Including tying thread, the Twenties Loop Series involves the use of only three materials. Two threads, and a yarn. The yarn is a light yellow or white polypropylene. This gives a small fly all the floatability it requires. The threads: one strand of black, one strand of white.

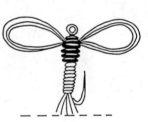

The tying style, like the Funneldun, reverses flytying logic, but needn't turn it upside-down. In an attempt to minimise tying stages and procedures, I abandoned the traditional 'front to back to front again'. Instead, my new direction is strictly 'front to back' only.

As far as maximizing every material and movement is concerned, the wing material doubles up as tail, the tying silk doubles up as a thorax and body - as does the whip finish which once again involves you tying off your fly at the tail end, rather than at the eye. And because it's a small fly, the whip finish is made a great deal easier, (and functional), for at the same time you whip finish you're also forming the body and tying in tails - three procedures condensed into one.

I promised simplicity.

————

Over-Here has a criminal dress sense. Kitted out like a snowman in mid-summer, in a white nylon shirt crackling with static and slacks a pale shade of wood ash, he is prepared for immediate helicopter rescue were he to stray from the river bank and lose himself in the Wild Wood. All he need do is lie down, arms and legs akimbo, making himself as visible in the dense scrub as a lone star on a winter's night.

Over-Here got his name because if you shared the river with him, before too long you'd discover where he was. 'Ere, over here. Is that a fish?' he'd shout at you.

You could tell how he got his passion for fish at twenty yards. He'd spent his life staring into goldfish bowls, or rather through them. His spectacles contained more glass than a Kew Gardens hothouse. If they had windscreen wipers attached, he wouldn't be able to tell you if they were switched on or off. He wouldn't be able to see them for all the glass.

But Over-Here's hearing was top-notch, and if he heard you coming, he wouldn't think of you as company. What he heard was a pair of eyes coming at him; sight he could borrow.

As you would quite rightly expect of a small, public-spirited group of flyfishermen, everyone on The Hollow was more than anxious to help him at all times. And one day in August, even though I was well out of ear-shot, I went out of my way to say hello when I spotted him at the top of the Marshes where he stood tilted forward gazing studiously at something he clearly couldn't see. Nobody had been near the water for two weeks. Everyone was on holiday, it was that time of year. I had the river more or less to myself, and I was glad of the company.

'Ere, over here. Is that a fish?' he shouted as he heard me walking towards him up the Broadwater. It was. But not what he was pointing at. He'd spotted a submerged fence post. I was looking at a large trout sipping at reed smuts along a stack of freshly cut weed just upstream a bit. For the first time that day I'd spotted a fish, rather than hearing it first. Over-Here would probably have heard it too if it hadn't been for the Broadwater Hatch ten yards below, where water thundered down into the hatch pool at a rate that sounded to me like thousands of gallons of water a minute.

To read the identity of reed smuts, you need a magnifying glass. A score of these tiny aquatic insects resembling tiny houseflies can stand on the nail of your little finger without it feeling like rush hour. Luckily for smuts, the trout have to squint to be able to pick them out, too. For this reason, collectively they have earned themselves the name 'The Black Curse', like some medieval pox. *En masse*, neither you nor the trout can ignore them because they come down in one long, continuous black sheet. At times like this, often once a day, all the trout has to do is close its eyes and steer an open mouth to the surface and suck them in. An imitation of a mating pair tied on a larger hook than a Twenties is a good pattern to try if you aren't able to overcome the fear of the fingersome. But even if you were to tie the pattern on a Japanese factory ship whale-harpoon, my fishing companion for the afternoon would still have needed my assistance when it came to seeing it on the water.

'There's another trout a little bit further up,' I informed Over-Here, dropping to my knees.

'Ere. Shall I try him with this?' He had a sedge on, the size of a turkey. I decided to be cautious. The last time he had asked this question, he had on the end of his line a Blue Dun he'd bought in Vienna, the size of somebody's hat. Before I had time to suggest something a little more effective, he had it over the fish, and the fish on the bank, in two swift moves.

'You can try,' I said, a hand in the thigh pocket of my trousers ready to pull out my fly box, as a precaution. But that day, I knew what this fish would take if he didn't go for the poultry. And sure enough, it didn't - although it followed it for a few feet with the turkey balanced on the point of his snout like a ball on the nose of a seal in a circus.

'Any ideas?' he asked. Code for 'Could you tie another fly on the line for me?'

By the look of it, the Boss had tied the turkey on the end of the line. A huge knot - the afternoon's work of a group of demented boy scouts.

Failure is not falling down, it's staying down. Even though you fail to raise a fish to your fly, if you don't put it down, you can still succeed. You just need to start again. I plucked the turkey off and attached a Twenties Loop Smut - something small, something black, just like the tiny black smuts. The answer was to fish a 'thing' with a 'thing' - something recognisable by its nothingness.

'Is it on yet?' Over-Here asked.

'It's on,' I said, giving the order to open fire. Out it shot in the direction of the trout. And up came the trout, its mouth opening up like the lid of a large enamel bread bin to breathe my insignificant smut off the surface. Persuasion with evidence.

'Has he taken it yet?'

'Not quite,' I informed Over-Here. 'Keep the rod down and to the side.'

I was waiting for the current to take the belly of the line and swing the hook home. The moment it did this, the trout exploded in our face.

'He's taken it!' we said in unison to a chorus of alarmed coots. The noise Over-Here had heard over the booming hatch was the sound of the fish taking the fly. For me it was the sound of the river taking over and taking the fish. Now, the fish took everything.

By now, the line was bellied out on the rim of the hatch. The fish had decided to go with the flow. Turning round, it headed off in the direction of the line. Under the bridge, down into the hatch pool below.

'It's over here,' I shouted, pointing into the hatch pool below. Over-Here was confused.

'How am I going to get the fish back up through the bridge?'

'You don't. Just keep the pressure on.'

I ran up and joined him. His line had shot under the bridge and was trailing in the hatch below. I told him to pull all the line off his reel and let all unconnected thirty yards wash away down into the pool. Reluctantly, he began to pay it out, very slowly. When he got to the backing I cut the line loose from his reel and away it went. The river hadn't just hooked the fish, it was now playing it.

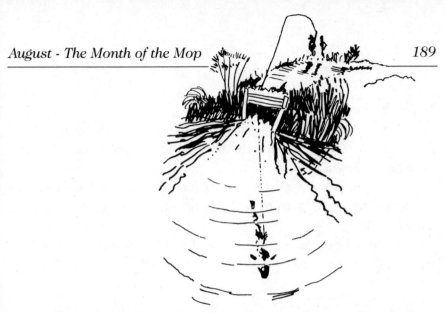

'Quick! Follow me!' I didn't give Over-Here time to think, time to ponder the madness.

We both dropped down to the Broadwater Hatch, to the back of the pool where it shallowed off. I waded out into the middle of these shallows where the line uncurled at my feet.

'Over here!' I shouted. Over-Here was there in a shot. I had all his line bundled in my arms. Speedily threading the line back through the rings of Over-Here's rod, I attached the end of the line onto his backing.

'Reel in! Like the Devil!'

Over-Here's wrist became a blur of action. The river had played its part. Remarkably, the fish was still on.

A bemused Over-Here inched the confused trout over to the spot where he was standing at the back of the hatch pool. The fish collapsed into his net. Over-Here collapsed onto the bank, panting like a foxhound. I thought I'd killed him.

Now some people like this sort of thing but it's not everyone's cup of tea, and thinking back, I can't honestly tell you if Over-Here enjoyed those action-packed moments or not. He never mentioned the incident again. At least not to me. I don't think he knew quite what had happened. They say shock can have that effect.

Certainly, after that episode I've never doubted the ability of any pattern in the Twenties Loop series to stay clamped to a trout's jaw with unforgiving tenacity. Nor have I questioned whether it has the same holding power as its counterpart on a larger, barbed hook.

All I know is that left with the latter, I'd never have had the opportunity to find out, for the fish would not have accepted a fly on a bigger hook.

And I also know that the next few times I saw Over-Here, or he heard me coming from over there, he never again gave me a shout.

If I'm to be honest, after what I put him through I think he preferred it if I stayed away. As far over there as possible.

September

SILVER CIRCLES

Most people have perfectly normal neighbours with two kids, a sensible estate car and a front lawn that's cut every Saturday. Nice people, who keep their music down low.

I have a rowdy rabble of head-bangers with hairy legs who thump on my bedroom window on warm September nights when I'm trying to get some sleep.

If I point an ear through my window in the direction of the river, I'm reminded that things aren't any more tranquil down there. Is that the noise of water slipping over the weir? Or is it the frenzied gnashing of silver, moonlit teeth under Sticklepath Bridge? The sound of my neighbours in the river snapping at members of the same family who are hammering on my window?

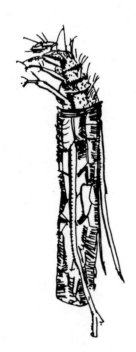

You get no peace and quiet living by a river. But it has its compensations. For a start, you have trout next door to you. And the trout under Sticklepath Bridge know exactly how to sort out those late-night window-rattlers. They eat them, hairs and all.

As their nearest sanctuary, all I need to do is switch a light on and I get all the sedges in the neighbourhood breaking my door down to escape the slavering jaws of the trout next door. Especially at this balmy time of year. Normally they slide in through a roof window left ajar in the bathroom. Once inside, they camp out on the high ceiling under their tent-shaped wings, antennae, like guide-ropes, trembling.

To be truthful, my door (and windows) are open to them. I don't exactly make up beds, but they like my company. They've had a lonely time. A year of acute insecurity, extreme neurosis. Twelve months of haunting the dark depths dragging their one-bedroom, pebble-dash bungalows across the cold, slimy river bed. One miscalculation, one slippery step, one faltering femur, and an avalanche of gravels alerts a sleepy trout to their endless wanderings. Perch a newly-released adult sedge on the back of your hand and this nervousness oozes out. Like a hairy jumping bean, one hop, one flap and he's somewhere else, just long enough to skip on to the next place, then the next.

Ask me candidly, as a neighbour, and I will tell you: sedges are not happy creatures.

For this reason, at this time of year I usually close the bathroom window, turn the lights off and take a break. I go to places where someone else does the sedge-nursing and I can get some fishing done. When I do this, I forget about the sedges at the bottom of my garden and start thinking about the sedge patterns in the bottom of my fly box. Could *they* be better behaved?

Now when I say 'well behaved', I'm not talking about *my* moral view on the nocturnal comings and goings of consenting adult sedges. I ask: do my artificials behave in the way trout expect them to? Do they look like adult sedges to a trout? Or more importantly, how do trout know my artificial sedge is an edible sedge?

An insect on the surface of a river offers four possible recognition features to the trout staring up at the sky. Let me peel them away so we get to the core - the one most relevant to the sedge.

The most evasive and elusive characteristic is colour. At the risk of insulting all those whose bible is the Pearsall's shade chart, the only colourful thing about sedges is their behaviour. You don't talk colours with sedges, you talk shades. But not only is the shade of one sedge merely marginally different from the shade of another species, one member of the same species can be a shade lighter or darker than another. Not just at different times of the year, or different locations, but on the same day, or night; on the same river, or lake.

Trust me. I've had bathrooms full of them.

And all this long before we start talking about how a trout beneath the surface sees them, with the vagaries and subtleties of light conditions at different times of the day; sun angles; flat sky; bright sky - not to mention evening and night; or how tying materials used to recreate colour can react differently under different conditions. And so on. The truth is, the flyfisher will never be able to be as certain as he'd like to be about how trout see the colours of his fly on the surface and the effect this colour, dominant or not, has on the specific feeding instincts, on that particular dining moment. In fact, the factors are so complex, the conclusions so incomplete, and the theories proposed so general and wide-spanning, that I would go on to say that even if trout were able to see colours through exactly the same eyes as the flyfisher, I doubt if the answer to this eternal problem would be any nearer being solved. And thank goodness for that. For if science were to overtake the art of flyfishing, and the River Test were to become the River Test-tube, then I would build a badminton court on the lawn of the Wild Wood Lodge and use my feathers to make shuttlecocks.

In short, if in your hand you have a sedge you brought home and you're standing in the kitchen at the blender mixing up seal fur to match the identical shade of its body, take my advice. Put the sedge back in a jar, and have an early night.

Len's
'moveable
feast'

Transparency is worth a study. Trout, and food photographers, are the only creatures that judge whether something looks scrumptious or not against a bright light. But what parts of the sedge stick out and fizz colour when looked at held up to the light? The answer is, not many. Bits of an adult sedge that aren't solid and opaque are hard to locate on a sedge with wings sloped over its back. Unless, that is, it starts to fuss and flap. Its antennae, perhaps? They certainly stick out, but I don't think they qualify. Let's move on to the next feature: shape.

Now we're starting to talk sense. You may not be able to tell the difference between the colour of a sedge and a daddy-long-legs, but hold them bodily up to the light and see if you can't spot the difference in silhouette.

Size also has to be a consideration. With no size reference, unless you're an entomologist, it's nearly impossible to tell the difference between a small and a great red sedge. But even more critical is something else.

Without doubt, the biggest attraction of the adult sedge to a trout is movement. Once hatched, a sedge motoring towards the bank in an attempt to lift-off presents the trout with the perfect meal-on-wheels. Movement puts it on the menu.

The sedge is one of nature's acrobats. Flytying niceties are lost in an explosion of energy; a flurry of flopping, flapping and pathetic paddling; anything to claw its clumsy way across the water. In doing so, the back edges of the wings tip down on the water surface in a folded position making the sedge as tempting to the trout as a water-skier wobbling over the jaws of a Great White.

So what pattern do I use to imitate this *movement* - for this at times is all an edible sedge really is to a set of gleaming, hungry teeth?

Along with flies knocking on my windows, I get flyfishers knocking on my door. These have included two illustrious sedge-experts from across the Pond.

I met the tip of Len Wright's rod long before I got to meet him. Standing in the middle of a wood fishing the Sheep Dip, a small side-stream on the edge of the Back of Beyond, you couldn't see him, but you couldn't miss him either. He was the thing at the end of the only stick in the woods that flicked backwards and forwards high above the tops of the trees. He later told me that the long rod helped him keep his fly clear of branches.

But much more important, a 10½' rod allowed him to mend the line more easily, curve cast better, avoid drag and animate his fly. For the wet fly fishing he did in the States, he could control the speed of the fly more sensitively.

His downstream presentation of a dry fly, incorporating the 'sudden inch' tactic, tweaking the fly a couple of inches in front of the nose of the targeted trout, is written up in his book *Fishing the Dry Fly as a Living Insect*. This killing tactic had began by imitating a sedge in motion. Len's Skitter Caddis pattern caused quite a stir amongst dyed in the wool purists. Len tells the story of bumping into the late Sparse Grey Hackle, the dean of American flyfishing authors, shortly after the publication of his book. 'Congratulations,' he said. 'I see you've written an entire book devoted to the ancient art of trolling.'

He gave me a trio of this pattern. I have them mounted, framed and hanging on the wall next to all the naturals that follow me off the river into my hall at this time of year.

Larry Solomon, co-author with Eric Leiser, of *The Caddis and the Angler*, also gave me some of his sedge patterns when I met him with the River God for lunch at Sticklepath Bridge. One of the flies he recommended was designed to do much the same as Len demanded of his sedges.

I know a wonderful hotel in the West Country, with more rivers and streams running through it than the cracks in my waders. Unspoilt by what some people might call progress, it was the sort of place that would have set Agatha Christie's imagination popping. The fishing was good, too.

At one time, I used to go and stay there quite regularly. But the management changed, and bit by bit it started to catch up with the rest of the world. Now I visit it only occasionally. Not as a hotel, but as a hotel water. There are fewer trout there now, but this gives it an edge - an edge I enjoy. Some would say it had become a very testing water. I'd agree.

A friend of Roll Cast was staying there with his son. Gripped by nostalgia, I arranged to join him there, but I only wanted the river. I didn't want to have anything to do with the hotel. I'd learned from experience the last time I'd dropped by, if the new chef finds out you've as much as stepped in the hotel and not sampled his cooking, he can get very excitable. His reputation is known locally. Milk, eggs, mail, furniture polish, you name it - everything that is delivered to the hotel is left on the doorstep. For this reason, I agreed to meet my host by the river.

One advantage that a rain-fed river has over a chalkstream has nothing to do with water, and a lot to do with wood. There's always lots of flotsam brought down by the flood and washed up on the bank. When I'm down on the river, I like to put two logs together, build a fire and fry up something for lunch. In a small knapsack I keep a tin kettle, a saucepan and a grill and some fire-lighters, a box of matches and a large plastic bag full of individual sugar, salt and pepper packs that I've kept from airline flights. I even had packs of soy sauce that reminded me of a memorable flight with Singapore Airlines. I'm fully equipped. No need for lunch, no need for tea. I'm the complete, self-contained, self-styled, self-catering independent river flyfisher/chef.

One thing I didn't know about the new people was whether they had a policy about lighting fires on the river bank. In the old days, I'd just light up and get the recipe books out. No-one complained, nobody bothered. Why should they? Well, I thought, the new crowd just might.

My host told me the new manager never went near the river. He wasn't a fisherman, he was a keep-fit freak and spent all his spare time in the gym in the nearest town. I wasn't worried, he'd never be able to tell I'd been there or not. On my trips to Alaska, I got the very best of training when it came to striking camp. The fishing lodge guides are ruthless about conserving the environment. Their attitude is military. To get on the bad side of one of these Tundra Tarzans, just flick a cigarette-butt in the river. You soon get a lesson on the chemical make-up and un-biodegradable silicon content of the filter. They all have to be saved to go in the bag along with everything else and be taken back. It's top priority. On the way back, if there's only enough room in the float-plane for either you or the rubbish bag - the junk travels, you stay.

About lunch-time, I laid out my two logs on the gravel, side by side near the river. I was well out of sight of the hotel, at the bottom of a steep bank. I lit up. Luckily the wood was as dry as a bone. Usually I get so much smoke North American Indians pick up my signals. But they don't reply or understand the message. When the flames finally took, I decided to go after a fish that had started to rise in the middle of the river. Half an hour later, I came back, flattened the charcoal, and started cooking. I'd just put the grill over the two logs when I took a look up the bank and saw the manager standing there in a track suit. Clearing the smoke from my throat, I introduced myself.

'I heard you were at the gym today,' I said trying not to cough the words out.

'They're redecorating. I met your friends. They're up in the hotel having lunch. We do lunches, you know.'

'I know,' I said. The manager shook something in his pocket as if to indicate he was a man in a hurry, turned and disappeared down the bank in a cloud a great deal darker than one of my incomprehensible smoke signals. But his message was clear. Ah well, I thought, it could have been the chef.

The first sausage had just hit the grill when the chef arrived with a snarling dog.

'We do lunches, you know,' the wild-eyed chef said, pulling his dog back on its lead as it prepared to launch itself on me as only dogs know how.

'I know,' I said.

'There's always a good fish over there,' he told me, pointing across the river to a small run under the far bank.

He walked off before I could reply. I was going to go on and tell him that I'd already tried to get across to that run earlier that morning, but even in chest waders, it was hazardous. But I think he already knew this. He'd clearly decided that if I wasn't going to come up to the hotel and sample his lunch, I probably wouldn't be wanting his homemade scones and cakes for tea, either - or his dinner. He'd wiped me out. If the current was to pick me up and whisk me down to the sea that afternoon, as far as he was concerned, it would be doing him a favour.

I did so much prefer the old management. Even so, I decided to sit it out. If August is about early mornings, September is about late nights. I'd come for the evening.

In the old days, I used to visit the hotel in June and July. One mid-summer evening, at owl's light, I remember being faced with a re-enactment of the Fastnet Race on the same part of the river I'd camped out on for lunch that September. I didn't have one of the sedge patterns Len & Larry had given me to try out in my box. So I had until the next evening to get together a sedge pattern with the floatability of a wine cork, the chugging determination of an Arbroath fishing boat and the succulent silhouette of a Kentucky Fried sedge. Lastly, and strategically, because there were hawthorn bushes in front, behind and all around where the trout were holed up in most concentration, I needed a pattern that wouldn't distress me too much if it got lost up a tree.

I'm no fan of expensive capes and top-grade American hackle brands, and never have been. I can't afford to be. Which is why at this time of year, when the surface film is at its stickiest and the things that trout eat tend to be glued to the surface, rather than bouncing merrily on and off it, a hair-shirt philosophy comes into its own. When it comes to flytying, it's goodbye hackles, hello hair. I go through this change of flytying style annually.

It's no accident, therefore, that one of the ingredients in my portable leather flytying box is a lady's fox stole which I bought in a junk shop. On account of the fact that it looked as though it

had been hunted down by a pack of Rottweilers, rather than hounds, it cost pennies, rather then pounds. Now I come to think of it, they held it at arm's length and donated it.

Of huge interest to me were the soft tails dangling from each corner. I clipped these off and used the rest as moth bait. There are two parts to these tails: the stiff guard hairs, and the under-lying, ground level fluff.

Sitting crossed-legged in the sun in the hotel garden, my back propped up against a yew hedge, I discovered that this soft fur spins thinly onto tying silk, fulfilling my first requirement. Above all, this pattern needed to be as lightweight and as agile as possible if it was to move with divine and deadly grace. This fur fluff can be lightly applied. Just enough to give the tying silk a five o'clock shadow.

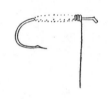

The long, stiff hairs pull off the other stunts I required. Firstly, the wings needed to be long and strong to outstretch the body. This is an important 'shape' recognition point when looked at from below, differentiating it from any other insect that may be passing over the trout. A blue-winged olive out on the tiles, a pale evening dun, or a token moth with wonky landing gear.

Secondly, rather than rest on it's hackles, up front my sedge pattern needed to stand proud on its tip-toes. At the rear, it needed to fall back and be propped up on its wings. A small bunch of hairs filled the bill. These stiff hair fibres could do both feats, yet stay well within my lightweight brief. The 'funnelled' hair represent *one* turn of hackle, not the four or five turns you'd need if you were to attempt to get the same effect using a hackle from off the back of the neck of a US gamecock champ. And it doesn't soften under stress.

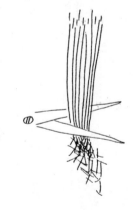

This makes for a super-strong, super-light fly that's super-easy to tie. A fly with no added extras, offering maximum buoyancy. A lightweight sedge pattern promising perfect floatability after two false casts, essential when you're fishing in strange waters in shrinking light.

That evening, I fished the wily, bushy-tailed Caddox - half-caddis, half-fox - across and down over the platinum rings and beads of mercury spurting from the late-late show of sedges at

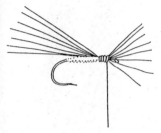

the edge of that clump of hawthorns. I had attached it on as light a leader point as I dared. It was a risk, but it made for more elegant animation. I didn't strip it. I chucked it out, dropped my rod tip and holding the line in my left hand, I lifted it up, bringing the Caddox towards me over the fish. If I'm on a still pool fishing blind, at the top of the lift, I drop my rod tip again, and retrieve the slack. When I've done this I start the procedure over again.

To add to its effect, I tied a Portland Hitch, or Riffle knot behind the eye. This is really a half-hitch, or if you prefer, a double hitch. The knot is tied on the side of the hook allowing the Caddox to swing down the stream hook first, eye pointing upstream. The line should come from underneath the hook, not over the top.

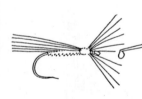

Now, in September, the technique hadn't lost its charm. Not on my first evening, at least. The cunning Caddox had a host of pound trout splashing, slashing and crashing mouth-first at it until I began to feel guilty at attacking another man's stre-am with such vigour.

As darkness fell and the thought of the long drive back loomed strongly, I made my shame-faced way up through the woods towards the orange peep holes of the hotel. It was nearly eleven o'clock when I walked over the croquet lawn and across the long shadows from the bar. One of the shadows was the manager. I could see him through the window, back-lit by a table light talking to the chef sitting on a stool by the bar. The two shadows standing next to them were Roll Cast's friends deep in the same conversation. I decided to march in, rather than grovel.

'How about that lunch then?' I asked jokingly, striding into the bar in my socks. The conversation shallowed.

'And a bed?' I added and about which I was serious.

They pulled the dust-covers off a single room in the attic for me. It was all I needed. I was thick with sleep and passed out before my head hit the pillow.

The next day the hotel notice-board informed me that I had been allocated the top beat, the one furthest from the dining rooms. A snarling piece of water, this short stretch was an aquatic Alps, a ballroom of rocks with streams waltzing round boulders, coming at you from all angles, all sides. It was better suited for hiking boots than waders. In June and July, this suits me fine. I simply fish the crystal froth in gym shoes and shorts. But hot summer days were coming to a chilly close; temperatures were dropping with the sun. Once again I had decided to fish late, so I was happy I'd brought my chest waders.

Only the English could have invented such ridiculous things as waders. Put them on and look at yourself in the mirror. Aren't they absurd? I read in another man's book the other day that it was a long time before our cousins across the Pond took to them. American stream fisherman were cautious. Waders did not happen overnight. They emerged slowly.

PoRtland
Hitch

Well-to-do City anglers were the first to take the plunge. These were the flyfishermen with private waters stuck away in the Catskills with no-one for miles around, so they could sneak behind a tree and climb into them without anyone seeing. They could even pay someone to keep watch.

In Robert Redford's film of Norman Maclean's book *A River Runs Through It*, you don't see the two brothers in the story pulling on their waders to go astream. It's not a film where you want the audience to get the giggles. These two bright young men let their old Presbyterian father wear the waders. When it comes to getting in the river, they just walk straight into it - trousers, socks, shoes, the lot. Anything is more sensible than wearing waders.

On The Hollow you don't really need to wear them. You can get by wearing Wellington boots, if you just want to keep the dew off. But if you want to fish the wilder corners, you need something a little more than knee boots. Ideally, something in-between. Something with enough rubber to cover your kneecaps to cross the shallows, or when you kneel. I found the very thing, in the most unlikely of places: Venice.

I say unlikely, but perhaps not. As we all know, Venice is

sinking. What I didn't know was that in February and March the water on all sides rises and they have the most terrible floods. Fortunately they're prepared for this annual event.

I was staying in a hotel right on the lagoon front, the Danieli. My first night, I got back to the hotel, picked up my key from reception and went to bed. The next morning, I got up and started to make my way downstairs for breakfast. The entire ground floor of the hotel was three foot in water. Carpets had been rolled up, furniture piled on top of tables and a plank stretched from half way down the stairs to the top of the reception desk which you walked over to get to the door. Dropping my key on reception, I stepped off the desk onto a drinks trolley on castors wedged in the revolving doors. The doorman pushed me round and I set off on a street network of raised planks, round the corner to St Mark's Square, eventually arriving at a shop that sold rubber boots.

This shop had everything in the foul weather footwear department. Knee-high, thigh-high - you name it. More importantly, they had the waders of my dreams: the 'something in-between' pair, stopping just above the knee cap, in chocolate brown, and weighing little more than a pair of carpet slippers. I snapped them up before they had time to say 'Buon giorno'. And I've worn them every day I've been on The Hollow ever since. But when I go to some rain-fed stream, I leave my boots behind. For tip-toeing through the violets on the banks of The Hollow, they're poetry. For exploring the hidden depths of a West Country stream, I pack a hot air balloon: my chest waders.

Now if you think thigh waders are ridiculous, chest waders really mess the mind. The Americans saw them coming from England before they arrived - and ducked. To counteract the sartorial insanity of chest waders, they speedily invented the neoprene waterproof body sock. If you look absurd in these, you don't go to your tackle dealer and complain, you go to your dietician. You can only blame your physique.

When you fish abroad, you can tell a British flyfisherman a mile off. He'll be the one with his head sticking out of the top of a green marquee with no guy-ropes, built to the same dimensions

as the Hindenburg airship. And just like the Hindenburg, they're disastrous. In the stream, the currents catch the loose rolls of rubber, billowing out at the sides. You'd be more water-dynamic wading out with a parachute dragging behind you.

But the strangest thing of all about chest waders is that as soon as you step into them, fix the straps, straighten them up, fasten the belt and put your oilskins on top, the first thing you want to do isn't go to the river and go fishing. No, the first thing you want to do is go to the toilet. Have you noticed this? Even though you've just been, you get all dressed up and what happens: you want to go again.

I remember telling a friend about this. I told him that if he ever gets constipation, he should go to the garage, unhook his chesties, put them on, put a jacket on top - and hey presto, he'll be cured. He won't be able to get them off quick enough. I met him on the side of the River Eden a year later. I was wearing my chest waders, just like last time. He was wearing thigh waders.

'Where's your chesties?' I asked, surprised to find him fishing the margins.

'I had to throw them out,' he told me.

I was intrigued. I've got mine until the day I die. This is another problem with waders. They don't walk away. 'How come?', I asked.

'Well, remember you told me that if I ever got a bowel problem, all I had to do was put on my chesties and I wouldn't be able to get them off quick enough?'

'Yes.'

'Well, I did. And you were right.'

The Alpine beat had fished badly during the day. I'd trickled a team of three soft-hackled flies round the rocks and through the passes with a small lead shot pinched on the leader below the top dropper and managed to trick two small trout into taking. I returned them both.

For the evening, I had my eye on a fifty-yard stretch of still,

quiet water right at the top of the beat. To be honest, I wasn't sure if this was the top of my beat or the bottom of the beat above. But after dark, out there in the wilds, who's to know? This beat was flat and meandering. For a rain-fed stream, the water ran slower than a carrier on The Hollow.

Just as I thought, as the sun dropped, the sedge began skittering across the surface. In the reflections of the fading sunlight, they looked twice as big on the water as they did viewed in the cup of my hand. The circles of the rising trout rocked the surface from one bank of the stream to the other. I fully expected to walk away within an hour, fed up with fishing too murderous to be fun. But this wasn't to be.

The day had been hotter than the day before and the sedges had appeared early, in full force. I threw my Caddox at the first rise I saw. From where I stood, perched on a rock shaped like the Matterhorn, it seemed impossible for any trout not to bust an artery to grab it. It looked so chunky, so meaty, I was all but leaping in after it myself.

I was still totally confident when it arrived back at my feet. Anticipation was mixed with disbelief. I threw it back. This time I lifted the tip of my rod enough to impart an itchy twitch just before it arrived at the trout's position. There was a swirl deep down, the surface heaved and I knew the trout was not only untempted by my fly, it was disenchanted by it.

This happened with the next trout I chucked to. And the one after that. I was stunned, then curious. The mystery was that although the river was a disco of skittering sedges, the trout were *sipping*, not slashing. This seemed odd. I bent down and looked at the surface.

No visible spinner. No upwing fly, in any stage of development. But along with the sedge I thought were hatching, the surface was peppered with sedge, dead and dying. At first I thought that these were perhaps sedges that hadn't hatched properly. But after a closer look, I couldn't find any evidence of shucks or sedges in semi-eclosion.

What I was witnessing wasn't a hatch after all, but a *fall* of egg-layers. And the trout, rather than chase after the active egg-layers dipping and skimming - the state that my well-briefed Caddox so cunningly imitated - they were waiting at the edges of the runs and under the banks of the dance floor picking off the weary boppers as they kicked helplessly in the film.

I needed a 'spinner' sedge. A spent sedge. A pattern *without* everything I had spent so much time incorporating into the Caddox. I wanted a lifeless sedge. But not one that looked like a twig.

Back at the collar box, a pencil torch held between my teeth, I screwed my vice into a log, put the log on my knee and pulled out my fox stole. Without actually moving the fly with my rod, the impression I wanted to give was of an egg-layer wriggling in an attempt to peel herself away from the surface film. Incorporating the super-long guard hairs on my fox-tail stole into the pattern, I got them to act as long-range surface tension distorters, imitating the shock waves emitted round the area of a struggling insect. At best they imitate the long, uncurled antennae of the exhausted sedge. As an egg ball, I tied in a short length of yellow polypropylene. As a body, I pinched a little fluff onto the silk. I took this from the base of the fox tail hairs I was to use for the wings. I then tied a small bunch of fox tail hairs two thirds of the way up the hook, in front of the body - points first over the eye, Caddox-style.

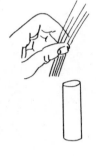

Instead of leg-length, I let these points stick out twice the length of the body. I then split the bunch pointing to the rear and tied them spent sloping back along the sides of the body. With wings in position, I trimmed the hairs up front, leaving a half dozen pointing out of the front of the hook. I pulled half of these hairs back so they splayed out behind and at the sides as well as at the front, holding them in position with a couple of turns of dubbed thread to form a thorax. Finally, I held the ones pointing forwards back to whip finish, letting them spring back on completion.

Knowing the fly isn't knowing how to fish it. The river was like a length of black velvet on my return, my eyes were suffering from torch shock, and the bats were out. Only a corner of the moon was showing in the sky, but this was enough. If it hadn't

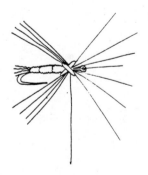

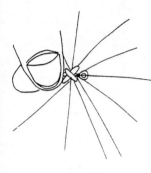

been for this, I would never have taken the two trout that I did.

It was this thin light surfing on the ripple of the rise-forms under the far banks that indicated that there were still two trout there at all. And having waded out and cast a fly in the right direction, it was this moonlight, rolling like mercury down the gutter made on the surface by my fly line, that told me where - and how well - my Film Star Sedge was performing.

As the hills got darker and eventually disappeared, it wasn't a matter of man-handling monsters from out of the depths, it was more a problem of taking pot-shots at athletes performing on an unlit stage. Rubbing the sleep from my eyes, I strained to make out the silver circles in the dark, trying to emulate the radar of a moth-tracking bat. My senses focussed, my muscles tightened, I concentrated on the tiniest details, checking that they matched my quest for precision. My hooks were super-sharp. I always carry a small file with me. While I'm waiting for a fish to show, or when I'm tense, I used to bite my nails. Now I clasp my hook between thumb and forefinger and sharpen it to needle-point sharpness. I can do it in my sleep. I probably do.

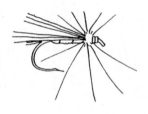

In the blackness, knowing that my tackle was honed to perfection, at the sharp end at least, gave me a strange comfort. It exaggerated my sense of effectiveness, giving me a glow of confidence in the icy chill of the late night sky.

There was a general feeling of pending excitement in the air. Only the flurry of aerobatic bats disturbed the charged atmosphere. I was no longer getting thumped on the head by agitated sedges. Those that had managed to escape were either shivering somewhere on the bank or floating past me, motionless, on the matt-black surface of the stream.

I scanned the area in front of me for a flash of platinum, a location signal from my hook point. But on the two occasions when I thought I'd made a semi-visual, super-sensory connection with my fly, the dark river opened up, wrapping the area at the end of my line in a ball of silver paper and rushing it away at the speed of a midnight trout.

Back on the brighter waters of my home beat, the Film Star Sedge is the only fly I ask to accompany me when I set out to the Marshes. Wide open to the night sky, these meadows catch the last glimmer of light to shine anywhere on The Hollow. Fishing the Film Star Sedge is a late evening tactic, a specialist tactic, and yet it remains a very special fly in my sedge selection.

For me, when the sedge arrives on the surface, it ceases to be a mystery. There is no excuse for complications. Nor, as the Caddox and the Film Star Sedge eloquently demonstrate, for complex tying procedures. Unless helplessly trapped, like the egg-laying sedges on my last two hours on the hotel water, of one thing I am sure: movement is the key to making sedges, and making them behave in a mouth-wateringly edible manner.

For someone who lives by a river, the sedge and movement - or occasionally the lack of it - can have more ominous meanings. Back home on my return from the West Country, the refugee camp on my bathroom ceiling hadn't shifted an inch.

———

The people in the Big House can sense the seasons changing. The snow comes in winter, the cuckoo comes in Spring, the leaves turn in autumn, and the fishermen's cars come, and go. With the end of September only a couple of weeks away, very soon the track down to the river will be silent and the river banks will be theirs again to walk around unchallenged. And at this time of year I can read a look in the residents' eyes, an expression on a face, a hand movement. It says: 'When are we going to be given our last trout of the season?'

It's a thought on The Hollow flyfisher's mind also, as the resolve of the trout remaining in the stream toughens, hard-baked by the sunshine of a long summer and latterly by a non-stop three weeks of clear blue sky, without a drop of rain.

I told Lady McFarlane I'd do my best when I met her walking back up the track with her dog as I was on my way down. I volunteered a trout, for she never asks for anything. Of all the people I give trout to, she's the one I most like giving to. But on

that still, featureless afternoon, I'd need to be lucky to get any fish up to the glare of the unyielding September sun at the surface. If not lucky, then highly resourceful.

The river was viscous. The trout, set in it like flies in jam, glared glumly into the middle distance, stony monuments to the hardest month of all. Needless to say, the flyfishing had been interesting of late. Not a single nose pushed through the rubbery surface during the day. Instead, trout joined the shoals of roach and dace, to gawp at the nymphs of small olives skidding along weed fronds, flipping head-over-heels and tumbling upwards to the surface. But not in any great numbers. It was time to rethink my approach. If only for Lady McFarlane.

I think Vincent Marinaro got it right when he said that what Halford did with the dry fly was catch more fish - and what Skues did with the nymph was catch even more fish than that. As for myself, as you will have gathered by now, I prefer to fish the fly on the surface rather than beneath, for no other reason than that this is what I *choose* to do - and because I never feel handicapped doing it. One aspect of trout behaviour that consistently creeps into nymph versus dry fly debates, and that remains constant and beyond dispute, is the fact that on hot, dry summer days, a trout feeding on nymphs at a depth of anything from a foot down, and therefore in mid-water, is rarely inclined to interrupt a fly on the surface. If this was not the case, if nymphing trout were happily drawn upwards to inspect every insect that passed over them, there would be no need for nymph patterns, no need for nymph fishing, and G.E.M. Skues would never have received half the book royalties he did. He might even have kept his rod on the Abbots Barton beat on the River Itchen from which he was unceremoniously turfed off for his heresies.

As fly-life fades in the summer, many trout leave their once rich and reliable Spring food-bearing lies and move to feeding stations better-suited for gorging on the more plentiful sub-surface food. These moves are a misfortune, not just for the dry fly man, but for the nymph fisherman also, because in the course of a normal day there are several occasions when it's better to lift a nymphing trout to the surface to take your offering. Quite simply because, by doing so, you immediately eliminate the problems that often make taking a trout on a nymph more demanding than on a dry fly.

Let me group some of these difficulties under three rough headings: the first is when it's better to get a nymphing trout to break the surface, so you can *see* and 'read' the take.

Probably the most common occasion it's necessary to do this is in slack water when, in order to cast your fly, you put yourself in a position where you can no longer see the trout, usually on account of reflected light. Under these conditions, because your nymph is moving at a slow, ponderous pace, the trout has ample opportunity to suck in your artificial and spit it out again in the time it takes a lightly-greased leader on the surface to travel an inch downstream on the flow. This being the case, any leader indication is likely to be subtle and unpronounced and will seriously limit your chances at the strike.

A second example of another 'seeing' problem is experienced when fishing to a trout nymphing under the far bank. The difficulty here is that, because of distance it's often impossible to detect a slight sideways movement of the trout, or tiny tell-tale openings and shuttings of his mouth, making the signal to tighten both inaccurate and largely guesswork.

The next group of difficulties I put under the heading 'presentation'. There are three instances of this problem that spring to mind. Instance one is when, in the case of open shallows, trout are likely to be scared, rather than stimulated, by the unnatural arrival of a sub-surface food-form - a nymph from out of the sky - and in order to get round this problem you cast way ahead of the trout, with the result that when your artificial arrives at the trout it's well below the horizontal plane of his mouth. Or, as is often the case with low-lying trout you can't see, it snags on the river-bed.

Instance two is particularly common on the wild, weedy stretch of river on the way up to the Firs at the beginning of the Marshes where trout frequently lie in mid-water directly behind a log, or beside weed-beds, fallen trees and similar obstacles. In situations like this, even though you handle a rod with lunging

accuracy, it's an impossibility to get your nymph high enough up in front of a trout to let it sink to his depth.

Instance three is the classic problem of successfully presenting nymphs to trout lying in mid-water beneath low bridges where, in the space provided, you are only able to manoeuvre an artificial a few inches above the trout and therefore, as in instance two, not high enough up to get your nymph to his depth. And, if you are fishing blind, not allowing enough time for your leader to straighten and become an effective take-indicator. As with the two 'seeing' problems, if a trout could be lifted to the surface, all these difficulties could be overcome.

The last category of problems, I file under 'rules'. There are some beats of chalkstream that I have fished where, during September, the rule is strictly 'dry fly only'. And I hear that often in this month, even though the fly-life returns, the trout seem slow and reluctant to feed on the renewed source of surface food during the day. At no other time is it more essential to bring a nymphing trout to the surface, for if you are to make contact with a trout, this is the only place etiquette allows you to make your introductions.

With Lady McFarlane awaiting her trout, frying pan at the ready, and her potential breakfast staring into a weed-bed as if it were a television screen, the leading question remained: Is it possible to lift a trout up to a dry fly when it's basking in a food-bearing lie or feeding in mid-water in a blinkered nymphing state?

The answer, of course, is: yes. But not if you think conventionally. Not if you are of the opinion that artificials tied on anything larger than a #14 are not a sporting method of luring chalkstream trout.

The fact is, dry flies tied on sub #14 sizes imitate only one thing. The one thing guaranteed *not* to tempt a trout in a nymph-bearing lie to the surface. Even though, as is often the case, naturals may be appearing in respectable numbers.

Taking into consideration the sort of food that trout in such lies are on the look-out for, any such imitation runs the very real and dangerous risk of being unnoticeable to the point of being invisible. And even if it was to catch a trout's eye, it simply doesn't warrant the effort it would need to pull himself up to the surface when he can trap similar sized food-forms in his mid-water position.

With this taken into account, the sort of dry fly I require will need to do something a little out of the ordinary. Unlike most dry flies, it must in some way distract the trout from what he is feeding on (nymphs), and then sell him the idea of feeding on something at a different level. Clearly, to do this, the fly will have to be large, with a distinct 'presence' about it that will first of all distract the trout, then hopefully, interest him enough to make him feel a trip to the surface is worth his while.

Lastly, as an added bonus, the fly must appear trapped to reassure the trout that, having made the extra effort, it will not escape before he reaches it.

With this as a brief, we're speaking about something no smaller than a #12 hook, something that's not alien for a trout during the summer to find glued to the surface film. This left me with one, or perhaps two, very clear options. Not river flies, but land-born ones. The bluebottle, and the daddy-long-legs.

The bluebottle - and the green-bottle for that matter - is a fly that has been around for some time in the flyfisher's armoury, but appears to have been largely ignored by most angling writers and, more significantly, most angler's fly-boxes I've peered into. Exactly why is hard to say. Perhaps on grounds of respectability, the fact that it is humbly born in unpleasant places and is the end-product of the maggot, and therefore cannot boast the same pedigree as those insects reared on the clean gravels of the chalkstream.

If this is the case, the more's the pity. But I suspect it has never won the popularity it deserves because no one has ever seriously considered its potential. This is a situation I dearly wish to reverse because, over the seasons, it has taken a significant percentage of nymphing trout in situations where, for reasons given earlier, a nymph would have been the obvious choice.

The pattern I recommend is a mishmash of several patterns.

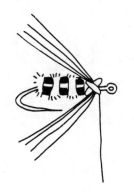

But there are no rules. In fact, this is an artificial few professional flydressers tie correctly for, like the Grizzle Mink that starts my season, the more chewed-up the finished effect, the better. You won't find it the best of floaters. This is essential, for the fact that it half sinks, I believe adds to its 'trapped' appeal. But to make sure it doesn't sink out of sight, I advise you to keep one in your floatant bottle. This way, when you come to use it, you'll find it will have soaked up so much floatant oil that if it caught fire you'd need Red Adair to put it out.

The first of my bluebottle imitations, tied with a cork body, caught me many nymphing fish - and the attention of the angling press when I first released it onto the the poor unsuspecting chalkstream fraternity weaned on the Halford ethic. The following month, it prompted an article by Richard Walker to put my case in perspective.

I remember putting off reading it at first. I was terrified. It was a good few days before I mustered enough courage to read it. I imagined that Walker would be attacking me for promoting the house fly as a serious addition to the ephemeropteran armoury. But everything he wrote turned out to be in defence of my observation. He went on to suggest two other flies that could be added to my 'big dries' category - the daddy-long-legs and the red sedge. He also suggested that instead of the cork for the body of my bluebottle, spun around with blue lurex, I should consider the employment of five or six strands of ostrich herl, twisted together over wet varnish on the hook (and then spun round with blue lurex), for this would work just as well. He also questioned the importance of wings. And, of course, he was right, on both counts.

I confess that until I'd taken my first half dozen trout on the bluebottle I had never had much faith in exaggerated or large flies on chalkstreams, apart from mayfly. It's hard to rationalize, but the bigger the fly, the more it seemed to give away my intentions. In short, I never believed for one moment that trout were foolish enough to be taken in by these big flies. But autopsies and my experience with the bluebottle - and for that matter, the daddy-long-legs - have altered my view, dramatically.

The daddy-long-legs, another damp location lover like the Spring hawthorn, lays its eggs in marsh areas, in decaying wood and fungi. For this reason, it is no surprise that we find it so close to the trout's heart if, that is, the way to a trout's heart is through its stomach. The daddy-long-legs larva has a rough, tough brown skin, and is known as a 'leather jacket'. But that is of no interest to a fisherman.

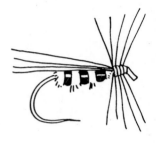

My imitation is simplicity itself to tie and incorporates two main materials. Garden-plant-binding raffia, and eight short lengths of brown nylon leader material that you might have lying around in the three to four pound category, knotted to form kneecaps on the legs. The combination of this, plus a couple of hackles, form the basis of a fly that sits in the surface film and is disturbingly attractive to even the most bottom-sucking trout. Trout cannot resist rising up and filling its mouth with this large leggy picnic. But it's not as easy as it sounds.

I have lost many a fish because I have not given special consideration to the size of the meaty chunk on the end of my line. For this reason, I have developed a unique style of striking. I call this the 'pause strike', for when a trout sucks in my mammoth offering, I drop the rod tip, let the line free from my left hand, and when the stream swings the loose line round forming a belly, I trap the line as it tightens between the forefinger of my right hand and the cork of my rod, letting the current wash the hook home. With a final uplift from my right hand to gather in any slack line, my trout now should be as well hooked as it ever will be.

Even with all the time taken during the 'pause strike' it is only rarely that I either miss the fish or I hook it in any place other than the jaw or the lip. I often wonder what a trout does with the daddy in its mouth to warrant such a delay in swallowing, for it seldom blows it out in rejection. Certainly not as many times as trout seem to do with imitations ten times smaller in size. Odd.

As a picture from Skues' *Nymph Fishing for Chalkstream Trout* eloquently suggests, bluebottles, like daddy-longlegs do lift nymphing trout to the surface more times than may be good for

them. The picture is of an autopsy of a trout's stomach. The dish is filled with olive nymphs and a single bluebottle sits amongst them. For me, this is picture-proof that 'Big Dries', as Walker christened them, are dry flies no dedicated nymph fisherman should be without.

———————

Lady McFarlane got her trout, in the end. In the bitter end. On the last minute of the last day, I crawled up the track for the last time that season, with the last trout of the season dangling from a stick. My mind was swimming with the trout I'd left behind. I was only able to leave the trout I hadn't caught because, as their home was also my home, I wasn't really leaving them.

The days were getting shorter, faster. The wheat fields were fixed solid in the landscape, like plates of gold. I had said my farewells to every trout I knew, every trout I'd missed, every trout I'd hooked and lost, or unhooked and released - with a very special nod of respect (and a final flick of a fly) to those I'd never been able to torment, no matter how hard I tried. Every inch of river bank had been trodden. Every corner had been investigated for the last time. Not a single watery, bank-side spider web, drenched by the first sodden autumn dews, had been left unbroken.

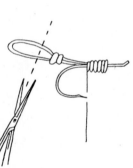

My last fish didn't come easy. The river was wriggling with rods, many of whom I hadn't seen since mayfly. One rod I had never seen before. He told me that he'd only come once all season. 'I had an hour to kill before the horse racing started. Anyway, I like the wet fly,' he told me, rushing back up in the direction of the Mad House and his car, at a gallop that would win him the 1000 Guineas.

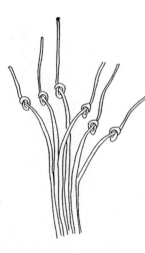

Over-Here was in his element. It didn't matter that he couldn't see fishermen, he couldn't help but bump into them. Accidentally-on-purpose we didn't make contact. I got within hailing distance a couple of times, but every time I saw him he was being well looked after by one rod or other. It was a good job he'd said his goodbyes and gone home by the time I eventually managed to get my last fish to take a fly.

All week, the bank-side vegetation had been weighed down with large cinnamon sedges. On Cemetery by the Withy Bed where in the final hours I'd staked out a fish in the two-pound bracket, they were rattling away like Flamenco dancers. On The Hollow, these frankfurter-sized sedges start hatching late on in the season, usually in the last two weeks of September, and they keep on hatching well into October if the weather stays mild. One October they flew off the river and up in the air so thickly, that guns out on the first day of the pheasant season might have been forgiven for shooting at them. And it was a shotgun I was beginning to think I'd need to get this trout lying tucked under the bend on Cemetery. Out of last-minute desperation, I attached the largest fly in my box to the end of my line.

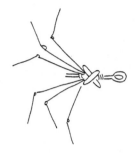

'Right,' I said, shaking a fist clenched round my frankfurter imitation, 'No more Mr Nice Guy'.

Rolling back my fingers, packaging the sedge pattern in the palm of my hand, I let the line whisk it away. Once behind my back, I shot it forward, squeezing the cork as if I was squeezing the trigger of a gun. The sedge hit the water with force, and my trout snapped out of its no-play coma and rose to the surface. A moment later with fear, with anger, with regret, with betrayal, the trout was buried in deepest weeds on one side of a dense bar of ranunculus. The side I wasn't on.

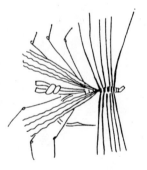

I went through all the normal, 'weeded-up' procedures. Walking above the fish and giving a yank, walking below the fish and giving a wrench, pointing the rod tip in the direction of the trout and giving the handle of the rod a healthy tap in the hope that if I couldn't haul the fish ashore physically, then I might be able to do it pyschologically, using sinister sound waves to freak him lose. I began to debate whether or not it was worth trying to wade in up to my waist to unravel the nautical knitting. It was the last half-hour on the last day of the season, what the heck. But I had a drier idea.

With no bridge between me and the hatch pool a hundred yards below, and not enough line or backing for me to walk down that far, I stripped all the line and backing off my reel and, detaching the line from my reel drum and letting it run free through the rod rings, I tied the end to a log and threw it at the trout. Not a flicker. It didn't budge an inch, but the log drifted downstream, as intended, taking my line with it. I followed after it.

With all the line between the trout and the log paid out, the log jolted to a halt and swung towards the bank at the bend on the opposite side of the river awaiting my collection. I kept on walking down to the Meadow Steam hatch, crossed over and walked back up to the log, whistling with confidence. Lifting it out of the water, I untied my line, fed it back down through the rings, knotted it to my reel drum and wound on the line as I walked back up towards the trout. I was singing aloud by now.

The trout wasn't expecting all this. Out of the weed it slipped into my waiting hand, onto the dew-covered bank, and straight into Lady McFarlane's deepfreeze, the door shutting softly on the season.

October

THE TROUT OUT OF HELL

'Imagine waking up in the morning knowing that's the best you're going to feel all day.' I think Dean Martin said this, explaining why he would never give up drinking - at least not altogether. And when it comes to flyfishing, that's the way I feel, too.

Some say flyfishing is a drug, and I wouldn't disagree. Every year at the end of the season, millions of flyfishers, like a million drug addicts, drop their habit and are expected to carry on living normal lives as if nothing had happened. What's a normal life when the fishing season finishes? Or perhaps the question is: How can you keep your habit going when you can't flyfish for trout any more?

Well, to start with, you can make sure you don't give your habit up - at least not altogether. Even if that means fiddling around with your tackle. Shifting it from your bag into a drawer, back into another bag, or a basket this time, and then back into yet another drawer, or another cupboard, in another room. If you're clever, you can keep this one going for months on end without boredom, or your wife phoning the doctor, but that's the tricky bit.

Then there's putting your silly, fly-festooned fishing hat on and looking at yourself in the mirror at regular intervals. Pulling it over the left side of your face is novel, the right side next, then the fun starts. Now you pull it right back so it sits on the back of your head like a drunken sailor, then forward so it sits over your eyebrows.

For the more practical and serious-minded, there's flytying. Or taking those unread fishing books from the shelf, sitting down and quietly reading them.

For me, thinking about days I've spent on the river is enough. But then I'm fortunate. Keeping in touch with the river doesn't take much. With or without a rod, I can still go down the track to the bridge, picking an autumn apple off the tree in my garden on the way for company, and walk around and stare at the fish I didn't manage to catch. For the first few weeks of October, at least, they're all usually still there in position - in the same position I left them on the last day. If not to fish for them, I can at least pay them a visit before they finally pack up and disappear into the thick autumn rain water, pair up and dissolve off to the redds, or get covered over by the blanket of leaves like children tucked up in bed for the night. It's hell and temptation, but it keeps me from crawling up the wall.

I have grayling fishing until the last day of December. I could go fishing for them the very first weekend after the trout season closes, but I don't. I like a gap before I go back down the track again, rod in hand. I welcome air between approaches. I go back sharper as a result. Anyway, October is not the best month for flyfishing for grayling. I leave it until the weeds have cleared and I can get level with the larger grayling lying deeper. But more importantly, I like to leave it until the first frost bites and the grayling get mean and hungry. I have a different relationship with grayling than I do with the trout and it takes a month to divorce myself from my main love affair.

As I say, I'm lucky. Kick-starting memories of the river to keep me sane is easy, for I never let them go. It doesn't take much to do this. I don't have to stretch my imagination, all I need do is to get up and stretch my legs. Rain, snow, sleet or sun; high water or low water, the river floods them back. Like a video on a loop, the river replays them for me. I visit a spot and a 'play' button is pushed, automatically. Every inch of river, every pool, every overhanging branch, every footbridge, every length of rotting camp-sheathing, every pebble, every scrape, holds a memory of one sort or other; good, and bad. Fragments of success, huge chunks of failure, I take these clips back with me up the track and re-examine them. Who knows? When the trout season reopens, turning them over in my mind just might make me a better angler. So at this time of year, when I set off down the track to the river, I set off down Memory Lane, pow-wowing with the cows as I go. Nothing changed there, either.

A mob of pheasants stood round-shouldered on a bale of hay in the field outside my kitchen window, black outlines against the bleached light of an early morning autumn sun. Released from the pens at the end of last month they had been scattered for miles around like refugees without food or clothing. Lanky, tail-less and tufty, snapped to attention by the first dewy chills of late September, only now were they starting to look like they'd found a tailor.

The Boss prowled past, logs replacing pigeons as back-seat passengers. Two pheasants on a gatepost by the side of the track barely looked up. The Boss could have put his hand out of the window and pulled them off the post like tickets from a machine at the entrance of a car park.

The summer finished suddenly. Nights lengthened. The tips

of the trees had been dipped in paint-pots of orange, red and yellow. On The Hollow, the beeches are the first to turn, then the ashes. The chestnuts follow soon after. Hawthorns, limes, sycamores, and crack-willows are next. Then, last of all, the oak. Like a house of cards, the woods collapse into the flames of autumn, ready to be charred black by winter.

On my walk, it's not just past fishing days that come to mind, it's memories of flyfishermen - and fisherwomen - I have shared the season with. And when I think back, I always feel the same way. The happiest flyfishers I know, the ones I like to fish with the most, are those who don't take their fishing too seriously.

I loathe the intense angler. The man who emerges from the bushes with clasped hands, a heaven-ward glance, and some tedious theory about the relation between barometric pressure and the emergence of *ephemerella ignita*. As a fisherman who lives by his river, I seem to be a magnet for this sort of person. They think I'm going to be like them, and they eat me alive. They think I pace the river bank in a studious pose, poised for the next trout-shattering discovery. In fact, I'm there to potter about, do a spot of fishing and generally enjoy myself. They waste no time (only mine) spilling their observations on why one hook is better than another, or the significance of the dark brown streak on the femur of *rhithrogena haarupi* in helping distinguish it from *ecdyonurus torrentis*.

Give me the angler who falls in the river, tells jokes passionately or, like the 94-year-old fisherman I met at Horse Bridge last summer, takes two hours to unravel his cast, spinning more yarns than he has knots.

Having led you so far through a trout-fishing season, I hope I haven't come across as an angler bent on ramming dry angling ideas down your throat. Or that I've lost sight of the fact that most of you, like me, fish for the pure fun of it. Catching trout and seeking to improve your catches is only a small part of that pleasure. With all this said, sometimes things that start off as light-hearted gags all of a sudden take on a serious complexion. It was only when I walked past the spot, in the white misty webs of October, that I realized that a party-piece I once performed to amuse my more eccentric fishing friends was a stunt that now has developed into a valid tactic against difficult trout in awkward positions. A tactic I call 'Fishing beyond your means'.

Most trout that manage to survive one season to the next do so by rendering themselves uncatchable. Few people would question that the trout most likely to survive in the stream are those that dwell in areas totally impenetrable to the angler's fly.

The trout that live in the centre of an overhanging tree that drags leafy boughs on all sides, for example. Or, more common and classic - and, at Sticklepath Bridge, the most infamous - is the trout that tucks himself deep inside the tunnel of a narrow-mouthed bridge. Although the combination of flyrod and fly-line is the most versatile and accurate method of presenting any bill of fare to any fish, it has its limitations in a cramped scenario.

The rod, even if short, needs room to whisk backwards and forwards. The process of casting demands relatively wide open spaces, even when roll-casting, Roll Cast style. It's these two factors that leave trout under bridges unmolested from one year to another, resulting in them becoming fat, deep, and highly desirable to every angler on the beat.

It was with a child-like curiosity (to begin with at least) that I set about attacking these trout, putting aside all convention and substituting a sort of cunning commonly recognised as unsporting within the starchy confines of chalkstream ethics.

Not immediately appreciated by most flyfishermen with two-piece rods is that they carry around with them, not just one rod, but two. The first consists of the two pieces put together. The second is a considerably shorter version. In fact, unless your rod is parabolic in design, exactly half the length: the top section. This top section, with very little extra skill, can be used to cast a fly relatively easily. Witness this for yourself on the lawn: with the reel at your feet and the line threaded up through the loops of the top section only.

That is the first trick in approaching trout in tight corners. The second step is modifying your cast so that you can cast a line within the confines of your sitting-room. In effect, developing a

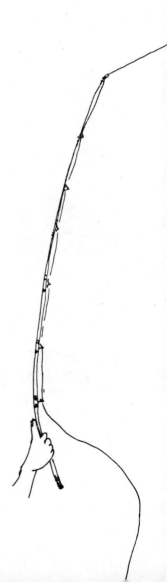

'non-cast', as I call it.

Most rivers, but sadly few sitting-rooms, have a downstream current. The mechanics of casting demand that during the back-cast, the weight of the line held mid-air behind you is counteracted by a forward push of your wrist which releases the line and shoots it forward like a spring.

From your position below the bridge, or in amongst the branches of the over-hanging trees, measure the distance between yourself and the trout by eye. Let this length of line float downstream from you on the current. When the push of water straightens your line, put into play the flick of the wrist you would normally use to propel the line forward, had it been behind you, in mid-air.

Throughout this operation, keep your rod low on the water and parallel to the surface. The tip of your rod should be pointing upstream after the follow-through, and no higher than the top part of the tunnel you're trying to get up into, or the branches you're trying to get under.

This casting technique won't win you any distance records. Largely because you don't have the facility, or room, to false cast. But it will keep your line no more than a few feet above water level and will whisk your fly up into that impossible position. Rarely will you need anything more than a five-yard cast to reach a trout tucked under a bridge.

The before and after of this tactic is just as important as the tactic itself. It must be well prepared and organised to avoid you becoming the central attraction of a six-foot grinner knot.

If you're in a wading position below the trout, and I find I usually am when addressing trout under bridges, pull off as much reel line as you think the trout will run off with if you were to hook him. You won't be able to pull line off again for a while, as you will discover. In my experience, trout under bridges are big and get super-angry when hoisted out of their cosy lies.

They do one of two things when hooked. They make a break downstream, see you at the back entrance and shoot back up where, shoulders down, they bear down with all the weight they can muster against you. Alternatively, they panic. Totally. Turning tail, they belt back out of the bridge into the water below you and, with the current behind them, they keep on going. Nine out of ten times this isn't the way they react. So don't pull too little line off the reel for tidiness' sake.

Very rarely do they take the upstream route and escape out of the front of the bridge. This is fortunate for you, but unfortunate for the trout for he'd break your line like a cobweb against the rough brickwork of the bridge. So, prepare yourself for a massive downstream rush.

Once you've piled the line in the water next to you, stuff the reel and bottom section in your boot, or wader, and pull the loose line through the rings of this bottom section so it flows directly out of the bottom ring of the top section. You're now all set to cast. If you approach the fish from the bank, lay the bottom section of your rod on the grass next to you and repeat the procedure above.

When the trout takes the fly, lift the top section high in the air. Holding the line tight in your left hand, pull this hand smartly down. This is your strike. With a three to four foot rod, it's hard to 'over strike' if you're to pick up the slack and pull the hook home. Once connected, keep the top section high above your head and start organising yourself so you can join the top part of your rod to the bottom section to be able to finish the play on a conventional two-piece rod.

Now all this sounds a bit tricky when you put it down in words. In practice, it's very straightforward, its success relying on very little more than common-sense. The hardest part is combatting the initial silliness of it all. It's hard to concentrate when you've got the giggles.

This summer I was fishing up on the Marshes with Roll Cast and the Academic. Nearest to the village, a tiny stream trickles down under the road runs for about two hundred yards along the bottom of the garden of a large, brick-faced Edwardian house, then stops dead above a hatch that feeds the Church Pool below. Even though you can wade this trickle in wellies, it is carpeted with wall-to-wall trout. Ravenous trout. A nymph only has to cough to start a feeding frenzy.

At the top of the stream there's a three-arched bridge with three deep tunnels. I waded up inside the middle tunnel to see what was inside. The water got dramatically deeper and licked the top of my waders. I'd hardly set foot inside when trout began pouring out behind me onto the inch-deep shallows below, with their backs out of the water and bellies squeaking on the gravels. In one panic-stricken lump, they swerved back upstream and shot into the tunnel on the far right.

The trout in this tunnel, terrified by the sudden influx of foreign trout, beat a hasty and equally nerve-ridden retreat, dashed out onto the shallows and, on seeing me, spun into the tunnel on the far left. The trout under this arch bolted out of the front of the bridge, did a sharp right and came flying back through the middle arch and landed back in the far arch. And so this game of musical tunnels continued until the shallows were whipped to the consistency of Jersey cream.

I came back later in the afternoon and made a more stealthy approach to a position behind the far right tunnel where the bigger fish seemed to live. Roll Cast and the Academic took up position on the bridge above me. The Academic was particularly excited being a past-master of the top section tactic. Roll Cast just wanted to watch me make a complete fool of myself. Well, that's what friends are for.

Since the channel was deep, I used a weighty Red Spot Shrimp to get instant depth. I have also found that a heavy fly is easier to lob up a narrow channel with a 'current flick', the mouth of the arch being barely five foot across and four foot high at its central point.

Stuffing the top section of my rod down my boot and organising my line, I let the shrimp trail in the current behind me while I got into my casting position - shoulder against the bricking, head poking up the tunnel. With one lunge, my shrimp shot up into the darkness, the rod ending up in a position where the tip was well under the arch. In the black of the tunnel, my leader sparkled on the surface like neon. It stopped and jabbed downwards.

I pulled everything up, smashing my rod tip on the roof of

the arch, but at the same time, connecting with a trout. As expected, all went slack. It was coming downstream at me.

I leapt into the middle of the mouth of the arch in the hope that, confronted with the sight of my knobbly knees, it would decide to remain inside, under cover. Instead, it shot between my legs to the delight of the Academic and Roll Cast above. Not one, but four huge trout thudded against my boots on exit. All four hurtling onto the shallows to escape. It was a good few seconds before I worked out exactly which one I was attached to.

If my trout had done what his companions proceeded to do, I would have pulled off the stunt. They bolted downstream, turning and spinning every ten yards for breath. This I could have coped with. However, my trout had other, more dramatic ideas. He decided to clear out of the stream altogether and began wriggling up the bank and out. While doing so, he hung my line up in a bush and it was broken within seconds. From my position he looked like a trout of two pounds. The Academic and Roll Cast, from their bird's eye vantage, disagreed. The trout was over three; and one of the other three was nearer four.

The next day I repeated the stunt. The exact same thing happened in the morning, and in the afternoon. In the evening, however, I hooked the biggie, but my line wrapped itself round the buckle of one of my chocolate-coloured waders as the trout made off downstream. I stopped that trout with such a jar, I thought the cracking noise was its neck breaking. But it was my line, snapped at the butt. All six pounds of it.

After this I spent a good deal of time perfecting my top section technique. Trout in other parts of The Hollow I'd never reached began to appear at my feet, white flags flying. At least, some of them.

———————

On the way up the track to the Boss's Cottage, you cross over a stream without knowing it. It's the end of the Meadow Stream where it curls round and disappears down a tunnel, slides under the track, burrows beneath the Nursery Stream and reappears out on the other side transformed from a gentle, crystal-clear meadow carrier into a mysterious dark woodland stream shadowed by silent alders.

What lives in this trout dungeon, those fifteen yards of deep subterranean grumblings, groanings and garglings, no-one knows. You can only peer up into it for the first foot or so before the light is snuffed out by brooding darkness. It leaves plenty to the imagination. Hang around the pool watching, as I did at the height of a hatch when every trout in the river was up open-mouthed at the surface, and you're wasting your time. Not a single slurp or secretive sip drifted out into the still air of the woods to reward my single-mindedness. But something had to be there. The tunnel had to hold trout, in the single, in the plural. In reality, or in the mind.

I spent many evenings sitting in the sweet, cool grass on the woodland side of the tunnel, gazing at the thin slit between the culvert and the gloomy waters swirling out into the pool, watching, waiting. This is the kind of communion with a stream and nature that gives fishing its enchantment. It's also the kind of madness that makes people talk about you behind your back. But it's these seemingly worthless hours that can, just once in a while, result in a fish that makes other anglers look foolish when you face them with the tale.

Accompanied by thoughts of the hugeness of the dividend if ever there should be a pay-out, I sat there often, quietly, alone, as the light faded, watching darkness fall and the water in the pool start to spiral in the wells of my eyes. In a trance, the closer I looked, the wider the black slit expanded, opening up to form a large cavernous void. Peeping down this rabbit hole and through the looking glass, the space seemed filled by the biggest trout of my dreams, finning silently up against the mossy brickwork, grey backed, with shoulders the width of a dog. Reaching for my rod, I blink and the entrance to the cave slams shut. It's then I realize that I had been under the spell of the trout that lived there, the trout that had become a sitting tenant in my brain; the trout from hell.

At the end of one long, sweaty August day, I found myself

back there resting in the cold grass amongst the alders. That afternoon I'd noticed that the weeds in the Meadow Stream which had been holding the flow back had been cut, dropping the water level by six inches. The slit had become a gap. Gap-enough for me to get a fly those critical, exploratory handful of inches up under and inside the dark hole.

On the other side of the alders, the last car door slammed shut at the Mad House. It crunched over Sticklepath Bridge, lights swooping round, lighting up the tops of the trees like a wartime air raid. The river fell silent.

Dusk plays strange games with the imagination. I sat trying to distinguish the different sounds of a departing day. Was that an owl hooting in the ancient woods behind me? Or was it a hellish howl from out of the tunnel behind the slit?

One thing was for certain. A trout living in that ghost-filled tunnel under the road could grow to mammoth proportions, certainly exceeding the size of any trout living in the sun-filled stream haunted by anglers. Perhaps even bigger than the image of the trout that had grown in my mind. Both pools, at the inlet and the outlet of the tunnel, held large communities of dace, roach and jaw-sized grayling, tailor-made to fill the waistline of the most savage monster from hell. I had no doubt of this. The only doubt I had was whether or not a fly would interest such a fearsome fish.

It was then that a hair-line circle ebbed out into the pool below. Something, underneath, had moved.

As if from Mars, I had picked up a remote, once-in-a-lifetime signal. There was life in hell after all. I dropped to my knees to pay homage to the brute that had finally decided to make contact and communicate after so many weeks of silence and expectation. And to thank him for giving me a 'sign'. But I also knelt to see if I could make out how far up the dank, dark, dripping tunnel the messenger lay hidden, for this could only be the trout of my darkest imaginations.

From the bank-side, I could see nothing. I had to cross the shallows below the pool and climb into the woods in order to get to the head of the far bank and into a position where I could stretch forward, twist my head to one side and peek, my ear at surface level. Cramped in this position in between two alders, I watched the faint arc of a second rise unfurl on the surface and waft out like a smell, followed by a bubble which burst, breaking the silence. My heart stopped dead.

Close behind, a cock-winged spinner trickled out from under the slit. It was a blue-winged olive spinner, blood-red and dying. My Dracula trout, cloaked in darkness, was up there silently sinking his fangs into any helpless spinner not lying crucifix-shaped on the surface. If I was to pull this trout out into the light, would it turn to dust in my hands? No - the light was fading fast.

I stepped back onto a ledge near where the pool drops away into its deepest corner. This was the only place to stand if I was to be able to get a fly up the tunnel.

Hanging limply from my sheepskin patch, I had a ten-ton sedge with a fat wool body. I pulled it off and, holding it to the sky, I tied it to the end of my line. I had decided that what I needed to cast up into the eternal night of the tunnel and onto the altar of the trout from hell wasn't an imitation of an insect. I needed a lamb.

Taking the top section of my rod from the ferrule, I stuck the reel and the bottom section in my boot and let the line swing loose behind me in the pool. Pulling the line forward, keeping the rod tip low, I let the sacrificial sedge slice through the bats now gathered over the pool and disappear through the Gates of Hell.

My first cast returned with the woolly sedge semi-submerged, cocooned in a net curtain of cobwebs. Once again, I pointed my rod top down stream. Guiding my line to the back of the pool, letting the current load it, I sprung my rod tip forward. The line shot up into the darkness like a rocket into a starless sky. An eerie echo, like a stone dropped into a deep well, was the only hint to suggest that the sacrifice had been accepted. I pulled tight, my rod lifting up into the warm night air, water showering onto my sweating face.

I may have been attached to the ghastly fish, I may have caught the moss that lined the inside of the tunnel - or some obstacle that was impossible for me to see. Whatever it was, it weighed heavy and lay motionless, as dead as night. I had it on for a good few seconds before the angle of the line rubbed against the concrete edge, frayed and snapped, dissolving my dreams into a fine mist of sinister spray.

It was a week before I got back down to the river again. The Boss was at the Mad House and I told him my tale. I don't meet many female flyfishers. For some reason there aren't that many. But the half-dozen I've come across have been some of the finest flyfishers I have ever known. One such lady fished The Hollow that season. She tied the prettiest, and tiniest flies. Even though her hands were bent and rougher than a crofter's. You noticed this the first time you met her, whether you shook her hand or not.

Apparently Claw-fingered Kitty had stopped by at the hell-hole that week. She was after a fish she'd seen drifting out from underneath the tunnel. It had taken up position close to the surface, head tucked under the slit. She'd slammed one of her small flies on the fish's shoulder. It turned and snapped at it, hooking itself momentarily in the gill.

'Did it have fangs?' I asked, wide-eyed and breathless.

'Fins?' the Boss replied. 'Of course it had fins.'

Immediately I knew that whatever size her trout had been, my trout was still in hell.

On slack afternoons, Claw-fingered Kitty and I would sit down and start talking. I learned a great deal from her little flies and the tricks she had developed to overcome severe arthritis in the joints of her fingers. She'd pick flies off the water, hold them up in front of my nose on the end of a pair of bent, twiglet-shaped pincers and I'd try and tell her what they were.

One morning Kitty and I were on an entomological expedition, camped out at Snowdrop Land above Red Gate Shallows. Kitty was cross-legged on the footbridge. I was by her side robbing the main highway of the river of its duns at stick point and holding them up in front of her for inspection. It all happened so suddenly; so quickly, Kitty didn't have time to cry out. Out of nowhere, a fox leapt onto one end of the bridge and in a cloud of musty smell was in and out of Kitty's lap, across the footbridge and half way across the field. Drop-jawed, we stared at the gap widening between us and the little red blob dipping in and out of the grass. In a low-pitched growl, I heard Kitty tell me 'Don't move.' Putting a hand on my shoulder, shotgun in hand, she hurdled across the bridge after the fox.

But it wasn't Kitty. She was still motionless beside me, watching the gamekeeper jump off the end of the footbridge and disappear into the space that the fox had filled moments before. He had appeared out of even thinner air than the fox.

It was five minutes before the whole event began to register. Two short bangs, followed by a third, more distant, thump a minute later, confirmed that the whole episode had been a reality.

Soon after, I decided that when the season was over, a good fireside job would be to get all my notes together and work out a simple stream-side guide to identifying upwing flies, dedicated to Kitty. You'll find these 'Vital Statistics Charts' at the back of this book.

From the very beginning I decided that identifying upwing flies was going to be fun. You might need to do a little work. But not too much, if you did it my way. I had no intention of dragging a mini space-lab with me down to the river, even though it was only a couple of hundred yards from the house. Bare essentials only, and this went for recognition equipment, too.

I took a cap, to catch my fly on take-off, or in mid-flight. Secondly, the smallest of Swiss Army knives - the manicure model. The tweezers I used to hold my fly by the head, the toothpick to part the wings and inspect them. This I hung round my neck on a leather bootlace. Next, I took along with me a low-powered magnifying glass. Mine is match-box size, and folds into a leather sleeve. Lastly, an empty film canister in case I needed to take a specimen home to check, double check, and check again. But first, catch your fly.

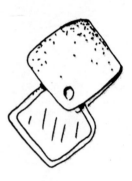

When you've done that, what's the procedure to tell you what member of the upwing family you have cowering in the palm of your hand? Where do you begin?

You start at the bottom. You pull my Vital Statistic Charts from out of your back pocket. You ask the fly: *how many tails do you have?* Answer: two, or three, as indicated in the first box. (If it's got one, you've caught a water rat in your net and you have a lot to learn.)

Next, the wing. In Box No.2, you'll find a forewing. All upwing flies have a pair of these. (Water rats don't. If you haven't already done so, throw it back.) Look more closely and you'll see that some have small parallel veins on the trailing edge of the forewing. In-between these veins are either one, or two shorter veins. These are an important identification feature, and they're circled.

Now look at your fly and ask: *how many wings do you have?* The answer will be two, or four. If the answer is four, these smaller wings are called hindwings and you'll find them in the next box. Now ask your fly: *what shape of hindwing do you have?* They will be either oval-shaped, or standing upright - with or without a little bump on the trailing edge. Alternatively, it will have a tiny spur-shaped wing that lies parallel to the body.

Flies with oval-shaped hindwings have two short veins on the edge of the forewing. Flies with spur-wings have one.

Next, size. You'll find this in the next box along. *Is your fly large, medium, small - or tiny?* You might think this was the first question to ask. But size can only be used as a general indicator. Size is relative, but relative to what? Much better to put your faith in practical features that are indisputable.

There's an emergence chart in Box No.6. This will put you right if you think you've found a mayfly in September. The last box gives you an idea of the shape of the nymph - what your fly looked like in a previous life.

One final, unboxed thing: *is your fly a boy or a girl?*

Female spinners pounce on a swarm of male spinners from above. To keep an ever-watchful eye out for them, the eyes of a male upwing fly, dun or spinner, pop out of the top of his head. The female's eyes are lost in the general make-up of the face and are not so prominent.

If you need a second opinion, the male has a small pair of claspers underneath its body, behind - and underneath - the tail. Males are generally smaller than the female of the same species.

Not all the upwing flies that you find on the river are mentioned in my Vital Statistics Charts. There's a reason for this. At the end of the last century, at the same time as Frederic Halford was checking through the proofs of the first edition of *Floating Flies*, a book of an entirely different nature was being published. It wasn't a fishing book. It was a cookery book, called *Why Not Eat Insects?* And why not?

Why not indeed. Whereas beef contains 17% protein, dried grasshoppers contain 50%. Termites even more. The fact is, humans do eat insects. Not here in Britain, perhaps, but in others countries, ants, locusts and a whole menu of other creepy-crawly fish food make up a nation's staple diet. But it isn't just

Europeans who find it hard to stomach the thought of eating curried cockchafers, bluebottle bake or centipede stroganoff - trout have their limits, too. In my observations, there are some insects that chalkstream trout stay well clear of, and therefore the flyfisher would be wasting his efforts trying to imitate them. I know an angler who did a great deal of research into this particular theme.

Is it a bird? Is it a plane? No it's the Plastic Surgeon - the mad flapping and buzzing noises in the air give him away. The unmistakeable sound of rustling newspapers and of brown wrapping paper being screwed up heralds the approach of this eminent surgeon in his olive-brown plastic mac. Billowing through the side-sedge and puffing out to touch the surrounding countryside, his mac suggests only one thing: imminent disaster.

When he doesn't wear his mac - during heat-waves, for example - he wraps it round his waist just in case it rains. When he does this, and when you can't hear him coming at you up the bank through a July heat haze, you can smell him. It's the sweet-smelling fumes of workmen tarmacing a road.

Now the Plastic Surgeon is one of those very precise sort of people who don't believe anything unless he's got evidence. So when I suggested one day that an imitation of the yellow may dun - which he thought was a mayfly - wouldn't catch him any fish because I'd never seen a trout eat one, I knew I'd said the wrong thing. Within seconds, he'd lifted one off the water and, pulling the wings off his specimen he popped it in his mouth. Tossing it around his tongue and squelching it on the roof of his mouth as if he was tasting a fine chardonnay, he spat it out and announced, 'You're right. It tastes of lemons!', and walked away.

Of course, he was absolutely right - which is why he is so eminent. And I can continue to state that I've yet to see a trout take a yellow may dun, even though hatches have at times been temptingly heavy.

While we're about it, I'd add the alder fly to that list of uneatables. And the super-seductive silverhorn sedges that hover so teasingly in spiralling clouds in shady corners of our summer streams never once hitting the surface to transform themselves

into trout-fodder. Not even to crash land.

One, two, three flies you need no longer have heart-attacks worrying about. At a stroke!

November

GHOST STORIES

All summer long, everyone up and down the river talked about 'white patches'. All this sounded like property-surveyor speak to me, but it wasn't. It was fishing talk. So what was everyone getting so excited about? What were these 'white patches' that stopped so many fishermen in their tracks and had them stooping and staring, singling out small areas of the stream and pointing with knowledgeable fingers across the river at them as if the meaning of life lay out there somewhere? I soon found out.

These mysterious marks in the river were plate-sized craters where silt had been wiped away to reveal pristine, polished gravels underneath - and often, a resident trout sitting on top. They helped passing anglers get a fix and locate trout.

This was all very well, but talk went on, and questions were asked - by me. Was it really the action of trouts' tails fanning the river bed that accounted for these give-away signs as everyone would have me believe? Here I wasn't a believer. Not even if you had brought me a basket of trout with half the underside of their tails worn away to prove the point. The question I asked was: which came first - the patch, or the trout? The chicken or the egg? I examined the egg first.

November was creeping up the river with an acid breath. The ginger and lemon side-sedge had finally collapsed, and on my way past the Firs, the birch branches tossed a handful of guineas at me, the last of their coin-shaped leaves. Egg-laying trout were starting to take up position in the Nursery Stream. The hens were getting ready to lay their pink-eyed eggs in the super-fine gravel where soon they would be covered by the white milt from one of the cocks swaying impatiently behind them. It will be January when the first of these eggs begins to hatch into something in the nests - the white patches scraped out by their mothers two months earlier.

When it comes to solving the white patch mystery, in autumn the trout comes first. It's the physical presence and mechanical action of the hen trout's tail that creates the white patch. But in the spring and summer months, the patch precedes. Let me tell you why, and close this chapter of mystery and uncertainty before we sink into winter.

I don't deny that during the season a large majority of the trout in the river have damaged tails, but they had this complaint when they were first introduced as stock fish. Rarely do I see wild trout with tail wear, even those I have caught by accident when out after grayling in the last days of the year. And surely, having been in the stream longer than stock fish, they should have all but rubbed their backsides out by the time they reach the size at which I caught them?

Heaping branches onto the Guy Fawkes bonfire, now almost the size of the wood shed in the clearing next to the Boss's cottage, I watched the first pairs of spawning trout getting to work in the Nursery Stream below the stews. Very quickly I could see why redd-scouring can seriously damage the health of a fin or two - and cock fish gnaw at one another in the wild as they do in stew ponds, I'm sure.

But trout lying on the river bed are hardly likely to allow themselves to be slowly mutilated in such a fashion. If I'm wrong, then why don't grayling, who spend considerably more time bottom-hugging, ever have tail wear? And what about barbel? And gudgeon? So, if not dug out by trout or any other home-making fish, where do these so-called 'white patches' come from? Who makes them? What is their meaning?

Underneath the surface of the stream is like a huge, silent pinball machine. Currents, not detectable on the surface, bounce off one another at different speeds and are channelled into tight areas. A trout, maximizing his feeding efficiency, will seek out points where currents meet and where food in the general flow is funnelled into a narrow space. Naturally these places are subjected to an increased flow compared to the area surrounding them. It's this push that sweeps the gravels and continually scours the bottom, twenty-four hours a day, seven days a week, until conditions - water levels or an obstacle - arrive to change the direction of the flow.

I see this happen on my daily riverside walks. Indeed, I've made it happen. I've watched trout follow these channels around. I've even pulled one out of its secure little lie under a bush so I could reach it with a fly by altering the underwater flow upstream with a log. This created a white patch that eventually induced the trout to come out and lie on it.

Observe for yourself. See if it's not true. Either a stone, a weed-bed, or an obstacle in the river will cause the current to form these ash trays. Not the tail of a trout.

But right now, the trout excavators were out on the shallows. Grooves were being carved, redds dug. In deeper water, bottom-huggers with perfect tails were hungrily haunting the well-defined polished food lanes like shadowy grey ghosts. Ghosts with purple wings.

———

Overnight, up on the Marshes, a hard frost had sunk its iron teeth deep into the heart of the Church Pool hatch at the head of Cemetery where the big grayling had tucked themselves away for winter. I sat in my study in a pool of warm morning sunlight, as though I was in the centre of a struck match, looking out across the white fields waiting for temperatures to rise above freezing at midday. In November, this is the time to go ghost-busting.

I thought back to colder grayling times. One winter in particular came back into my mind.

Whatever the season, whatever the weather, I normally put aside an hour to walk by the river. That winter day, I skated on it. England was somewhere under snow. Fingers of ice on the edges of the smaller side streams had spread out, meeting with a frozen handshake in the middle. The newspaper headlines that morning read: ARCTIC CONDITIONS FOR BRITAIN, with rumours of treacherous roads in high and remote areas. Thick with cold and a brain like a sack of cement, I set off over the hills to Amesbury in a darkening late afternoon sky. I couldn't cancel. At long last I was off to meet the voice at the end of many a phone call.

It had been a clear night. Apart from a fifty-yard stretch of solid ice-blocks made by tractors compressing snow at a farm turning, I had arrived safely; my heart, finally out of my mouth, tucked back in behind my ribs.

The man behind the 'voice' turned out to be taller than I had imagined, his hair longer than in photographs, and whiter. He was seventy-one but his eyes gleamed like a young man's. A green tweed suit concealed a slight stoop, the result of gazing into a river over his Pezon Michel and swinging a scythe. He spoke clearly and steadily, a soft Wiltshire accent adding a breathy buzz to certain words. I talked about pheasant tail nymphs, he talked about pheasant tail 'niffz'. As the man who devised the pattern, this detail stuck. That evening, fins bristling, Mrs Sawyer hung on her husband Frank's every word. We were discussing which female olive spinners crawl underwater to lay their eggs. I stretched forward to give him my Sunk Spinner pattern, a lightly weighted pattern I originated to imitate these deep-stream divers, but Mrs Sawyer got there first. Intercepting

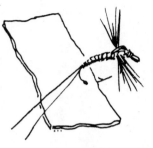

my gift, she pinned it to a piece of card, and swung back to her lie.

'Why not fish weighted mayfly nymph patterns on chalkstreams? Damsel nymphs? Alder larvae grubs?' I asked the man who had taken nymphs to places Skues had dared not go. Or, at least, wasn't permitted to.

'If a man gets pleasure from fishing a mayfly nymph on a chalkstream, good luck to him,' Sawyer replied. 'But if he's doing it to give me pleasure, I'd prefer him not to.'

'If you could live your life over again, would you do the same thing?' I asked.

'I've always said I may not have been wealthy. But never once have I not been wealthy - in my mind. I have spent my time doing something that has interested me every day, every month of my life.'

And what about grayling? He told me that one year he'd netted out twenty six thousand grayling from his six-mile stretch of the River Avon. Had his attitude changed?

'Yes,' he replied emphatically, reflecting a reformed view. He told me he'd stopped fishing for trout. If he took a rod out now, it was grayling he was after. 'They're more sporting than stocked trout.' But in truth, he was happier taking a gun out into the woods, rather than a rod onto the stream.

I'm no river keeper, but I know most of the other Bosses up and down the valley - and they sort of know me, and in a neighbourly sort of way, they trust me. As a result of this, if I ask, they let me onto their beats once or twice at the back-end of the season to help keep their grayling in check. They know I won't sneak an off-season trout into my bag. It would be like being asked to their house and nicking a cup of sugar. And they know if I catch a trout by mistake, I only borrow it for a very short time. I use barbless hooks, exclusively, all year round. And they know I have 'The System': a rubber thumb grip and a pair of blunt-nosed, groove-free pliers. I can get a trout out of a pickle faster than he got himself into it - without him having to leave the water, and without getting my fingers wet on a cold November morning.

With the trout season well and truly finished and the weed beds withered away, I set off up the valley to the grayling shallows with a jug of my teeth-staining tea and a job to do, and I get down and do it. For a morning, I'm a hired gun, a professional. I have a specific brief, targets to reach, a deadline, and a quota. For this reason, I developed a method to reach these targets. An empty basket would mean I wouldn't get asked back again. It's not really in my interest to give away trade secrets - but then what can I lose? If Frank Sawyer had kept his Killer Bug to himself he wouldn't have had anybody helping him thin out the number of grayling on his river. His job would have been harder and that twinkle in his eye would have dulled.

On some trout streams, netting, or stunning, must be used. That's as may be. But I don't like the concept of mass slaughter, or relocation, on any stream - to any fish, to any animal. But *judicious* culling, carried out by rod and line, on a stretch of river that is clearly over-crowded, is beneficial to spawning trout. It also increases the graylings' chances of survival. I've fished too many heavily-populated grayling rivers not to note that a few dozen grayling taken on rod and line is no threat to the survival of strongly established shoals.

I tell you this, for I'm not a killer of grayling, of trout - of anything. In particular, not of wild fish born in the stream. We haven't inherited them from our grandparents, we're borrowing them from our grandchildren. I quote this often, for I don't want to lose the initial chill of its cold logic that shivered down my spine when I heard it for the first time. So, unless I'm sent on a mission to the killing-fields up river, I do what comes naturally: I return them. Come with me now this frosty morning, north - to Alaska.

Iliaska Lodge is an hour's fight west of Anchorage in the Iliamna drainage area. In July on the Newhalen, the Copper, the Upper Copper and the Upper Upper Copper, you fish small dry flies. A Caddox, for example. Rainbows herniate to ensure their taste-buds make contact with this chugging feast. This is truly 'big fish' fishing with small flies.

But go there at the end of August, and the style changes so

dramatically you think you've gone to the wrong place. In fact, you have. For as soon as you arrive, they fly you somewhere else. The Moraine, the No-name, the Upper and Lower Talarik. Here you're fishing for salmon-egg-hungry rainbows of up to twelve pounds that have followed the huge shoals of sockeye up out of Lake Iliamna on their journey from the sea to the age-old river spawning beds. Four million sockeyes enter the drainage system between the middle of June and the second week of July. That's a million salmon a week. The largest run of salmon in the world. To get to these rainbows, you cast over the backs of the sockeyes - many of them undergoing serious head-butting sessions from rainbows trying to get eggs to spill out onto the gravels.

Fishing an egg-pattern called a Glo-Bug is one of the most highly specialised and demanding sorts of wet fly nymph-fishing you can do. For the gravels are red, orange and pink with spawned eggs and you have to get your pattern right to a marauding rainbow's mouth, just as it is opening. Landing it on its nose isn't good enough. You have a one in a million chance. This requires Apollo Spaceship accuracy if your egg is going to touch down in the crater of a rainbow's maw.

1 part

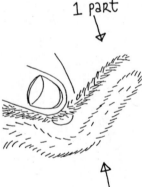

5 parts

Now this behaviour isn't exclusive to Alaskan rainbows. At the end of May, at the bottom end of the Back of Beyond (which I lie in bed thinking about in January, counting the female pike swimming under the Old Iron Bridge to get to sleep) low water conditions bring the spawning coarse fish high up river. Roach, dace, chub and bream. A barbel has been spotted, and a carp. I was watching the bream when I saw something I hadn't seen since my last trip to Alaska: two trout hungrily circling the egg-laying bream. Up river at the Doctor's Cottage, I lent over the rickety footbridge at the end of a ford watching the water pound

Pull down hard!

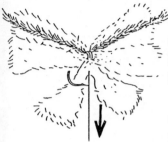

down the Red Gate Shallows. Thrashing on the surface in between the weed-beds was a shoal of roach and dace, and more bream. Each shoal had a trout mopping-up round the edges.

This restaurant closes down for summer holidays at the end of May, beginning of June. But it opens again at the end of the year. This time it's the trout's turn to have their friends round for dinner. Trout eggs are on the menu. And one of the first uninvited guests round for hors d'oeuvres is the forever-curious 'lady of the stream', the grayling. And I'm right there too.

Straight away I must tell you that my approach to fishing egg-patterns on British streams is entirely different to rivers in Alaska. For a start, I don't fish the redds - not even if there are grayling grouped amongst them. I keep well clear. My job is to preserve the trout population, not harass it.

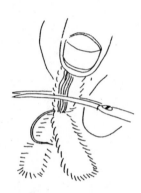

Grayling on the shallows seem to take my Glo-Bug pattern instinctively, even though they may be several hundred yards from the nearest spawning trout and never have had the chance to roll a soft-boiled trout egg round their pallets. What's the attraction?

Through the ages, flyfishermen have claimed that the grayling is partial to brightly coloured flies. Here's another theory I don't support, but neither do I reject it. I just note that nearly all the renowned Yorkshire patterns have a bright red or orange tag fizzing at the rear like a lit firework. And this feature isn't restricted to patterns associated with the rain-fed Northern grayling rivers, either. A much respected, indeed revered, local fly is the Terry's Terror. This was devised by an angler called Cecil Terry about the time I was knee-high to a pair of waders. Today, it's still getting its feet wet.

———

Sheltered from everything the November Downs could throw at you by a mattress of alder and hawthorn, there isn't a more pleasant place to tune into the rhythm of the twists and rises of a grayling than back on my home beat, on the broad shallows at Snowdrop Land, directly opposite the Doctor's Cottage.

Tucked under an alder, a small shaky bench provides a Royal

Box view. Here you can sit, eat your sandwiches, drink your sloe gin, sup your evil tea and glow. Then, sticking your hands down the tops of your waders out of the cold, you can watch the surface break open through a cloud of warm, steamy, bedroom breath. It's best to spend time doing this, before uncorking your fly. For much more important than taking your pattern from the rings and casting it out, is a careful consideration of the precision demanded of your presentation. If, that is, you are to address one of the thin bubbly rings on the surface correctly, and understand its relation to the grayling's position on the gravels below. This is essential to its downfall, for a grayling does not rise directly upwards and take a surface fly ahead of this position. She will always drift down and lift up to a fly passing over her. And this position will always be one directly behind her. If your fly isn't perched on this imaginary tight-rope that she has marked our above her she will not move an inch either side to make an interception and suck it off the surface.

More than pattern failure, not being able to place your fly on this line is why ninety percent of the time grayling don't rise to your fly. Accurate presentation is that crucial. But if, perchance, you do seduce a grayling up to the surface, an artificial moving independently from surface currents is the most common reason why grayling miss.

Because matching the drift of the hatch is infinitely more important than matching the imitation, the bench mark of success in surface grayling fishing isn't fly pattern, but fly position.

Grayling may be fussy about the position of the fly on the surface in relation to their position on the river bed, but fortunately - unlike trout - grayling rise as if on tracks, with great consistently and regularity.

Earlier in the month, when there had been spasmodic hatches of lunch-time winter olives blowing off, to address a rising grayling on the far bank opposite Snowdrop Land, I climbed off the bench and slid into the water below the last fish at the tail of the shoal. If I knew exactly where this grayling was lying on the gravels, I marked her position alongside a piece of sedge, an overhanging branch, or a tuffet and cast my fly three feet above this spot.

If, however, all I had to work on was a rise, my approach differed slightly. Taking into consideration that a grayling intercepts a fly on the surface three feet below her position on the gravel, I chucked my fly three feet above this rise, six feet in total above it. For this reason my leader is always two or three feet longer than my normal dry fly leader - a length of fourteen foot. This extra length is usually tippet material only.

If the grayling were on the surface in the faster flow in the centre of the stream, I would cast down and across, at a forty-five degree angle, making sure that my downstream dry fly arrived at the grayling dead-drift. Unlike trout, grayling will not accept Len Wright's induced 'sudden inch' tactic, or a fly skating on tip-toes. Before she leaves the river bed, a grayling is careful to make sure that her prey is firmly fixed to the surface film. On arrival at the surface, she doesn't want to find that her fly has flown. From my position above the grayling, I raise my rod tip before the fly lands, and lower it to release the slack I need and to ensure a long drift.

teal
hackle
tips

If not a dry fly, I use a small, lightly-weighted nymph on rising grayling if I am wanting to avoid problems of drag and line exposure. This way I let the current and the grayling catch it on the swing. A grayling normally registers acceptance of the nymph with a classic wet fly bang on the rod tip and an accompanying surge beneath the surface.

When dry fly fishing during a hatch, the 'tease cast' is my favourite stunt to trick surface-rising grayling - using my favourite grayling dry fly: the Funnelmozie. This 'now-you-see-it-now-you-don't' tactic involves a degree of psychology, for you play mind-games with the poor unsuspecting grayling you've set your sights on.

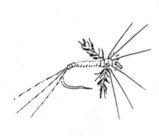

Once a grayling has been selected, rather than casting directly at her with the aim of her grabbing it, you wait until her attention is grabbed by a natural. When this happens, you aerialise your line, keeping it airborne with false casts and the correct amount of line curled up in your hand ready to shoot the fly on command. The minute the grayling begins to move downstream after the natural drifting over her, you place your fly three foot above her starting position on the gravels while her mind is preoccupied. When she returns to her position, she arrives just in time to catch a glimpse of your fly a fraction of a second before it passes over her, having been oblivious to your presentation. This gives her no time to question the pattern or any other discrepancies in the drift so far. The grayling isn't taken on your fly, she's taken in by your deceit.

This isn't a tactic for difficult grayling, for me it's a strategy for all surface-feeding grayling and, occasionally, for metronome-feeding trout. But it depends on a thorough understanding of the rhythm of the grayling rise - when it rises, how it rises - and where it takes a fly in relation to its launching pad.

When the widening circles of surface activity are over and the river has become blank; when it comes to addressing grayling in a clear run of shallow, weed-free river like the flat, black water opposite the Doctor's Cottage, serving up an egg is my preferred method of attack.

The peak of the grayling season is September through to December, with November the pinnacle month. By then regular hatches of fly have ceased, and I bring out my nymphs. Far from being choked by toxic fumes of acid steaming off dead leaves smouldering on their dining-room floor, grayling feed harder now. But their feeding times are more regimented. They're concentrated into shorter periods - or rather one single period: lunch-time. If you can't cram your lunch in a flask, get stuck into a big breakfast.

The November grayling-gorge isn't guaranteed. Firstly, it's dependent on water levels. In particular, on the amount of rain that falls in October. I was reminded of this as I sat in my study biding my time until midday and looking out over the frosty noses of winter wheat poking through the ashen fields. Heavy rain and ploughing in our valley don't mix. Often, if there have been weeks of rain preventing drilling, as soon as it stops, ploughing begins. This can shake up a cocktail with a lethal tinge, fouling the water. This, perhaps more than anything, affects the grayling and the grayling nymph-fisher, for the river rarely recovers until

the Spring.

But that Saturday, the river was clear. I had spent the morning at the top of a ladder placing the last few branches on the bonfire, now the size of the Boss's cottage, and still growing. At midday, with a streak of orange sun in the sky, I set off down to Snowdrop Land. Sun, or sun-flashes, are essential if you're going to spot the large shoals that tend to accumulate at this time of year, and then to fish with the necessary accuracy for shallow, cross-stream nymphing techniques with the living egg, and lastly to strike swiftly and sharply in order to penetrate the rubbery grayling lip.

Under the far bank, across from the Doctor's Cottage, a grayling rose. A thin circle ebbed out wearing a bubble on its bald head telling me it wasn't a trout.

On this short stretch, the current flows thick and even, down and across, like a velvet curtain stretching from my side of the river to the other. Here in two or three feet of water, the grayling lay huddled together, soundlessly, beneath the protective arms of four elm trees. Long dead, but not yet buried - leafless every season, summer and winter - these old soldiers provide a consistent and comforting sense of safety in the shape of an impenetrable mesh of brittle twigs and branches which they cast over the shoal. For a grayling holding ground there, it's as good as being tucked away in the darkest corner of the deepest pool.

Midway across the flat, the dark green curtain parted to reveal a thin backbone of pebbles and gravels carved into the river bed. It was hard to detect, but an invisible and complex flow-force stemming from one or other of the footbridge posts above, directed an influential underwater current down this lane with single-minded determination. And with it, this conveyor belt carried a wide selection of objects of desire to tempt out a grayling nursing a rumbling belly from under the elms. Looking across the river through the gap in the curtain, I watched a procession of ghosts busily flitting backwards and forwards across this high street paved with gravels.

The most important tools in grayling fishing aren't rods, reels, lines, tippets - even flies. They're eyes. Your ability to see, and also to notice. 'Yes, I can see the grayling. No, I didn't notice it had seen me.'

Grayling have subtle ways of telling you that they know you're there. By and large, if a grayling sees you arrive on the scene with a crawl in your step, she may not bolt away. She will shift slowly into reverse and back off gently downstream, inches at a time. In fact, she's telling you that, for the moment at least, you've been well and truly rumbled. The flash of a highly varnished rod, a dragging leader or an unpaletable pattern is enough to have her gliding down the gravels, in reverse.

This doesn't automatically mean you've lost your chance. Grayling are much more than a strategically positioned trout waiting inches from the surface to give its next prey the closest of inspections. A grayling shoots up from great distances to grab what she thinks may be edible. She has little time for inspection parades. The decision is made in advance from her lowly position on the river bed. Split-second calculations - judging the distance from target, speed of surface flow (faster than in the bottom inches), angle of interception - all of this often leads to understandable miscalculations. And then there's the lip factor.

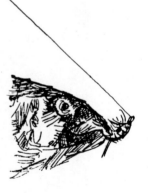

The top lip of a grayling protrudes over the bottom. Not the best design for trapping food that can't be rootled off the bottom, or sucked off stones. With all these physical, mathematical and aeronautical calculations whizzing round the brain cells of our poor river ghost, it's not surprising that a minor disturbance in the shape of the arrival of an angler on the bank nearby, is not considered a long-term threat. To begin with at least.

Grayling have short memories, they're quick to forgive and forget. Unlike a trout, it's unlikely that a grayling will move back to her original lie (which *is* an indication that a trout may be back on the feed). But that doesn't mean she won't feed again for a long while. I've often taken a grayling on my second attempt, a short time after she's backed off. Second time round, however, she'll quickly tell you if she's going to fall for the same trick twice or not. She'll turn on the current, mainsail and spinnaker hoisted, and she'll be off with the wind and your hopes behind her. If a grayling starts moving backwards, back off.

Across the channel where I've fished for grayling on La Loue in the Jura, arguably the best grayling river in France, they call grayling *ombres* - shadows. This is a more descriptive name than ours. Although 'grey thing', which was presumably the original thinking behind the name, is not unapt. On their own, grayling are hard to spot. To find them on the shallows the French don't look for fish, they look for shadows, mobile shadows. I look for ghosts; same thing.

A grayling, whether on the feed or not, will patrol her area more regularly than a trout in a carefully chosen and cherished lie. In a shoal, grayling are constantly playing musical chairs. If one of them makes a fast move, the music starts and they move around in unison. The panic over, the music stops, and they all stand still. My advice is to look for the large shadow of a shoal. Or, in reflected light, look for an ever-increasing circle on the surface, often with a bubble in the centre sitting like a cherry on a cake. It was this that alerted me to the shoal I was about to address early that November afternoon.

From a position well behind the last grayling in the shoal, below the elms of the far bank, I tied the egg onto a light-gauge point. Two pounds; for two reasons. Heavier line results in more rejections, and should a trout swing in suddenly and intercept, it breaks free with no problems, rubbing my barbless hook free. He's got a better chance of survival this way. Perhaps better than having to fight it out with me before I can slip the hook.

About four inches from the egg, I pinch on a tiny split shot. A size that makes casting easy. If it swings round your head when you cast, it's too heavy and a bit too dangerous. In Alaska they sell the perfect product, called 'Water Gremlins'. This is shot you can pinch on, and off. They have little wings. Squeeze them and the shot drops off and can be re-used. Essential when you are working a stretch at a variety of critical depths.

I mark out the shoal of grayling, and position myself on a spot directly across from them. I get as close as possible without trampling on their fins and cast a short upstream line - just enough to allow the egg to sink onto the gravels. When my egg reaches the bottom, I lift my rod tip high in the air to shorten my line so that I am in total contact with the shot and can feel it tap-tap-tapping over the gravels. You should be tuned in to every bounce. Meanwhile, I'm also watching the tip of my reel line for movement, or the end of my hollow, tangerine-coloured, floating Shockgum section, four inches down from the leader butt. I like the end of either to hang just above the surface. A 12-14 foot leader allows me to do this.

The method is both tactile and visual, which is why it is so deadly. A grayling just has to blow a kiss at the egg and it's registered. When I first started with this method, I added a tiny line indicator to the leader. Half, or even a quarter of a sticky-backed Day-Glo take-indicator is recommended. If you can be bothered, do what Roll Cast introduced me to. He takes a half inch of floating line, bores a hole through the core with a dubbing needle and threads it onto a section of his leader.

The largest grayling in a shoal takes neither the advance nor rear position. She plonks herself wherever she decides. Smaller grayling surround her like body-guards, with food-tasters up front intercepting in-coming meals. That afternoon, I had singled out my target from amongst the clan swinging in and out of position under the elms. The smaller grayling were the biggest problem when it came to tempting her - or rather him. For he was a hefty, charred male, smouldering black, crimson and purple. The other problem was knowing that the egg had been taken by a member of the lunch party - and was not snagged on the bottom.

I was using a medium-weight Gremlin, categorised #BB on the polythene pack. In a gentle current, in three foot of water, this rig plunged my egg straight into the main artery of the lower level flow. This allowed me to fondle every inch of the river-bottom with enormous sensitivity as, tapping away like Fred Astaire, my egg swung through the shoal immediately opposite me.

Keeping the rod tip high, I stood mesmerised, watching the Shockgum strip sway backwards and forwards like a pendulum in front of me just above the surface, my egg on the gravels below. Every second cast, the tangerine tip was yanked down to six

o'clock. Simultaneously, my left hand pulled the line it was
holding down in the same direction, coinciding with the action of
my right hand which shot the rod tip up to twelve o'clock. But
there was no resistance. No fish, no twig, no tin can, no bicycle
wheel, no brass bed at the end of the line to let me know what
had interrupted my egg's progress. Even when I moved a couple
of paces higher up to a position where the reflected light was
eliminated and where I could watch the back end of the shoal
reach out and react to my little shot-eyed pinkie, it was
impossible to tell whether one of the grayling that had swooped
into the path of the egg had taken it in her mouth, or had just
rolled it round her eye with great caution.

With this style of short range, down-and-across egg fishing,
it's advisable to concentrate your full attention on either a
grayling you can see, or the tangerine tip - never both at the
same time. Otherwise you go cross-eyed, and the grayling slip the
strike. I have always found watching the line tip, rather than the
grayling, more reliable.

With trout I play it the other way round. But then you can
see a trout's mouth open and close, a shoulder turn - the whole
procedure is in slo-mo. With a grayling, it's a blink. The take is
impetuous. It's all over in an instant.

The grayling's low-level egg-assault mirrors the lightning
reaction and the procedures she goes through to mug a surface
fly. The decision to attack needs to be immediate if she is to drift
back and up to the surface from a deep-down position to snatch
her prey in time.

Once again, the mouth is at the heart of the problem. In the
shallowest of waters, with an uninterrupted sideways view of the
take, the grayling's mouth, like a hidden trap-door under her
chin, conceals any movement and evidence of it ever having
opened and closed again. In conclusion, you may *think* you've
seen a grayling take your egg as you watch them both swing
across the gravels, but it's only when you invest your
concentration on the tip and see it dip that you *know* she has. Or
you've caught the bottom.

I may not have taken any of the sub-elm grayling as yet, but

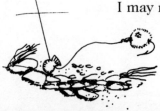

the egg bouncing through the shoal had caused great interest and excitement. The shoal had started Scottish country dancing. Even the big old sour-puss I was after, lying there like a brick, was starting to lift instinctively in time with the other grayling as the egg was checked-out on its way down to him over the pebbles. Eventually, the tangerine tip dipped. I struck and swung a small grayling to my ankles. Running my blunt-nosed pliers down the line, I slipped the egg off the point of her silver nose and led her out of the watercress that lined the bank where I had taken up position. It's not often you find the fly inside a hooked grayling's mouth. More often than not it's on the snout, or hanging from the side of her mouth, the side nearest your bank.

Unconcerned, the big grayling was now going through the motions of every grayling that tipped up to take the occasional nymph or shrimp, like a football coach playing out every move made by members of his team on the field. It had to happen - and eventually it did. Through the crack of reflected light, I watched. With a spectacular rush, the large grayling shot forward. Sweeping his food-tasters aside and parting the shoal, he sucked in my egg just as my rod tip hit twelve o'clock and I was about to clear the lift to recast. The final inches of the upward movement of my rod completed the tactic, hooking the grayling well and truly.

A grayling caught accidentally on a mayfly in June is a different grayling to one taken on an egg in November. For a start, the latter leap. Twice my grayling made an ungainly twirl, flopping rather than leaping, out of the water. You may mock, but in its way, this protest is every bit as impressive and heart-stopping an action as that of any angry Atlantic salmon. But shortly, the burnt-out male, the shade of a nasty bruise, came to my heels and I ran my blunt-nosed pliers down the line. He had all but digested it. The mouth had clamped down on the line and was shut as tight as the lid on a biscuit tin. A gentle flick on the nose calms any grayling (however miffed), and I prized it open with my thumb and forefinger.

Gazing like a dentist into the square hole of his mouth, I could see teeth. A row on the roof of the mouth behind the lips, pointed backwards. Now I never used to imagine grayling having gnashers, but they do. I was reminded that grayling aren't soft-mouthed vegetarians one December day some years back when I was out after pike. My livebait cupboard was bare and I couldn't get hold of any sprats. I caught a grayling on a cold, metal #5 Mepps. The next week, while out after pike again, I hooked a grayling in the mouth on a small treble sunk into the back of a salted sprat. Watch out! The 'lady of the stream' bites! If not an egg, why not a chicken?

Right now, I can't guarantee that Frank Sawyer isn't turning in his grave as I write, but I think not. The egg has too many similarities to his weighted nymph. It's made to the same brief. Firstly, it's easy to tie. Secondly, the style of fishing demands no great circus performances. And thirdly, it's effective - when you get the hang of it.

At this time of year, it's the alders that play the sneakiest game. One minute the branches are curling with leaves, dark green and coniferous. The next, they're sick, stripped and naked. No death throes, no spectacular transition hues for the alder. If there are, then I'm always looking the other way and I miss them. Their sudden death leaves the valley black and hollow.

By the last week of November, there wasn't a single leaf left on any of the trees. The weather had turned bitterly cold. The frost had licked the fields white every morning for two weeks. A north-easterly wind ran a freezing tongue over the roof of the Wild Wood Lodge as if it was an ice-lolly.

Inside, we shared the house with plants. They stood in pots in the hall like a classroom of schoolgirls, leaves tied in tidy bunches. At the fireside, the basket was filled to the brim with ash logs. Thrown off the back of the Boss's pick-up in block form, they cut like Caerphilly cheese. Outside, the log stack was piled high with an assortment of elm, oak and alder all squeezed up to the top of an old barn door which I lift up on the rim of the fence in the Secret Garden at this time of year and prop up with a post driven into the ground. This arrangement is enough to hold off the rain showers from the Downs and snow flurries that occasionally puff over the top of the Big House from the north. Putting on my scarf for the first time since last winter, I held it up to the empty golden sky and peered at the thin white light through two new moth holes.

On my way up to the Church Pool, I cut through Robin's Wood past a dormitory of beeches ready for hibernation and dripping like taps onto a thick-piled orange carpet of frosty leaves. It was midday.

Where the sun had been able to skip round the deep blue shadows, it had begun to thaw. I wondered if the heat of the next two hours, the warmest time of the day and just above freezing, would seep down into one of the holes where I was hoping I might find one of the large grayling that had eluded me during the summer months.

I arrived at the hatch pool with a sore ear. It was bitter cold and the Marshes were streaked with yellow and dotted with tiny willows with orange fingers. The little colour that remained on the river bank was kept alive by the watercress which looked as fresh as ever, just as if it had been bundled up in the summer and stored in a deep-freezer. I was happy to see it thriving, and the shrimps were happy to live in it, thriving also.

Rodless, the week before, in clearer water I had watched the grayling patrolling the river bed below the hatch, dashing in between decayed leaves that rolled out of the depths and down the sparkling gravel lanes dug out by the first flush of winter water, like drunks in the streets at closing time. A large blue male encased in a slimy stocking of mucus tipped up the ends of these leaves, turning them over one by one as if checking to see they were dead.

Grayling don't eat decaying leaves, but shrimps do. And at this time of year, the shrimp is the most important source of grayling food. In fact, it's on the menu all the year round. But more so in November when there is very little else in the nymph category on offer. A relative newcomer to the chalkstream angler's fly box, the shrimp is of great culinary interest to the

deep-lying grayling, and of even greater practical use to the cold weather flyfisher with a mission to get his artificial down to murky depths. For no other aquatic food form, apart from the mayfly nymph, has the bulk to carry the weight needed to do this other than a shrimp on a #10 iron.

Whereas the 'rolling egg' technique is essentially a shallow, fast water technique, fishing the shrimp is a tactic for addressing grayling (and trout) well out of reach of Netheravon nymphs - in deep water, trundling rather than fizzing.

As I watched two transparent female grayling evolve and dissolve chameleon-like, gliding over the gravels in a deep run near ten courses of bricking that backed out of the hatch pool, the need for a large food-form to imitate, capable of concealing more than just a modest amount of weight, became top priority. The tactical problem posed by these late-season grayling enclaves is that you have to manoeuvre flies into tight, awkward corners and get them to voyage to the bottom of the stream with the sort of plunging accuracy known only to Jules Verne.

There is little we need know about shrimps, other than that they are quite content to make their daily rubbish collection rounds, twenty-four hours a day, seven days a week, three hundred and sixty-five days a year. Wherever an obstacle collects old leaves, in particular watercress debris, here you'll find the scavenging shrimp. All they ask for is highly oxygenated water.

When it comes to mating, the male shrimp carries the female to work with him, and I noticed that several of the females that I scooped out of the stream contained a luminous red blob tucked tight into their bellies, seemingly held by their legs. At first I thought they were some sort of parasite, or mite. As did the River God when I first pointed this out to him. But now we are of the opinion that they are the first stages of an egg sac.

Once the eggs have been laid, the females cart them about in a brood pouch close to the gills beneath the middle of the body and they can be seen clearly as an orange or red spot. This observation led to the development of a pattern that over the last ten years has earned itself an unparalleled reputation on south country streams as a fault-proof, fully-tested winter grayling

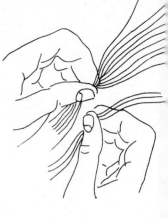

pattern. Even though, in truth, it began its life tempting rain-fed river trout sheltering in muddy pot-holes tucked into the banks of early season streams in full flood, in the valleys of southern Wales.

Against the dull olive colour of the shrimp, this sac glows as brightly as a farmhouse window on a dark hillside. Nature, I decided, had provided the flytyer with a wonderful way of illuminating his shrimps in the bleak dungeon of a trout hole. Or for that matter, a limey, dark-green grayling grotto tinged by black clouds and the excesses of the ploughed fields of October.

Bob Preston, the man who developed the very first plastic-backed, lead-bearing shrimp, using fluorescent-pink seal's fur pinched into olive of the same, was a riverkeeper in the Salisbury area, where Sawyer developed his 'deep water' shrimp imitation, the Killer Bug. But even the Killer Bug simply didn't go far enough, in a downwards direction, to tackle the slower, deeper, funereal stretches on The Hollow, of which we have many.

The Red-Spot Shrimp, as it is now known, is tied big, on a #10. Even a small grayling's mouth is an inch across. Don't let anyone have you believe that the 'ladies of the stream' don't have big mouths. They'll swallow a mayfly in June, they'll wolf down a juicy fat shrimp in the winter. And remember that sprat? The fatter and juicier the better.

How much weight you incorporate into the hump of your Red-Spot Shrimp depends on two factors. The depth of your quarry and the pace of the flow. The grayling by the bricking were lying in water at a depth of six foot, but they were gliding on the current to the back of the hole to take food in water depths that ranged from three to four foot. Bellies on the bottom, cushioned by leaves serving them up the occasional shrimp, they weren't lifting an inch. They were there for the duration.

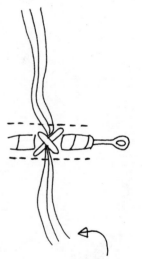

DFM Wool
TRim flush
on completion
of fly

All the holes behind the thundering hatch pool were cloaked in a milky haze. Flat light made visibility impossible. A chilly breeze shivered down the river. I was fishing blind, whether I wanted to or not.

When greased-line fishing, an understanding of the invisible grayling rise to the nymph is as important as understanding its position on the river bed in relation to its rise when taking a dry fly from the surface. The grayling 'take' needs a close examination, for it's more complicated than simply a yank on a greased leader lying on reflected light. The grayling strike is a bang, then a draw.

No matter how long your leader, or how hefty your lead, you will rarely be able to deliver your shrimp at gravel level at great depths in the same way as you are able to roll an egg, led doggy-fashion and held down in position by a shot weight in two or three foot of water. The shrimp *is* the weight and liable to lift from the bottom into the sub-surface drift, anything up to a foot off the gravels.

When your shrimp approaches a grayling, she will see it and rise quickly to intercept. Her various fins may play many different parts in her attempts to manoeuvre in and out of a myriad positions, but ultimately it is the grayling's large swim-bladder that controls the upward and downward motions, regulating the rate of ascent and descent. When a grayling rises up to the surface, the tell-tale bubble she leaves to commemorate her expedition is nothing more than her extruding air to facilitate her descent. It is not the grayling breaking the surface with her head. She rarely does this.

On reaching your shrimp, the moment she takes it in her mouth, she will use her pectoral fins to brake. At this point, your leader will indicate the collision. Rather than drag, the leader will shudder as if an electric shock has passed through it. Your strike should be immediate, for momentum and swim-bladder carries the grayling upwards with a nymph she cannot release. For fractions of a second she is as good as washing it into her mouth. If your shrimp is semi-accepted, you have just time to tighten. She will sink back down to her position as quickly as she rose up. Her descent is registered by a long draw on the leader. This is when a grayling normally rejects your nymph if she doesn't like the smell, taste or look of it.

As mentioned earlier, grayling don't 'turn' on nymphs. Their large dorsal fin doesn't allow them much manoeuvrability. However, in an emergency, it will spin her round for a dash downstream. Which is why grayling tend to do just that when hooked. That fin against the current doubles a grayling's weight force.

This 'direct drop' theory, as opposed to a 'turn of the fin take', is continually being reinforced each time I catch a grayling. Eighty percent of all the grayling I catch are hooked in the centre of the snout. Sometimes in the gill, or pectoral fin if my strike on the 'bang' is late, but lucky.

I selected a heavyweight candidate from my biscuit-tin full of shrimps and positioned myself below the hole alongside a clump of ochre sedge rattling like a dance troupe of women in taffeta ball-gowns. I was resigned to the fact that if I was to get the small car on the end of my line delivered to the door of the grayling in the hole, I would have to fish blind, and I made sure that I had the most sensitive indicator system possible to let me know exactly what was happening to my shrimp beneath the curtain of reflected light.

When rolling eggs, I use a standard 12-foot leader with an 18-inch 22lb butt needle-knotted to the end of my floating line. The butt is then connected to an 18-inch strip of floating Shockgum. From here to the tippet, the cast tapers down at 12-inch intervals from 15lb, 12lb, 10lb, 8lb, 6lb. To this I connect a two-foot length of 4lb line - and then the tippet: a two-foot length of 4lb, or 3lb super-fine, pre-stressed nylon. My Gremlin is clipped on just *above* the knot joining the 4lb nylon to the tippet. In actual fact, without the shot, this is my normal all-occasion leader.

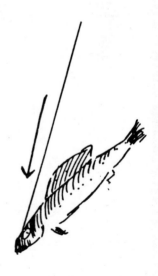

When I need to lengthen this to fish a shrimp, the extra goes just above the tippet, a two, three - sometimes four-foot length of extended 4lb. I used to add this extra to the butt, but the thicker the line, the slower it sinks. The finer the line the faster it cuts through.

The preparation of the leader butt is essential if the grayling take is to be registered and correctly translated. I dress it two ways. One using muscilin grease, the other using my fingers. I wind the first four foot of my leader butt tightly round my second and forefinger and anoint it with grease, using the thumb on the same hand to rub it in. When I pull the line free, the leader butt has a tell-tale curl. This acts as a float. When the shrimp is intercepted, the greasy loop straightens, my left hand flies down at the same time as I pull the rod tip up, and contact is (hopefully) made. All of this is done from a position directly behind the grayling. But first, I have to get the shrimp out there.

A stillwater angler will tell you how to cast using a 16-foot leader. The length of leader isn't the problem, it's the weight of the lead-filled snow shoe at the tippet end. Holding the shrimp in between the thumb and forefinger of my left hand, I move the rod tip backwards and forwards, going through the 'motions' of a cast - all the time working my leader through the rod tip, aerialising the reel line. When I have a rod's length through the end ring, I release the shrimp from between my fingers as the rod tip passes behind my right shoulder. The line snatches it away on the back-cast.

The shrimp landed two-foot above the top of the bricking where the shallows shelved off and dipped down into the hole. I dropped my rod tip to water level and calculated the speed of the plummeting shrimp, watching the leader sink into the pit leaving the greasy loop curling on the surface. To straighten the cast and resume direct contact with the shrimp, I raised my rod smartly. This also imparts movement to the shrimp. This is the first crucial part of the whole procedure. Any bump, bang, pull, yank or judder that follows after this is probably a grayling. I always strike, instinctively, at this point. If there's not a grayling flopping at the end of the line, I have not wasted my effort, for this acts as induced take No.2 - and on the end of this second lift I felt a grayling.

It was the one wearing the shiny, dark blue overcoat I'd seen digging in the leaves. First, he turned and rampaged through the small shoal in the hole. Then, rushing the shallows, he dived deep into the white water in the centre of the hatch pool where he spent the next few minutes boring down in an attempt to burrow into a clump of submerged branches. My Shockgum twanging like a guitar string, I tried to steer him out of the current and bring him to the watercress at my feet. But with one last almighty rush he dived deep down to the flinty foundations of the bricking where he knifed my point.

No matter how careful and gentle you are in your approach, you will never be able to empty a deep grayling grotto with a heavily-weighted shrimp, as you can so often do on the shallows with a lightly-weighted nymph If, that is, you're careful to start at the back of the shoal and work your way forward. Grayling will tolerate a great deal of disturbance, but they have their limits. A lead-filled nymph is ideal for addressing a single grayling in a hole, but not a shoal of grayling in a panic.

It was already starting to get dark at 3.30pm. The village threw up a brownish light all over one part of the sky. A vampire night of mist began to gather and my ears tingled with cold. As I walked back through the woods to the track, the pines hissed in the Firs and temperatures fell. Late afternoon dissolved into evening; evening became night - all in the time it took me to get home.

In the field in front of the Wild Wood Lodge, the cows had been rounded up and were gone. In their place, a herd of warm, fat sheep. In passing, I baa-ed at the spooky, woolly-white shapes in the darkness.

In a hot bath with a whisky, I lay watching the ripples push out across the water, shock-waves of my heartbeat. My kneecaps rose up like sunset-pink icebergs. The skin of my fingers holding the glass on my chest crinkled. Half-dozing, I thought over my day. With December only a day away, I hoped they might have replaced the cows with turkeys.

December

THE RIVER'S WAY OF TELLING YOU

Against a back-drop of snow, the young pheasants stood around a hay-bale abandoned by the gate into the sheep-field posing for their portrait like an Edwardian shooting party. A chilly couple of weeks had helped them dump their fluff and sprout a sensible deck of feathers. In full kit, emerald chins resting on puffed-out golden breastplates, they flashed jewels of colour under a thin sun with the magnificence of a Pharaoh's entourage. They looked an impressive group.

It was the gamekeeper whose feathers were more ruffled. The shooting season had got off to a slow start. When I stopped his Land Rover to say hello, he threw himself out of the window at me mouth-first, snarling like a wolf. Eyes watering with rage, veins popping out of a scarlet forehead, he was blind with frustration. Slim totals had nothing to do with the drives, of course. His new guns just couldn't shoot. As he drove away, he pointed at the sheep and asked me if they'd settled in. It was then I realised just how blind with rage he really was. He'd thought I was one of the lads from the farm, the same size as me, also with a beard. The latter had been the only feature he'd been able to make out through the steam rising up from under his collar.

On the brighter side, the Boss brought with him news of a happier sort. It had been a good couple of months for the ducks. Totally at peace with himself as usual, he invited me to help myself to a brace from under some old sacking thrown in the back of his pick-up. This I did, giving them a good sniff-over first.

He told me how he'd recently taken his tape recorder up-river to the park on the neighbouring estate where he'd done some recording. At the next duck drive, to bring more ducks down to the decoys, he'd hidden his Land Rover in the woods, pushed the tape into his cassette and turned the volume up full blast. Apparently, along with ducks, the recording featured pheasants, owls, pigeons, Canada geese and, at one point, an InterCity train, generously sprinkled with short bursts of 'James Last's Greatest Hits' that hadn't been completely wiped off the tape. I guessed it wouldn't be long before this tape joined everything else of incalculable value, bunged in the back of his pick-up.

The December woods were sweet with wood smoke spiralling up from the pyres below Horse Bridge. The growling of distant chainsaws no longer came from woodsmen in amongst the poplars. With the felling job complete, this sound now could be only one thing: the Boss in his woodshed. Dry bones of branches piled high were all that remained of the poplar plantation. Wood ash hung in the air like suspended snow. The foresters had left in a hurry.

At the top of the track, the stack of poplars - once as big as a house - had vanished too. Six thousand tons of wood in total. But the gaping hole on the south side of the river had begun to reorganise itself. Alder had been planted. Whippy, four-foot high saplings sheathed in red PVC knee-high socks, these new residents were jostling for positions. Released to the open sky for the first time in twenty years elderberry, hawthorn, sallow and a million bushes, grasses and thistles no longer lay dormant. My ignorance of the names of all the trees and plants closing in on all sides of the new plantation heightened my impression of their profusion. Suddenly, sometime last summer, the undergrowth had detonated. Fifty acres, once filled with the smell of two-stroke, the sound of cracking tree trunks and the air smoking with yellow sawdust, were now engulfed in a chaos of vegetation.

Now, this new landscape was lying asleep under a thin veneer of powdery snow, half-covered by bracken and a dark brown blanket of a thousand ambitious, exotically mis-shapen weeds with no names, preparing to spring up in front of my very eyes. But not before Christmas.

The year was hurrying to an end.

The bare trees made The Hollow look so small, so insignificant, so easy to explore, so vulnerable. Underneath thin seagull-grey clouds, the river rolled over in its winter bed with freeze-dried leaves heaped on the river bank, like an old badger in hibernation. As black as Indian ink, occasionally streaked with flashes of blue and white light, it slid silently though wood and water-meadow; travelling incognito, fusing with the low hanging sky. This was the river telling you that the time had come when it wanted to be left alone again, to run back into itself. After heavy rains from ten-ton clouds, she had pulled the curtains tight shut. She was closed for fishing - of any kind, in any form.

The grayling shoals had disappeared as mysteriously as ever, just like they always do at this time of year. A few remained. A token half-dozen had been picked up one cold Saturday afternoon on maggot sonar lowered into the impenetrable waters by a handful of lonely coarse-fishermen exiled from their warm homes by their wives.

For the grayling, the signs of the river were clear. They all pointed in the same direction, and the exodus had begun. A whole species had packed its bags and vanished. In so many weeks, they'd wiped themselves clear of the river. Not even the electro-fishing probes, later in the month, could pick up more than a handful. These were all returned, one by one. Where the grayling go, we do not know, yet every year I fear the same thing: I take a rod out and come back with no entry to put in my record book. Brandling, maggot, Red-Spot Shrimp, red worm pulled from the warmth of my steaming, oven-hot heap of decomposing grass cuttings - you can't say I don't give it a good try.

At this time, I fear the worst. I fear it's the end. As the river fish most sensitive to any form of pollution, the grayling is the first to turn over. I begin to ask apocalyptic questions. That rain in October? The treated fields of winter wheat? The insecticides, the glyphosphates?

But I know in my heart the grayling will be back. They always turn up again. Sometimes in the Spring, sometimes later. Severe drought, severe rain. Numbers might tail off, but the river returns them all back safely, one way or another. As if they had never left in the first place.

As the year comes to an end, weary, well-trodden thoughts return. Emotions unconnected to any one particular event in the past, present or future; good, bad, or indifferent. They manifest themselves as a sinister sensation that floats around the fishing corners of my mind like a dulling fog. I like to think I know what it is. It's a self-induced anaesthetic that produces a numbness - an insensibility - to the pain of not being able to flyfish. It affects the side of my brain that controls my body; the hand, the wrist, the arm and the shoulder, and a select number of other minor fishing parts of my anatomy that I didn't know I had. Just occasionally it results in a complete lack of consciousness, a coma, a catalepsy, should my mind start to stroll down to the river unattended. In truth, it's a safety valve - and I welcome it.

Not surprisingly, with all this bottled-up expectation fanned by frustration, December is a sad month in my book. For a start it's a month when nobody passes the Wild Wood Lodge. Even the people in the Big House are dug in deep behind shutters and doors. This emptiness makes The Hollow a strange water to me.

But December has its distractions. There's Christmas. There's New Year - then the year's gone. The last hurdle is cleared.

December is a month to keep warm - and to think thoughts that will keep you warm. Even at their most remote in my memory, rivers, streams, fishing places have a way of clinging to my thoughts like old lovers. As I gaze into the flames of winter log fires night after night, I walk the banks thinking of them. As I do so, my mind travels beyond tactics, tackle and the tying of flies. I consider other ways of preparing myself for the season that lies barely three months away. As the Boss constantly reminds me as soon as the festivities are over 'It'll soon be mayfly.' And he's never wrong. I am already preparing for it. Outwardly, and inwardly. As the flames of the fire form shapes, the shapes become bushes on the other side of the stream and as the heat from the fire reaches a familiar temperature, my mind drifts up with the smoke, across the field, through the Hole and onto the river.

Down there, the afternoon air is still sticky. Just as it was before I had drifted off to sleep. The small curve in the river bank cradles my back with a comfort that has me trapped like a fly on a fly-paper. I found this cosy dent in the bank several seasons ago. I guard it jealously.

River-side armchairs rarely make good fish-watching stations. I searched long and hard to find one that was. A bean-bag tuffet on the Snipe Stream had been dismissed on the grounds that it set me too high up on a pedestal in full view of the trout I wanted secretly to observe. The moss-upholstered tree stump just down from Horse Bridge was too far back in the woods. I had to squint to see the river.

The bunker, with my back to the Wetlands, facing the Ashes, fitted round my body like an old leather-patched tweed jacket.

Furthermore, it 'offered discreet and comprehensive views over a highly select and desirable beat of trout fishing'. I sometimes wonder how an estate agent might describe my observation post. But right now, it isn't for sale.

Most anglers aren't clear when they talk to you about why they flyfish. They fumble at it, with many false casts. In truth, most fishermen, fly or otherwise, fish to get away. From people, their family, their house, their work, their town, their city, their problems. I'm no different. On many occasions, my grassy space-capsule has blasted me far from the world - and other fishermen. No-one strays to this part of the beat without giving ample warning. The joviality of the Mad House might be in another county.

The whole procedure of preparing for a day in my bunker takes on a schoolboy magic. My flask that isn't taken to the river, it's smuggled. The brew that it contains isn't drunk, it's sipped secretly, as if I really shouldn't be doing it. The very worst thing that can happen is to be found. If a fisherman stumbles across me, the spell is broken and I allow myself to be grumpy. This is why the most favoured season-within-a-season - the mayfly - is my least favourite. The river may be heaving with trout, but the river banks are also crawling with flyfishers, and their guests. On the worst days, there might be half a dozen.

In my tight little hole, where the river telescopes itself into a tiny area and the world seems no bigger than a pocket handkerchief, I notice strange things happen to me, physically and mentally.

At times my body becomes so relaxed and calm I don't feel attached to it. Only the faint pulse of my heart beat reminds me it is there. Often I feel I could drift away, like a puff of pipe smoke, and look back at myself lying in this dip. It's an odd feeling. Like dreams in which you fly.

Simple things like eating a biscuit become a hugely enjoyable experience. Tying a fly on the end of the line is done with more than the necessary care. My rod, my fishing pockets and everything inside them becomes astonishingly precious. Even though I am not a particularly tidy or precise person in the things I do, I constantly check to see if everything is in its right place and set out correctly.

But this isn't the only change I observe in my behaviour. Normally boisterous and impetuous by nature, I find myself gripped by an intense calm in the bunker. My mind is silent. With my vision restricted to what I can see through the crack in the curtains of two clumps of comfrey, I find my thoughts focused. I can feel a knife-edge in my powers of concentration. I feel curiously effective.

Watching the river nudge a stalk bent over in the water, I think over the times when I'd longed to feel like this. I look back at experiences that had confused me at the time. Fishing days when, for seemingly no reason at all, things went wrong. When I flunked an easy cast, struck too soon, misjudged the distance between myself and the fish, walked past fish I should have spotted. All simple things that need never have happened. Things that normally don't present problems.

I think over times when I failed to catch a fish, not because of lack of skill or knowledge, but because I just hadn't performed what I knew I was capable of doing - at the time I needed to do it.

I remember fishing a twenty-yard stretch of the Wild Water, the stream nearest my house, but not one in which I wet a line very often. Overgrown, overhung with trees - and skinny - it is filled with small trout and is more of a spawning run than the haunt of resident leviathans. The water runs fast below a footbridge and small fish had moved up out of the fizzing tumble into slack eddies between alder bushes to suck at olives. The water is crystal clear. To get a fly between the branches into the eddies is no easy matter.

But that particular day, I was shooting my line into the holes as if the branches didn't exist.

The trout were all small. I had nothing to lose if I tangled up. I had merely to wade out to retrieve my fly. I was fishing for fun. With rare, almost super-natural regularity, I rose all six little trout in this short stretch without a hitch, returning them to their lies untouched by human hand with a flick of a barbless hook - none the worse for this temporary inconvenience.

Just below the alders the stream begins to meander lazily through a clearing down to where it joins the main river by the Game Hut. Here there are no bushes or obstacles on the banks to snag a cast - and no problem with drag. The pace is even from one side of the bank to the other making it a dry fly duffer's paradise.

Mid-stream a big, black head pushed the surface open and took a fly, leaving a bubble to mark the event.

This was no small trout. I could see it on the gravels. I'd never seen a trout that size in this small carrier before. My eyes popped out on stalks. My body shuddered as if I'd shifted straight from top to bottom gear. The rogue trout rose again. The surface rocked.

'This trout is as good as caught,' I thought to myself. 'All I have to do is be careful. Very careful.' I prepared myself and my tackle.

Nervously, I picked at my fly. When I was after the small trout, it didn't matter that it was water-logged and flat-hackled. It mattered now. I dried and permed it. My leader had weed hanging at the knots. This hadn't worried me earlier. It mattered now. I pulled line from my reel, calculating the exact distance to the last half-inch, piling each coil neatly on the ground ready to cast. I normally just let it fall around my heels. Usually this did fine, but not now. I was anxious all over.

I began to doubt my ability to catch the trout and the more this doubt set in the more tense I became. What little confidence I had oozed and evaporated in beads of perspiration.

I took up position. Was this the best place to be? No. I moved two steps backwards. The trout rose again, shifting three foot to the right to take a fly.

'This trout would snap at a sock if I threw one in,' I muttered through clenched teeth. This should have reassured me. Instead I doubted myself more.

I started to cast. 'Lightly does it. Ever so softly,' I told myself. My rod waved back and forth. The line felt unnaturally slack. I wondered when I'd ever cast like this before. Never, I concluded.

Suddenly I had found a new style. It didn't feel comfortable. My concentration side-stepped. I began thinking of the cast, not the trout to which the cast was aimed.

'This isn't the cast I caught these six little trout with,' I thought. But I couldn't remember what I was doing then. My thoughts seemed to have been somewhere else at the time. I tried to get my cast more natural. But the more I tried, the slacker the line got and the more my uneasiness intensified. I let the line shoot out. I gritted my teeth and drew in my shoulder blades as the fly headed out for the trout. I feared it would slam on the surface. Surely it was going to?

It didn't. But it was a close thing. It landed near enough to its target to rouse interest. The trout moved in its direction, open-mouthed. I was rigid. But by now I had already resigned myself to the fact that the fish would never be mine.

The trout took the fly with all the confidence I seemed to have lost. As it did so, my mind raced through a myriad of striking equations. Should I count to three before tightening, say 'God save the Queen', or just let the current wash the fly into the trout's scissors?

I was talking aloud now. But to whom? Who was I giving instructions to? Who was taking them? Who was questioning whose ability?

I had split in two. One half of myself was yelling at the other half and my hand was getting confused. It knew how to strike. It had done it six out of six times, ten minutes earlier, without directions. Now it was stalling, waiting for my mind to take the decision and give the order 'Now!'

My mind was in no state to do anything. Meanwhile my hand squeezed the cork as if it were sponge.

Somehow, my rod lifted up and I felt a wobble at the end. For a split second, I had my confidence back and, as if released, my hand tightened instinctively. But too late. There was a jerk, a knock and the trout and I were no longer connected.

Just as I feared. I'd lost the trout.

I kicked myself all the way back through the Wild Wood, over the bridge and across the field home. But there were plenty of excuses to let me off the hook.

'Wise old trout that,' I remember thinking. 'Just got the strike wrong. Easily done. I knew the cast was a little funny. Just bad luck. It happens to everyone.' There were so many things my mind could blame my hand for.

Back in the bunker, I smiled to myself and peered at the sun. Since that day, I've thought hard about the event and others like it. I now see it all in a new way, in a different light.

Why did I fish well one minute and not the next? Why did my casting style suddenly change? What made me strike too late and tighten too hard? Why did I miss the big easy trout handed to me on a plate, yet catch the small difficult trout surrounded by jungle? How many times do things like this happen? Hundreds? Thousands? It had to be thousands. Why did they happen? What were the excuses? There were thousands of these, too. From weather conditions to the number of tails on the fly pattern.

So many things to blame.

On the carrier, what were the difficulties that stood between me and those trout?

With the small trout, the obstacles were branches. But what about the big trout lying out in the stream? The sitting duck? I was stumped. I re-examined my day, looking for clues.

Strangely, although I could remember every detail of the build-up to fishing for the big trout, I couldn't remember anything about how I felt or what I did fishing for the smaller ones. Only that the feeling was good. It took a lot of skill to get the fly through the branches but it seemed to come easily. I pulled off the stunt without a care in the world. The more the trout came to the net, the easier they seemed to get. I had hit some sort of high.

Looking back I couldn't help feeling that I could have caught those trout standing on my head. I was casting as if programmed to do so. I never thought to question my actions or interrupt my flow. It hadn't mattered. Everything just seemed to be going fine. And I had kept it going that way.

I remembered a story I'd heard about a woman whose child was trapped under the wheel of a car. In an attempt to save her son, the woman lifted the car up to free him, a feat only possible by two grown men. When asked what she had been thinking of at the time, the woman couldn't explain, other than that she only had one thing on her mind - to save her son. She never once considered whether or not she *could* lift the car.

Like the woman, I had managed to concentrate my mind on one thing, never once questioning what I was doing, or fearing that I might lose a fly. Nothing interrupted the flow of simply *doing* what I knew I could do. It just all came together in a moment of great calmness.

I now realise that it was my state of mind, more than any tricks of the trade I may have picked up over my years as a flyfisherman that took those small trout against the odds. It was when this state was interrupted that I found myself faced with problems much harder to overcome than branches. Obstacles that face me constantly as a fisherman. Things in the way that lose me more trout than wobbly casts or poorly matched artificials. Hurdles inside *me*, not out there on the river. Tension, uncertainty about my ability, fear of failure. Even fear at the sight of the big trout. All things that unsettle the quiet, confident mind.

Back in the calm of my trout hole, I looked down at myself and saw a different fisherman lying in the grass to the angler trembling over that monster in the carrier. I was no longer a flyfisherman who believed that skill alone, even understanding and what you read in books, is all it takes to make one man a better angler than the next. Or myself a better angler on one day than on another. There was so much evidence.

Why, when sent out to catch a trout for supper, did I invariably come back empty-handed when I should have filled a basket? Why, when surrounded by people hauling out trout, did I seem to catch less the more I tried to keep up? Why, having put a fish down with a splashy cast, did I always seem to cast perfectly to the spot after the fish had gone? I knew that there was no ready solution. I looked at how my fishing had changed. How the challenge and the things that stood between me and the trout had shifted.

I no longer go with my mind intent on catching fish, or filling baskets. I'm no longer obsessed with catching fish. Maybe it's my imagination, but I seem to catch the same, if not more.

I no longer carry a net. If I don't mind not catching fish, why worry about landing them? Maybe it's my imagination, but fish never seemed to drop off any more than usual.

I prefere to fish the tiniest of flies: dry flies - without barbs. Maybe it's my imagination, but they seem to lodge themselves like grappling irons, at least as well as any other.

The ash trees stopped whispering and fell silent again. A wide circle ebbed from one side of the river to the other. The trout I had been waiting for pierced the tranquillity of the afternoon with its nose. Without taking my eyes from the spot, I reached for my rod.

I didn't get up to cast, I did it sitting down. Never for one moment did I imagine that my fly would catch the tree behind me. I knew it was there, but I also knew I could get a fly between the gap in the branches, and bring the back-cast forward quickly.

A line, a leader, a fly hissed through the hot air with ice-cold confidence. Even before the fly touched the water the trout was as good as in the grass next to me, lying there dreaming in the orange glow of a winter fire.

A cigar with one puff sucked out of it bobbed past me as I made my way up the Fly Lane to the Sticklepath Bridge. The river was the colour of sheet metal and just as featureless.

There's only one person I know who thinks the tobacco in a cigar is ruined once it has had smoke strained through it, and who, for this reason, only ever has one puff per cigar. Picasso was somewhere upstream from me.

I found him standing in heavy frost outside the door to the Mad House. Rod in hand, his breath made clouds as dense as any bonfire smoke in the pink sky. An unfamiliar oilskin concealed the characteristic blue and white banded sweat-shirt, like the one worn by the twentieth century's greatest artist. All summer long, he had worn this to go fishing. On his feet the toes of his waders, curled up like Aladdin's slippers, confirmed it was him.

Picasso had been down after grayling, or pike, or cold-nosed roach - anything. Anything just to be by the river again. A superlative fisherman, he was one of the most competent rods on The Hollow. He'd fished long and hard all season and had ended up catching the biggest fish of the year. A fish touching on four and a half pounds. An exceptional fish, if only because it was caught outside mayfly time on a small dry fly, on a hot summer afternoon, on a day when even the most regular rods had decided to stay at home watching cricket. I do love the unpredictability of what is so often made out to be such a predictable sport. I remember shrieking with delight when he presented his record fish to me. We had The Hollow to ourselves that day. I had wanted to rush up the track to the Wild Wood Lodge and bring back a bottle of champagne to share with him. Looking back I wish I had, I only wish I had.

Now, under the river's broad white sky, we walked up to the Marshes for a last look just as evening dropped on the meadows, Picasso's Arabian slippers failing to punch quite the same quality of hole that I was thwacking into the icy puddles. The river smelt old. She was tired.

In the distance the village smouldered with mist and log fires.

'Funny thing, fishing,' Picasso said to me with great conviction. 'People have been fishing these streams, interrogating their contents, waxing lyrical about them for over a century, yet the mystery lingers on - unsolved.'

As we walked the river, the spell was still as powerful as it had been that January day when the Boss first marched me around. The river still felt as if I had discovered it for the first time.

'But the bank's a little lower,' I said. 'We must have walked it that many times!'

Picasso nodded. 'May the challenge of the chalk be with us - forever.'

We passed by a spot just up from the Firs where last August

I had caught 'the fish with no face'. A trout with its head stuck in a clump of ranunculus, that had been feeding so ravenously it would have taken a mouthful of my hat. I had spent all morning serving up shrimps so succulent my tummy rumbled every time I tied a bigger pattern onto the end of my line to try and get down and reach it. I managed to get the trout on for a couple of seconds, but I never managed to pull its face out from the weed-clump. In the end, I just had to go back up to the Wild Wood Lodge - to eat something.

I didn't return until the next day - and the trout was gone. Someone had visited the trout after me in the afternoon and managed to administer an impossible cast to this semi-subterranean fish. Who else but Roll Cast? He got his fly into that impregnable, impenetrable position and the trout scoffed it in one, turned, but instead of ripping off upstream or down, it did a right-angle and headed straight for the bank where Roll Cast stood, loose-lined, with mouth wide open. The trout hit the turf at such a high speed, Roll Cast assured me that it could only have been identified by its dental records.

'New developments in chalkstream fishing are all about moving little differences around.'

If Picasso wasn't able to get a fish out of the river, that December day he was hell-bent on pouring his soul into it - and all over me. Picasso could make pausing for breath a spectator sport.

'Ask any creative person,' I said. 'Look at the circumstances that have resulted in some of this century's most creative thinking. The narrower the guidelines, the more imaginative the solutions. The Pheasant Tail nymph was born on chalk.'

Picasso looked at me in disbelief. 'You don't find the chalkstream code restricting?'

'I find it challenging. The more things are alike, the more interesting their differences become. And the greater the challenge.'

Even if nothing was to change - even if we were to get trapped in a time warp, stuck with the same old rod, reel, box of flies and tactics, it would still be fun. Flyfishing is something you can never totally learn. Even though you're still flyfishing when you're ninety.

'And this,' I told Picasso, 'is why I fly-fish. I sleep soundly knowing that I'll never discover just how good a flyfisher I can be.'

There are days when I walk the river bank saying to myself 'I know enough,' knowing that I'll never know everything. But the next day I find a new, better way. Something I thought I wouldn't need to know, but do.

'How often do you come to this river just to *catch* a fish?'

I hung on Picasso's question. 'Quite often. Unless I can't catch one, which is often. Then I change the remit, slightly. Then I'm happy just to be out on a sun-filled meadow on my own - or with someone I have something in common with.'

'Like "fishing"?'

'Something like that.'

This all seemed to make sense to Picasso with thirty more fishing years on the clock than me. For him this was what chalkstream fishing was all about. Escaping, not fishing. A river was a magical place where he could hide away, lose himself, become a little boy again - in the company of other little boys with similar aspirations. Like me.

'When an artist sees a sunset, he wants to paint it. When I see a river, I want to fish it. But I don't pay for the fishing. I buy peace and quiet; that's what I pay for - until it's time to move on to somewhere else.'

'Why would you ever want to move on once you've found that place? '

'You just know.'

'How will I know when that day has come?'

'You'll know. It'll be the day your memories and imaginations of the river are better than the reality of actually being down there. This will be the day you rethink.'

'Or write a book?'

'Or write a book. You're a permanent fixture here now, so answer me this. What will keep making you want to return to this same chunk of river day after day after day, in years to come?'

I had the answer ready, even though I'd never given it a second's thought.

'To check it's still there.'

That first season, Picasso gave me a glimpse into the future. It is now exactly twenty years since I first set up home on the river bank, and my relationship with The Hollow is just like a relationship with an old friend, and every bit as rare and precious. You don't need to ask favours; you never fear being let down; you can communicate in silence. The most valuable thing is to know your old friend is still there - so you keep checking.

———————

Golden light retreated from lengthening shadows. I arrived back from the river wet, cloaked in a late evening mist and smelling like an airing cupboard. I spent the evening putting the Christmas tree up in the hall and tossing fistfuls of tinsel down on it from the cat-walk.

The next day, my wife, my son and I went to the Christmas service in the village. Children rustled around in dressing-gowns, bathroom towels wrapped round their heads and silver halos made in the school art class. A nativity play, I decided, sponsored by Bacofoil.

We walked back along the canal. A small hatch of blue-winged olives accelerated off the Fly Lane as we crossed the Sticklepath bridge. No need to take one home for closer examination. A trinity of tails confirmed their identity beyond any reasonable doubt.

At the New Year's party at the Wild Wood Lodge we crammed seventeen people round the table in the hall. Vincent had come over from Paris and we had fireworks indoors, and out. The Boss and his wife dropped by with their daughter and her boyfriend. They had all got invitations, but there had been so many other parties to go to in the village, and they'd been to them all. Lady McFarlane should have been there too, but she had left earlier in the day to spend New Year with her family in the West country. I helped her load cardboard boxes full of teddybears, dolls, party hats and crackers destined for her grandchildren.

As the final minutes of my riverside year slipped away like water under Sticklepath Bridge, I thought back to the summer that I thought would never end. The trout I thought would never stop rising. I couldn't keep my mind off them. I was already planning what I would do next season. It'll soon be mayfly time.

Out in the blackness of the Secret Garden, I leaned over the wall and listened to the river slide through The Hollow, out of one year, into another, the sky a broken net of stars above me.

Across the Marshes, the village clock struck midnight through the frozen air. For the man who lives by the river, the trout season closed. I blinked - and a new season opened. The challenge of the chalk is forever.

Gnats & Bolts

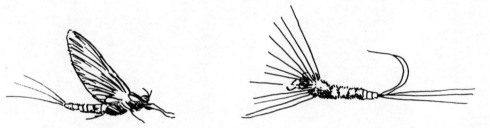

GNATS & BOLTS

I've tried to keep as much of the dry details out of the text as I can - until now. Watch out! Here comes the dry, the damp and the wet fly pattern tying details to supplement the tying procedures illustrated throughout the book. And the promised 'Vital Statistic Charts' I compiled for Claw-fingered Kitty.

Before I divulge - a word.

The patterns itemised here (and described throughout the book) are not a selection of complete pancake, down-beat vegetable noodle flies. They have been well tested. By myself, and by other people. Some people I know; many I don't. In this country, and on other rivers; both in Europe and in America. In fact, come to think of it, on rivers in places I'd give my hind teeth

to visit myself! And adopted by people I'd like to meet one day.

Yes, I can honestly say, my babies are better travelled and more socially active than I am. They've certainly caught more fish than I have - and probably had more fun! And it was me who did all the hard work!

But suffice to know, I have been using each and every one of them on my little beat for years. Some of them, for over 15 years. The Funneldun, for example, first fluttered off the vice in the late 70s. The Grizzle Mink hasn't had a haircut in two decades. And it won't be long before the phone rings and they tell me the Deerstalker has turned up in cave drawings. New patterns, yes; prototypes, no.

Drawing another breath for a moment - a warning.

While getting together my first division team, a curious statistic emerged. Almost fifty per cent of my chosen few make a dramatic break from the ranks of conventional fly-tying procedures. They demand you abandon the most fundamental and elementary tying procedures of all. One rarely challenged - ever since the first flyfishing code was laid down by a woman in England, back in the fourteenth century. Dame Juliana Berners was her name. It goes something like this: Tie in the thread near the front of the hook; bring it back down to the bend; wind it back up to the front again (tying in materials as you go). It's what I call the 'front-back-front-again', or 'Two-way street' technique of tying a fly. The 'street' being the shank of the hook.

It's the first thing flytyers learn. Something I've been doing from Day 1 at the fly-tying bench. As if programmed to do so. You could say it was the second vice I was sold - after the first one I bought, still screwed to the breadboard on my bench.

Now I'm not saying I was screwed, too. The 'Two-way street' technique is still a valid method of tying a fly. Half my flies are still tied this way. But in time, I began to see things differently.

In an attempt to simplify and minimalize flytying procedures, incorporate the hugely underestimated thorax (something I believe passionately to be an important part of a fly's outline), give me the option of tying big flies on small hooks (and therefore further concealing the hook and, therefore, my

duplicity) and make the whip finish easier, I developed a 'front-back', or 'One-way street' approach to tying flies. A novel method made radical on account of the fact that you drive down this one-way street backwards!

When tying a fly, instead of setting off near the front, travelling down to the bend and returning up at the front again, I start where conventional flies end up - right up against the eye. Then I move on down - but I don't come back. I keep on going. I head off down the hook shank with my silk, tying in wings, hackles, body materials, thoraxes, tails, as I go - finishing off at the tail with the flourish of a whip finish knot. And that is the end of the tale.

As explained in Chapter 2, this idea first surfaced when I was developing the Funneldun. It reappeared again shortly after with the Suspender, sneaking its way into several other patterns as I got more confident with this way of tying and it began to make more and more sense in a variety of different applications.

The test of time - the only true arbiter of whether you've hit on a genuinely good idea, rather than just a duff, cranky one - has transformed what started off as a minor fly-tying tactic into a major one. And for me at least, its influence continues to grow.

To conclude: by now I can guarantee that all the patterns listed below (in order of appearance) come up to scratch. By this I mean that they are flies that have had all the bugs shaken out of them - and they're ready for action!

Lastly, a word about hooks. Use them. But if you're catch-and-releasing, make sure you snip off the barb with your blunt-nose pliers. There are still far too few barbless hook designs available in the world. But this, I predict, will change.

Bon voyage!

EXCITING CLADDINGS

TWO-MINDS NYMPH   **pages 17-18**

Hook:	12 d/e, barbless
Thread:	crimson
Tail:	bronze mallard breast feather fibres
Body:	beaver pelt fur. Don't clip guard hairs!
Rib:	fine gold wire
Thorax:	deer hair fibres
Wing case:	same deer hair fibres folded over thorax
Hackle:	points of same deer hair fibres folded back again under the thorax

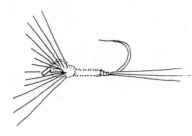

FUNNELDUN   pages 39-43

Hook: 14-18 u/e, barbless
Thread: colour to match hatch
Thorax: light coloured fluff from roots of
              mink pelt hairs
Wing: grey mallard, widgeon or teal breast
              feather fibres (optional)
Hackle: cock - colour to match hatch
Tail: cock hackle fibres - colour to match
              hatch

FUNNELSPINNER   page 45

Hook: 14-18 u/e, barbless
Thread: colour to match the hatch
Thorax: dark coloured fluff from roots of
              beaver pelt hairs
Body: soft dub - colour to match the hatch
Hackle: cock hackle - colour to match the
              match
Tail: cock hackle fibres, or white nylon
              paintbrush 'microfibetts' filaments -
              colour to match the hatch

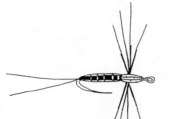

SUNK SPINNER   page 50

Hook: 14-16 d/e, barbless
Thread: crimson
Tail: two hare whiskers, or white nylon
              paintbrush 'microfibetts' filaments
Body: fine red copper wire
Rib: close turns of flattened 4lb
              monofilament nylon
Thorax: three cock peasant tail fibres
Wing: cream badger, tied spent

DAMP SPINNER   page 49

Hook:	14-16 d/e, barbless
Thread:	crimson
Tail:	two hare whiskers, or white nylon paintbrush 'microfibetts' filaments
Body:	fine red copper wire
Rib:	close turns of flattened 4lb mono-filament nylon
Thorax:	three cock pheasant tail fibres
Wing:	White Zelon (or strip of clear plastic) to lie back over body

GRIZZLE MINK   pages 53-54

Hook:	14-16 d/e, barbless
Thread:	brown
Tail:	bunch of grizzle cock hackles
Body:	mink pelt fur, including guard hairs Don't clip!
Rib:	fine gold wire
Hackle:	ginger wound through grizzle cock hackle

FUNNELHAWTHORN   page 79

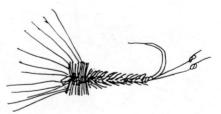

Hook:	12-14 u/e, barbless
Thread:	black
Thorax:	black seal fur
Hackle:	black cock hackle
Legs:	black 'Hairabou' strands, knotted
Body:	black silk
Tail:	small bunch of black cock hackles, clipped short

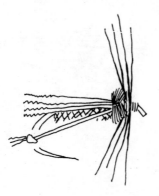

HAWTHORN   page 78

Hook: 12-14 d/e, barbless
Thread: black
Body: black cock hackle, clipped and palmered
Rib: silk
Legs: black 'Hairabou' strands, knotted
Thorax: black ostrich herl
Wing: white polypropylene yarn
Hackle: dark red furnace

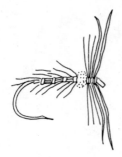

WATER CHICKEN (DRY)   page 95

Hook: 16 d/e, barbless
Thread: yellow
Body: light olive mohair, picked out
Rib: fine gold wire
Thorax: light coloured fluff from roots of mink pelt hairs
Hackle 1:   light dun cock hackle
Hackle 2:   two turns of a large greater wing covert feather from outside of moorhen wing

WATER CHICKEN (DAMP)   page 96

Same as dry version, but without the support cock hackles

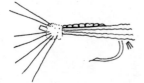

FUNNELGNAT   pages 102-103

Hook: 16-20 d/e, barbless
Thread: colour to match the hatch
Thorax: soft dubbing - match the hatch

Wing:	white polypropylene yarn
Body:	soft dubbing - colour to match the hatch
Hackle:	colour to match the hatch
Tail:	hackle fibres - colour to match the hatch - clipped short

ANDELLE   pages 104-105

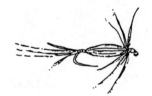

Hook:	10-12 d/e, barbless
Thread:	brown. Use thin gold wire at tail to transform dun to hatching nymph
Tail:	three cock pheasant tail fibres
Body:	ochre/yellow polypropylene yarn
Hackle 1:	(wing & nymph skin) three turns of summer duck breast feather. Or teal, or grey mallard breast feathers dyed light olive
Hackle 2:	large brown partridge neck feather

DEERSTALKER   pages 122-123

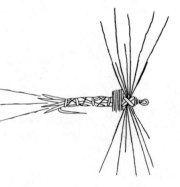

Hook:	8-12 d/e long-shank, barbless
Thread:	black
Tail:	three cock pheasant tail fibres, dyed black
Body:	deer hair, bleached white
Rib:	black silk & silver oval wire
Thorax:	black cock hackle, part-clipped
Wing:	remaining unclipped thorax hackle & red furnace hackle, tied spent. Or remaining thorax hackle and dark blue dun hackle, split tied upright

WHITE SOCK   page 128

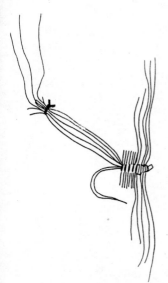

Hook:	14 u/e, barbless
Thread:	black
Tail:	three long, soft black horsehairs
Body:	white, mixed with a few strands of yellow polypropylene wool
Rib:	black floss
Thorax:	black cock hackle, part-clipped
Hackle:	remaining black thorax cock hackle wound behind a large dark blue dun hackle

YELLOW SOCK   page 128

Hook:	14 u/e, barbless
Thread:	brown
Tail:	three short, soft reddy-brown horsehairs
Body:	yellow polyropylene wool
Rib:	brown floss
Thorax:	dark ginger cock hackle, part-clipped
Hackle:	remaining unclipped dark ginger thorax hackle wound behind two turns of summer duck (or substitute) breast feather

ORIGINAL SUSPENDER NYMPH   page 153

Hook:	14-18 d/e, barbless
Thread:	colour to match the hatch
Thorax:	light coloured fluff from roots of mink pelt hairs
Body:	colour to match hatch
Hackle:	colour to match hatch

BWO SUSPENDER   pages 161-162

Hook: 14 d/e, barbless
Thread: hot orange
Thorax: dark coloured fluff from roots of
                beaver pelt hairs
Body: dirty olive wool
Hackle: dark-centred Greenwell cock hackle
                wound round nylon pouch
Tail: three bronze mallard breast feather
                fibres, short

BWO DUN   pages 166-167

Hook: 14 d/e, barbless
Thread: orange
Thorax: dark coloured fluff from roots of
                beaver pelt hairs
Body: light olive polydub (Orvis)
Hackle 1:   two turns of dun hackle
Hackle 2:   two turns of a large greater wing
                covert feather from outside of
                moorhen wing

RUSTY FUNNELSPINNER   page 165

Hook: 16 u/e, barbless
Thread: hot orange
Thorax: light coloured fluff from roots of
                mink pelt hairs
Wing: blue dun hackle
Body: 50% ginger seal fur, 40% hare fur,
                10% hot orange seal fur mix
Tail: three white nylon paintbrush
                'microfibetts' filaments

Twenties Loop Caenis   page 184-185

Hook:	20 d/e, barbless
Thread:	black & white
Wing:	white polyropylene yarn
Thorax:	black thread
Body:	white thread
Tail:	white polypropylene yarn

Twenties Loop Smut   page 188

Hook:	18-20 d/e, barbless
Thread:	black silk
Wing:	white polypropylene yarn
Thorax:	black floss
Body:	black silk
Tail:	black floss

Caddox   page 199

Hook:	14-16 d/e, barbless
Thread:	brown
Body:	fluff from roots of fox tail hair
Wing:	stiff fox tail guard hairs
Thorax:	fluff from roots of fox tail hair
Hackle:	points of stiff fox tail guard hairs

Film Star Sedge   pages 205-206

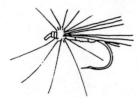

Hook:	12-14 d/e, barbless
Thread:	crimson
Egg sac:	yellow polyproylene yarn, clipped short
Body:	fluff from roots of fox tail hair

Wing:	stiff fox tail guard hairs
Thorax:	fluff from roots of fox tail hair
Antennae:	points of fox tail guard hairs

BLUEBOTTLE pages 212-213

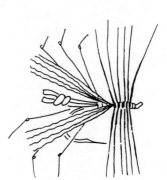

Hook:	10 d/e, barbless
Thread:	black
Body:	three black ostrich herls plaited together
Rib:	two liberal turns of wide blue lurex ribbing
Wing:	white polypropylene yarn, split (optional)
Hackle:	black cock hackle

DADDY LONGLEGS page 214-215

Hook:	12 u/e, barbless
Thread:	fawn
Body:	khaki garden raffia, looped, knotted, clipped
Legs:	six lengths of 3lb sepia monofilament, knotted
Wings:	yellow polypropylene yarn
Hackle:	ginger and red cock hackles

GLO-BUG pages 241-242

Hook:	16 d/e, barbless
Thread:	orange monocord
Body:	5 parts 'Cream Delight' or 'Baby Pink' Glo-bug floss.*
Eye:	1 part 'Flame' Glo-Bug floss* (* The Bug Shop, 3342 Dodson Lane,

Anderson, California 96007, USA - or
from Orvis)

FUNNELMOZIE   page 244

Hook:	16-18 u/e, barbless
Thread:	crimson
Thorax:	hare's ear fur
Wing:	two teal breast feather hackle tips
Hackle:	red cock hackle
Body:	light coloured fluff from roots of mink pelt hairs
Tail:	two bronze mallard breast feather fibres

RED-SPOT SHRIMP   page 255

Hook:	12-14 d/e, barbless
Thread:	orange monocord
Body:	strips of wine bottle lead dubbed over with 90% olive mohair, 10% hot orange mohair, picked out after ribbing
Rib:	gold wire
Back:	2 x strips cut from plastic bank coin pouches, or stretched strip of beer (6-pack) plastic
Egg sac:	DFM DFM red wool/Glo-Brite 5

VITAL STATISTICS

Thanks to Claw-fingered Kitty, I offer you the simplest way to upwing fly-spot. With accuracy. With the secret at your finger tips.

Now at last those infuriating little upwing bugs that flit enticingly over the snouts of all those trout you want to catch, and land anonymously and unannounced on the point of your nose, can be identified. At the flick of a cap - and a lunge of a toothpick.

How to use these charts is self-explanatory. But in case you need reminding, you'll find a full explanation on pages 231-232.

The medium olive, small dark olive, iron blue and pale watery on an identification parade on the back of your hand can look remarkably similar. Even under the magnifying glass. For this reason, I have added an eye-shade chart under the appropriate Vital Statistics chart. I find this very useful when I need a bank-side identification that can to hold up in a picky trout's court.

All the equipment you need to activate the Vital Statistics charts is some form of head gear (however silly), for catching your specimen - and a Swiss Army Knife. The tiny manicure model is recommended. The one with a small pair of tweezers and a tooth-pick. The tweezers you use to hold your specimen; the toothpick you use to separate the wings, allowing you to give the tiny hindwings tucked away at the roots of the larger wing a darn good seeing to.

I also carry a small low-powered magnifying glass around with me. It's a little larger than a book of matches, and slips into a leather sleeve. This is all I need to get an even closer look at those tell-tale wing veins, hindwings, or any other feature that has me squinting.

An empty 35mm film canister is also worth slipping in to your pocket. You may want to take a specimen home for a more detailed analysis.

The dotted scissor line isn't there to encourage you to vandalise this end section of the book. It's there to indicate that the charts can have a practical use outside the constraints of these two covers. I suggest that you photostat the chart pages, put them in a plastic sleeve, slip them into one of the pockets of your favourite fishing jacket and take them with you to the river.

Even though you don't have to be a scientist or a scholar of ancient languages to be able to identify one upwing fly from another, I've included the Latin nomenclature of each fly (in brackets), as well as the common riverside user-friendly name. It won't help you recognise the fly on the bank, but it can help you confirm your identification at home if you need to consult more hefty tomes to help verify your identification.

But the first thing to identify is a friend with a photostat machine.

––––––––––

LARGE DARK OLIVE (Baetis Rhodani)

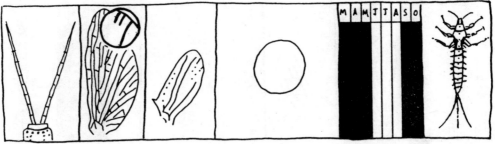

MEDIUM OLIVE (Baetis vernus, tenax)

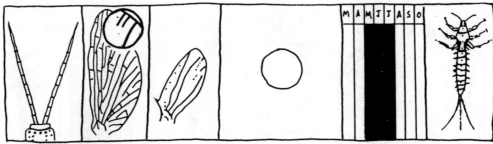

👁 DUN ♀ GREEN ♂ BROWN SPINNER ♀ BROWN ♂ BROWN

IRON BLUE (Baetis pumilus, niger)

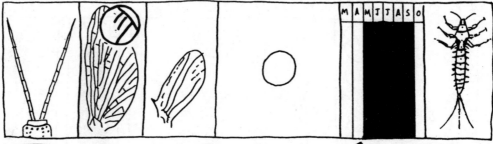

👁 DUN ♀ dull GREEN ♂ BROWN SPINNER ♂ dk. RED ♀ black

PALE WATERY (Baetis bioculatus)

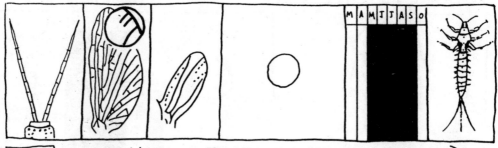

👁 DUN ♀ light GREEN ♂ lemon SPINNER ♀ dk. BROWN ♂ lemon

SMALL DARK OLIVE (Baetis scambus)

👁 DUN ♀ black ♂ brick <u>Spinner</u> ♀ black ♂ Red brick

SMALL SPURWING (centroptilum luteolum)

LARGE SPURWING (centroptilum pennulatum)

PALE EVENING DUN (Procloeon pseudorufulum)

MAYFLY   (Ephemera danica, vulgata)

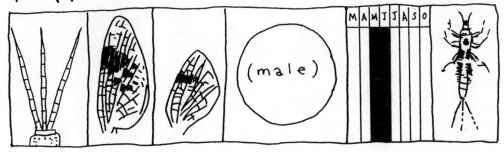

BLUE-WINGED OLIVE   (Ephemerella ignita)

CAENIS   (caenis Robusta, horaria)

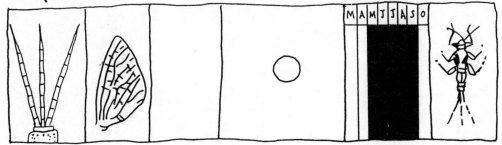

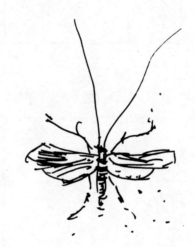

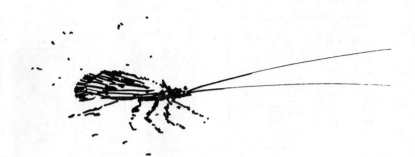

CADDIS CALCULATOR

GRANNOM (Brachycentrus subnubilus)

• Fawn-grey wings • Green egg sac at tail of female	10mm	M	A	M	J	J	A	S	O	plant

MEDIUM SEDGE (Goëra pilosa)

• Day-time • Dark, greyish-yellow wing with circle	12mm	M	A	M	J	J	A	S	O	stones

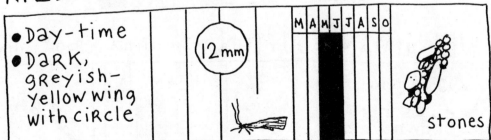

SILVER SEDGE (Odontocerum albicorne)

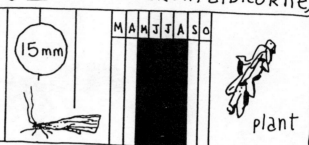

- GREY-BROWN wing
- Antennae, longer than wing

15mm

| M | A | M | J | J | A | S | O |

plant

CINNAMON SEDGE (Limnephilus lunatus)

- slim, cinnamon wings — with no markings

14mm

| M | A | M | J | J | A | S | O |

plant

LARGE CINNAMON SEDGE (Potamophylax latipennis)

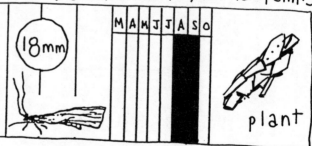

- similar to CAPERER
- pale patch on wing

18mm

| M | A | M | J | J | A | S | O |

plant

WELSHMAN'S BUTTON (Sericostoma personatum)

- Day-time
- chestnut-brown wing
- golden legs

14mm

| M | A | M | J | J | A | S | O |

sand

GREY FLAG (Hydropsyche instabilis)

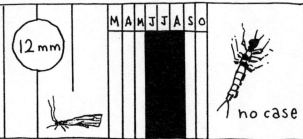

- Day-time
- Grey wing
- Antennae, same length as wing

12mm

M	A	M	J	J	A	S	O
			■	■	■		

no case

SILVERHORNS (Athripsodes/Mystacides)

- swarm in circles over water
- Antennae, 3x body length

8mm

M	A	M	J	J	A	S	O
		■	■	■	■		

sand

GREAT RED SEDGE (Phryganea grandis)

- reddish-brown wing
- black bar along centre

25mm

M	A	M	J	J	A	S	O
			■	■			

plant

CAPERER (Halesus radiatus, digitatus)

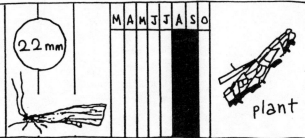

- Yellow-brown mottled wing
- Black eyes
- orange-brown legs

22mm

M	A	M	J	J	A	S	O
					■	■	

plant

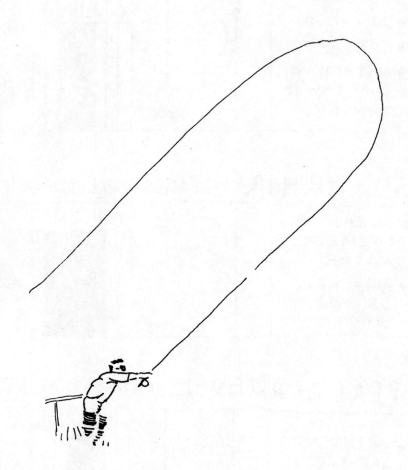

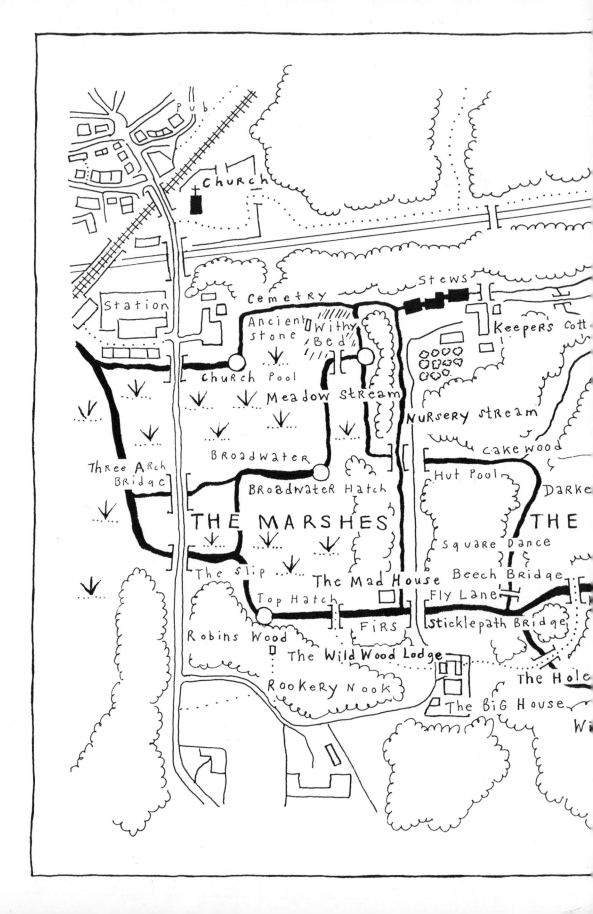